CW0096810G

THIRTY-SIX MURDERS
& TWO IMMORAL EARNINGS

THIRTY-SIX MURDERS

& TWO IMMORAL EARNINGS

LUDOVIC KENNEDY

P

PROFILE BOOKS

First published in Great Britain in 2002 by
Profile Books Ltd
58A Hatton Garden
London EC1N 8LX
www.profilebooks.co.uk

Copyright © Ludovic Kennedy, 2002

1 3 5 7 9 10 8 6 4 2

Typeset in Minion by MacGuru
info@macguru.org.uk
Printed and bound in Great Britain by
Clays, Bungay, Suffolk

The moral right of the author has been asserted.

All rights reserved. Without limiting the rights under copyright reserved above, no part of this publication may be reproduced, stored or introduced into a retrieval system, or transmitted, in any form or by any means (electronic, mechanical, photocopying, recording or otherwise), without the prior written permission of both the copyright owner and the publisher of this book.

A CIP catalogue record for this book is available from the British Library.

ISBN 1 86197 354 3

Often in the past when the prisoner has gone into the witness-box and the jury has had an opportunity of contrasting the voluble incoherences which every question – even the kindest from his own counsel – touched off, with the lucid and well punctuated flow of statement taken at the police station, they must have known that the police account of the way in which the interview was carried out was nonsense.

It is the general habit of the police not to admit to the slightest departure from correctness.

Patrick Devlin, *The Criminal Prosecution in England*

If 99 per cent of all convicted prisoners have been rightfully convicted and 1 per cent not, that means that in a prison population of say 50,000 (omitting those on remand) no less than 500 shouldn't be there.

David Jessel, former presenter of *Rough Justice* and now a commissioner for the Criminal Cases Review Commission

To Gareth Peirce,
doyenne of British criminal defence lawyers, whose sustained
and untiring work behind the scenes on behalf of the innocent
and wrongly convicted – among them the Birmingham Six, the
Guildford Four, Cooper and McMahon and George Long – has
led to large numbers of them seeing their convictions quashed
and liberty restored.

AUTHOR'S NOTE

The thirty-six murders for which innocent people were convicted, punished and in most cases subsequently cleared, some post-humously, are apportioned as follows:

Year	Location	Numbers of dead
1932	Hopewell, New Jersey, USA	1
1949	London: 10 Rillington Place	1
1952	Whiteabbey, Northern Ireland	1
1952	Croydon: rooftop of a warehouse	1
1969	Ayr: 1 Blackburn Place	1
1969	Luton: car park	1
1974	Birmingham: The Mulberry Bush and the Tavern in the Town	21
1974	Guildford: The Horse and Groom	5
1974	Woolwich: The King's Arms	2
1978	Deptford: an alleyway	1
1992	Belfast: New Lodge area	1
TOTAL		36

(The two immoral earnings were those allegedly paid to Stephen Ward by Christine Keeler and Mandy Rice-Davies, for which Ward was convicted against the weight of evidence.)

CONTENTS

ILLUSTRATIONS

Picture Section 1
'Judicial Pronouncements It Would Have Been Wiser Not To Have Made'

Picture Section 2
'A Gallery of "Noble Cause" Practitioners'

Picture acknowledgements
Associated Newspapers: 10, 16, 18, 21; Belfast Telegraph Newspapers Ltd: 3, 19; *Express and Star*, Wolverhampton: 20; *Glasgow Herald*: 4, 5, 23, 24; Pacemaker Press: 13; Popperfoto: 1, 8, 12, 14, 15, 17; Topham Picture-point: 2, 6, 7, 9, 11, 22

ACKNOWLEDGEMENTS

I have many to thank for information or advice:

1 In the Judicature of England and Wales
Lord Alexander of Weedon; Lord Bingham of Cornhill; the late Iris
Bentley (sister of Derek Bentley); Sir Louis Blom-Cooper, QC; David
Calvert-Smith, QC (Director of Public Prosecutions); Hugh Callaghan
and John Walker (two of the Birmingham Six); Eileen Callaghan,
Sandra Hunter and Kathleen McIlkenny (wives of three of the Birm-
ingham Six); Richard Ferguson, QC; Lord Gifford, QC, and Michael
Mansfield, QC (counsel for the Birmingham Six at their failed 1988
appeal); Alastair Logan; George and Chris Long; Dr James McKeith;
M. J. Trow; Lord Woolf.

2 In the Judicature of Scotland
Joe Beltrami; the late Nicholas Fairbairn, QC; Lord McLuskey; the late
Patrick Meehan; the late Lord Stewart.

3 In the Judicature of Northern Ireland
Lord Campbell of Alloway, QC; Father Desmond Curran; Iain Hay
Gordon; General Sir Michael Gow; Margot Harvey; John Linklater;

General Murray Naylor; Peter Smith, QC; Dr G. M. Smith; Colour Sergeant Mark Swift; E. R. Telford.

4 In the Judicature of the USA
Barbara Broccoli, Mark Falzini (Curator of the Lindbergh Archives at the New Jersey police headquarters at Trenton, New Jersey); John Runyon (Curator of the Hoffman Papers at the East Brunswick Corporation Museum, New Jersey); Anthony Lewis (*The New York Times*); Anne Morrow Lindbergh; Anthony Scaduto.

5 In the Judicature of Canada
Terry Blocksidge (Press Attaché, Canadian High Commission, London); The Association in Aid of the Wrongfully Convicted (AIDWYC); Gaston St Jean; Win Wahrer.

6 In the Judicature of Australia
Evan Whitton, barrister.

While grateful for advice and information received from the above, I must stress that they are in no way responsible for the opinions expressed, which are entirely my own.

Lastly, my grateful thanks to my editor, Peter Carson, for masterminding the whole project through from commissioning to completion, to my copy editors, Penny Daniel and Sally Holloway, for their meticulous corrections to the text, Nicky White for her industrious photographic research, and to my secretary, Louisa Morrison for seemingly endless transpositions from the original typewritten text with illegible handwritten amendments to computerised perfection.

PROLOGUE

The starting point of my lifelong obsession with miscarriages of criminal justice may be said to have been the library of my grandfather's house in Belgrave Crescent, Edinburgh.

My grandfather, Sir Ludovic Grant (after whom I was named), was the holder of a Nova Scotian baronetcy first conferred on a seventeenth-century ancestor who had been made Scotland's Attorney-General as a reward for having helped to subsidise a scheme enabling Scottish emigrants to form a colony in Nova Scotia. My grandfather, when I first came to know him, had been Professor of Public and International Law at Edinburgh University, where his father, Sir Alexander, was Vice-Chancellor. So in one way, I suppose, it could be said that the law runs in my blood.

For most of his life my grandfather was very happily married to my grandmother, Ethel, whom I called Ga and he called (although I don't know why) Old Muckrake, yet to whom he wrote a series of affectionate and touching love poems which are now in my possession.

Between the ages of about eleven to fifteen, I used to spend a part of my Christmas holidays at Belgrave Crescent. I always looked forward to my visits, for they meant a respite from the presence of my mother, with whom I never had a satisfactory relationship. Both Ga and Grandad seemed as fond of me as I was of them, for, my mother being their only child, they looked on me as the son they never had. ('My dearest old cocky', he used to begin his letters to me.) Theirs was a compact, well-ordered household, run by two women who had shared their lives for many years: Helen, the maid, who was always dressed in black, with a white pinny and a headband in her grey hair; and Bessie, the cook, whom I used to visit on most mornings for a spoonful of black treacle and – if she had the time – a game of cards, at which, she told me years later, I was inclined to cheat.

Thanks to Bessie we ate well, although the meal I treasured most was tea. At a quarter to five Helen bustled in with a trayful of crisp brown toast, flapjacks, drop scones, treacle scones, oatcakes and, to spread on them, Patum Pepperium and a honeycomb of heather honey in a wooden box, followed by shortbread or buttered gingerbread; and on another tray two silver teapots, one of Indian tea, the other of China, and, to replenish them, a silver kettle of boiling water resting on a flaming spirit lamp.

In my earlier years (say, eleven or twelve), after Helen had cleared away, the three of us would play a card game called Old Maid, the object being not to be left with the Queen of Hearts when all the other cards had been discarded. When Grandad found the Queen in his hand, he would clear his throat and tut-tut in a very marked way – a signal that he was going to try and pass the card to me, which made me quite hysterical with excitement.

By the time I reached teenager's estate, I had made a very interesting discovery, one which, though unknown to me at the time, was to influence a large part of my future. Exploring my grandfather's library in search of information about murders and adultery – to a 14-year-old awesome and thrilling subjects illustrative both of the weakness and the wickedness of grown-ups – I found on the very top shelf, reached only by a step ladder, the handsome red volumes of *Notable British Trials*, published by William Hodge of Edinburgh. Murders and adultery proliferated in many of them, the study of which proved infinitely more rewarding than rubbers of Old Maid.

And every day after tea from then on, having watched a character who looked like Robert Louis Stevenson's Leerie come down the crescent to light the gas lamps, I would mount the step ladder, perch on its top step and sit entranced for hours. One day it might be the trial of Dr Buck Ruxton, the Parsee doctor from Lancaster who believed (wrongly) that he had made his children's nursery maid pregnant, then, having murdered both her and his wife whom he also wrongly believed had been unfaithful to him, chopped them into little pieces which he deposited in the Moffat gorge in Dumfries. He was duly hanged. Another day it would be the trial of Madeleine Smith, the attractive and sexy 20-year-old daughter of a prosperous Glasgow architect, who took as her lover a clerk from Jersey named Pierre L'Angelier, then, tiring of him, was suspected of killing him with arsenic. The crime and revelations that surfaced at the trial shocked middle-class Glasgow. The jury brought in a verdict unique to Scottish Law: Not Proven, which can mean, We think you did it but there is insufficient proof, or, We are convinced you did it, but you are young and attractive and we do not want to be responsible for hanging you.

Another sexy trial was that of Oscar Wilde for sodomy. He was convicted on the evidence of a chamber maid at the Savoy Hotel who said that she had found excrement on the sheets of a bed that Wilde had shared with Lord Alfred Douglas.

I was a great romantic in those days, in some ways still am, and what fascinated me about these trials, and others like those of Charles Peace, Steinie Morrison and Dr Crippen, was on the one hand the sheer depravity of those charged and the dreadful things they had done, and on the other the majesty, panoply, mystique and, as I saw it, immaculacy of the criminal law. I never doubted for a moment (who did?) either the integrity of those taking part or the correctness of the verdict. That policemen in the witness box could lie through their teeth and suborn other witnesses to do the same, that judges could show bias, never occurred to me. And when a murder trial reached its apogee in the terrifying ceremony of the judge receiving the black cap and pronouncing sentence of death, I thought that events had come to their inevitable and proper conclusion. Here was wickedness punished, virtue applauded, justice done. If anyone had passed an unfavourable comment on British criminal justice in those days, I would have stoutly defended it. It was the finest in the world – everyone said so, particularly those who had never studied any other system. An added bonus to my reading was that the general editor of the series, a Mr William Roughead, also lived in the crescent and sometimes my grandfather would invite him to tea. For me it was like meeting God.

After the Second World War I embarked on a career as an author and journalist, first as a newscaster with ITN, later as presenter of the ITV current affairs programme *This Week*, and then as a reporter on the BBC's current affairs programme *Panorama*; and it was in the course of these activities that my rose-tinted view of the immaculacy of British criminal justice was shattered. Over the years since then I have come to the conclusion that the adversary, or accusatorial, system of justice which we and the Americans, Canadians and Australians share is an invitation to corruption: by the police (who, once the prosecuting authority in this country, in order to secure convictions and gain promotion have an inbuilt disposition into deluding themselves that a suspect is guilty, but lacking sufficient proof, take it on themselves in what they see as a 'noble cause' to fabricate additional prosecution evidence); and collusion by the judiciary, many of whom are prosecution minded, in accepting too readily the word of police witnesses – an attitude which the police are not slow to exploit. Yet the judges face a dilemma: if they were to regard police evidence as no more reliable than that of other witnesses, police morale would crumble; and our system relies on a tacit understanding that the judiciary and the police are mutually supportive.

The police fabricate evidence in several ways. One of the common-est, and undeniably the most effective, ways is to bully or cajole the sus-pect into making a confession which is often false, so that common sense juries, ignorant of the circumstances under which the confession came to be made, refuse to believe that any defendant could ever bring himself to admit to an offence unless guilty of it. In most murder cases, interrogations are conducted by two officers who, Lord Devlin avers in his book *The Criminal Prosecution in England*, must convey to suspects the certainty of their guilt – and if they do not, he says, they are of no use.

The interrogation is likely to begin with a set of friendly questions on neutral subjects with which the subject can agree (television pro-grammes, sport, etc.) so that his confidence is gained. Then there will be a gradual shift of direction to the offence in question, one interroga-tor staying with the friendly approach ('We've got all the time in the world, so just relax until you're ready to tell us what happened. You'll feel better for it when you do, and we'll see you're all right afterwards'), the other hostile ('Just listen to me. We know you did it – we've got scores of witnesses to prove it – and you know you did it, so why don't you stop wasting our time and admit it?')

Then the two officers may take a break for tea, leaving the suspect alone in his cell and, whether guilty or innocent, confused or bewil-dered. Often, when the officers return, they will have exchanged roles, the formerly hostile one now friendly, the friendly one unsympathetic – which confuses the suspect ever further. Interrogations may con-tinue, with short breaks, for several hours until a stage is reached when the suspect, by now thoroughly brainwashed, begins to wonder if the police officers are right, that he did do it. (In reading police accounts of false confessions I have lost count of the number of times that the phrase 'From what you say it looks as if I must have done it' occurs.) What makes the suspect finally crack is that the interrogation seems to be without end, the same line of questioning being continu-ally repeated, the same technique of carrot and stick, on and on and on. In the end, even the most strong-minded of suspects (and many are of low intelligence and poor moral fibre) is liable to crack, the pressure to conform becoming finally irresistible. Again, one phrase occurs regularly in police reports after the suspect has signed his 'confession': 'It's a great relief to get it off my chest', meaning no more than, 'It's been a great relief to bring all that bloody questioning to an end'. Later, when the suspect has regained his senses, he retracts the confession. But by that time it is too late: the damage, irrevocably, has been done.

While it is true that since the introduction of the Police and Criminal Evidence Act in 1984 it is now unlawful for an interrogation to take place in a police station without the presence of a solicitor or without the interrogation being taped, there is nothing to prevent a similar interrogation being held elsewhere – at the scene of the crime, the suspect's home or the back of a police car where, police officers can falsely claim, the suspect admitted his guilt. It is regrettable that the 1993 Royal Commission into the criminal law, chaired by Viscount Runciman, should have given the green light (three commissioners dissenting) to the admission of confession evidence, even when unsupported by other confirmatory evidence (which under Scottish law is a statutory requirement).

Other methods of faking evidence are: putting words into the suspect's mouth ('Who grassed me, guv?' being the old standard catchphrase to epitomise this); planting incriminating evidence in the suspect's pocket; persuading witnesses to lie (again in what is seen as a just cause); and prisoners who were cellmates of a suspect claiming, in exchange for a promise of remission and/or money, that the accused had admitted the charge.

There is a very good example of this on page 170 in the Luton Post Office Murder case, but another occurred quite recently and is therefore fresher in the public mind. It is what has become known as the Josie Russell Case, the case surrounding the little girl whose mother Lin and younger sister Megan were murdered in a frenzied hammer attack in July 1996, after which Josie herself made an amazing recovery, and for which one Michael Stone was arrested. At his first trial, in

October 1998 at Maidstone Crown Court, it was revealed that Stone had protested his innocence in thirty police interviews, but then, like a number of innocents, had gone on to 'confess' to no fewer than nine fellow prisoners. The prosecution discarded seven of these as unreliable, but put forward two as prosecution witnesses: Barry Thompson and Damien Daley. Both were police informants, but with this difference: after the trial, at which Stone was given three life sentences by a majority verdict, Thompson found he was unable to live with the thought that he could have helped put away an innocent man for the rest of his natural life and admitted he had told a pack of lies, as a result of which Stone applied to the Appeal Court for a retrial. That left Damien Daley, who at the retrial in September 2001 repeated the story he had told earlier of his cell being next door to Stone's and of their sharing a cracked heating pipe through which Stone admitted to him responsibility for the murders of Lin and Megan Russell and for the attempted murder of Josie. This scenario is one of the oldest police ploys in the business and is strikingly similar to the one involving Thomas Weyers (see p. 170).

Daley seems to have benefited, too, according to a series of impressive articles in the *Daily Mail* by journalist Jo Ann Goodwin. She says that when Daley first met Stone in Canterbury prison he was on remand on charges of assault, arson and affray, but that these were mysteriously dropped later due to 'insufficient evidence'. Further charges against Daley of arson made in February 1998 were also dropped the following June. Then, in September 2000, when Daley and another man appeared at Maidstone Crown Court on charges of actual bodily harm and affray, the other man was sentenced to twelve months' imprisonment while Daley was acquitted 'due to lack of identification'. As Goodwin says, 'He appeared to be leading a charmed life.'

And that is not all. A month later, in October 2000, Goodwin took a call on her mobile phone. The speaker had a South Coast accent. He told her his name was Damien Daley. He sounded terrified and said he needed help. 'What I said in court wasn't true, they told me what to say.'

Goodwin asked who told him what to say, and he replied, 'The police. It was all lies, all bollocks. Now I'm fucked either way.' Goodwin arranged to meet the man the next day, but he never showed up and did not get in touch again. She has no way of knowing whether it was Daley who called her, but has no reason to doubt it. At any rate this evidence was tendered to the court hearing Stone's appeal and could have lent weight to the decision of the court to order a retrial.

So Daley repeated his evidence at the retrial: that Stone had confessed to the murders along the cracked heating pipe between their two cells and had related to him in lurid terms how Lin Russell and her daughters were whores and bitches, slags and paupers, and how at the scene of the attacks he had enjoyed the best orgasm of his life. Goodwin, who has spoken to Stone many times since his first conviction, comments that this sort of language does not sound remotely like him. However, the prosecution warned the jury that, without Daley's evidence, Stone had no case to answer and so, for whatever reason, they again brought in a majority verdict of guilty – but a verdict that rested on the evidence of a convicted criminal, and sowed doubts in my mind about that evidence having been allowed. Just before being taken down Stone screamed at the press box, as Michael McMahon had done at Lord Justice Lawton in the Luton Post Office murder case (see chapter 6), '*It wasn't me. I didn't do it.*'

There is a further point worth mentioning. When, after the verdict and sentencing, the jury were told of Stone's appalling record, including his obsession with hammers, they must have congratulated themselves on finding him guilty. But it is possible that it was this evidence of 'system' that led the police into targeting Stone in the first place, in what, as it turned out, made a very unconvincing prosecution – no forensic or ID evidence, nor any obvious motive. Also, according to a report by Lynda Lee Potter in the *Daily Mail* Dr Russell, Josie's father, has serious doubts about Stone's guilt, so does Goodwin.

By all accounts Stone is a deplorable character – 'unlovely and unlovable', Goodwin calls him – but his guilt or innocence is another matter. I have not looked into the case deeply enough to form a view on it one way or the other, which is why I have not included it in these pages. But if Stone's solicitors think it worthwhile submitting his case to the Criminal Cases Review Commission, the commission might well decide on one ground or another – the admissibility of Daley's evidence, the dangers inherent in the police practice of placing grasses and alleged murderers in adjoining cells linked by water pipes – to refer the case back to the Court of Appeal.

In my autobiography, *On My Way to the Club*, I describe how my dearly loved naval captain father was unfairly reprimanded and court-martialed for not having quelled more harshly a minor mutiny by some reservists. Some reviewers and columnists have seen this as the unconscious springboard for my books on miscarriages of justice. They may be right, they may be wrong, I don't know; in any case, I don't think it much matters. What I do know is (a) I cannot imagine anything much worse happening to one than to be punished for something one has not done and (b) I have continued to write about miscarriages because so long as they continue our system of criminal justice, despite some improvements, is still in urgent need of reform.

1

CRAIG AND BENTLEY
1952–92

The first case I came across of the police putting words into the accused's mouth, with devastating consequences, was the infamous Croydon rooftop murder of a policeman on 2 November 1952, featuring Christopher Craig, aged sixteen, and Derek Bentley, aged eighteen. They were a strange pair. Craig, although younger, was the dominant of the two. As other boys of his age collected conkers or foreign stamps, so Craig collected weapons; in his bedroom he kept a veritable arsenal of pistols, knives, knuckledusters. He also liked to watch gangster films and, being illiterate, have his friends read to him the works of the children's author Enid Blyton. Aware of Craig's evil influence, Bentley's parents had forbidden him to see his friend any more, but it had no effect. Bentley was illiterate, had an IQ of 66 and, according to one psychiatrist, the reasoning powers of a child of four. He had also been bombed out twice during the war, suffering head injuries that had led to epileptic fits.

On this November night the pair were observed by a local resident breaking into a confectionery warehouse. Craig had armed himself with a loaded revolver, Bentley with a knife and a knuckleduster which Craig had given him. The police were called and a posse of men was sent to apprehend them. Seeing the policemen coming, the boys retreated to the roof. The police followed. The passive Bentley offered no resistance and was taken into custody almost immediately. But Craig, full of hatred for other policemen on whose evidence his brother Niven had just been sent down for twelve years for armed robbery, shouted at them, 'Come on, you brave coppers', and began firing his gun. One shot slightly wounded one officer and another struck PC Sidney Miles between the eyes and killed him stone dead.

At his trial Craig claimed that his only object in firing was to frighten the police. This may well have been so, for to have killed PC Miles so cleanly and accurately would have required a prolonged and steady aim which in the darkness prevailing was clearly not feasible. Also, a ballistics expert testified that at the estimated range (39 feet) which separated Craig from Miles, the gun was so faulty that even in daylight accurate firing was not possible and any shot aimed straight would have gone several feet wide (Craig admitted having sawn a piece off the barrel). It was therefore a sheer fluke that poor Miles happened to be in the path of the bullet. None of this excused Craig in law, for he would have been deemed to know the likely consequences of what he was doing. Nor, according to the police, did he show the slightest remorse: when told of Miles's death he said that he 'wished he had done the fucking lot'.

Yet by far the most damaging evidence against the defendants was that provided by three of the police officers on the roof, Detective Sergeant Fairfax and PCs Harrison and McDonald, who agreed that, just before they heard the shot that had killed Miles, Bentley, who was now in custody, had called out 'Let him have it, Chris' – a phrase that came to be associated with the case ever afterwards and became the title of both a book and a film. The meaning of this has been debated ever since: most people, including the jury, assumed it was an invitation to Craig to open fire; apologists for the pair interpreted it as a plea to hand over the gun. Yet what is clear today, on a balance of probabilities – and maybe even beyond reasonable doubt – is that the words were never said. Craig's counsel, John Parris, called them 'an utter fabrication'.

In court each boy denied that they had ever been said, and while many observers may have thought, 'Well, they would, wouldn't they?' Craig was quite emphatic about it.

'Are you saying,' counsel asked, 'that you did not hear that ["Let him have it, Chris"]?'

Craig replied firmly, 'Bentley did not say it.'

'Three officers heard it in the darkness from different points of the compass. Are you saying he did not say it?'

'I am saying I did not hear it. And if they heard it they have better ears than mine.'

If it was only a matter of the denials of Craig and Bentley against the word of three police officers I would not be saying with such assurance that the phrase was never said. But there was a fourth police officer on the roof of the warehouse who was never called to testify. His name was Claude Pain, and he only came to public notice in 1989, nearly forty years after the case, when he was eighty. The man who accidentally found him was a teacher and writer called M. J. Trow, whose wife was taking driving lessons from Pain's son Ray, a qualified instructor. Ray told Trow that his father had participated in the action on the Croydon rooftop but had a different story to tell from those of his colleagues. Just how different Trow found out when he went to interview Pain. Although on the roof with the other three during the shooting, he was not invited to join them as a prosecution witness. This was because neither in his notebook nor in his deposition for the trial had he said anything about Bentley shouting 'Let him have it, Chris', as the others had done. Yet he was only a few feet away from Miles when he fell dead, and subsequently helped carry his body to the ground. 'I did not hear Bentley shout those words,' he told Trow. 'If he had said them, I would have heard them. He did not say them.' Pain added that his conscience had been troubling him because he had not spoken up publicly before.

So if, as I believe, Craig, Bentley and Pain were right in their denials that Bentley had said the fatal words and Fairfax, Harrison and McDonald wrong, one has to ask how this came about. One does not have to imagine that when the three officers sat down together to prepare their depositions and discuss the evidence they would give, they consciously and deliberately agreed to put into Bentley's mouth words they knew he had never said. It does not happen like that. More likely, in my view, one of the officers remembered the words said to have been uttered in the Appleby Case of 1940, in which two men had also been accused of the murder of a police officer. This officer, having just been shot, said he had heard Appleby shout to his accomplice before he fired, 'Let him have it.' Probably, therefore, one of the three officers on the roof, without mentioning the Appleby Case, had said to the others something like, 'Am I imagining this, or did I hear Bentley shout just before Craig fired, "Let him have it"?' And the other two, perhaps grateful for the lead, and such being the power of self-delusion, would have agreed that, Yes, now they cast their minds back, they were sure Bentley had said something of the sort. Let us not forget that the death of their much loved and respected colleague Sidney Miles had traumatised them (the shot that had hit him could equally well have hit one of them). Deep in the unconscious they wanted a life for a life if it could not be extracted from the defendant who had killed Miles because he was under the age of criminal responsibility, then his partner in crime would do just as well.

But, as I wrote in the introduction to the book that Trow subsequently published,[1] Pain could not be of their number. Yet he had felt the death of Miles no less than the others and there could be no question of his disassociating himself from their evidence. He knew that if he did, he would become a pariah in the Force. Pain had only two years to go until he retired and, as he told Trow, 'Some very funny things were going on in those days, Mr Trow. I could be hit by a car or anything.' For their part, his colleagues denied that there had been any other officer on the roof with them. Pain was thus airbrushed out of history, and after the trial his notebook and deposition 'disappeared'.

There are two other reasons why it is unlikely that Bentley said, 'Let

---

1   *Let Him Have It, Chris* (London: Constable, 1990).

him have it, Chris.' He was a follower not a leader, and to have urged Craig to open fire on the officers while he was under arrest would have been quite out of character. And nobody ever heard him address Craig as anything other than 'kid' or 'kiddo'.[2]

If the pair had been hoping for a fair trial, they were to be grievously disappointed. The trial judge was the Lord Chief Justice, Rayner Goddard. While most High Court judges are men and women of learning, understanding, good manners and good sense, Rayner Goddard was the great exception – one of the most unsavoury characters ever to mount the English Bench, a bully and a sexual deviant. At Marlborough College, says one of his biographers, it was the custom for new boys to do a turn for the rest of the dormitory, sing a song or recite a piece of poetry or prose. Goddard, aged twelve or thirteen, gave them the death sentence ('… taken thence to a place of execution and there hanged by the neck until you are dead. And may God have mercy on your soul').

I met the old bruiser once, when he was already Lord Chief Justice, at a small dinner party given by the historian Arthur Bryant and his wife Anne at which, apart from my wife and myself, Goddard was the only guest. I much looked forward to the occasion, being then quite ignorant of his character, and hoping to be entertained by some gems of judicial wisdom and wit. Disappointingly, and despite being in mixed company, he regaled us over dinner with a succession of embarrassingly unfunny risqué stories, then, pleading work commitments, departed.

After Goddard's death his clerk, Arthur Smith, told John Parris (Craig's counsel) that on the last day of a murder trial he would bring a fresh pair of trousers to the robing room, as Goddard was in the habit of ejaculating into his current pair when sentencing a prisoner to death.[3]

---

2   Which means that if Bentley did say the words, it is just a coincidence that in the only two twentieth-century cases where two men were accused of the murder of a policeman, Appleby and Bentley uttered exactly the same phrase. At Bentley's trial PC McDonald tried to salve his conscience by agreeing that, although he had heard the phrase being said, he was not sure who had said it.
3   See John Parris, *Scapegoat* (London: Duckworth, 1991).

While not wishing to linger on the mechanics of this, I have to say I find it hard to believe that at his age his ejaculation was spontaneous and can only conclude that, with the bench protecting his lower half from the eyes of the court, he did his business unseen, a repetition perhaps of nights in the dorm at Marlborough, an affirmation of life in the dispensation of death.

A lifelong believer that violent crimes should be met with violent punishments, Goddard, who was a firm advocate of the rope (for women as well as men) and the lash,[4] told the House of Lords that in his view 'murderers should be destroyed'. On being informed that a man found guilty of murder had been declared insane, he pronounced that he thought it 'quite proper' that he should be hanged. Another time, when two delinquent brothers were up before him, he commented that what they needed was 'a good larruping'. 'What they want is to have someone who would give them a thundering good beating and then perhaps they would not do it again. I suppose they were brought up to be treated like little darlings and tucked up in bed at night.' It then transpired that their father, who was even more brutal than Goddard, had beaten them almost every night and that this was a cause of their delinquency, not an effect.

To say that Goddard had it in for Craig and Bentley at their trial is not to exaggerate. Long after the event a young lawyer called Anthony Samuelson, who had been present throughout, wrote, 'The thing that stuck in my craw and has stayed there for two decades was the injudicial and partisan manner in which Goddard said what he said.' One example he gave was the meal that Goddard made of the knuckleduster

---

4   'The Lord Chief Justice,' the Bishop of Stepney, Dr Joost de Blank, once told an audience of girls at Queen's College, Marylebone, 'has been canvasing for the powers to order flogging as enthusiastically as any usher at a Victorian charity school.'

Craig had given Bentley, which had been found in his pocket but which he had never used and most likely would not have known how to use. The knuckleduster was a court exhibit and in the course of his summing-up Goddard called for it to be handed to him. 'Have you ever seen a more horrible sort of weapon?' he asked the jury. 'You know, this is to hit a person in the face with who comes at you.' He tried to fit it on to his hand. 'You grasp it here, your fingers go through – I cannot quite get mine through – and you have got a dreadful heavy steel bar to strike anybody with; and you can kill a person with this, of course.'

Then he fingered a spike attached to the knuckleduster. 'Did you ever see a more shocking thing than this? You have got a spike with which you can jab anybody who comes at you: if the blow with the steel is not enough, you have got this spike at the side to jab.'

Next he called for Craig's sheath knife.

'One wonders really what parents can be about these days, allowing a boy of sixteen to have a weapon like this. Where is that other knife [the one found on Bentley]? You can feel it, sharp and pointed. What is he carrying that with him for in his coat, not even with a sheath on it?'

And then he came to the crucial evidence about 'Let him have it' which both the accused denied had been said but which three police officers were sure had been said.

'Are you going to say they [the police] were conspicuous liars? Because if their evidence is untrue, these three officers are doing their best to swear away the life of that boy. Do you believe that those three officers have come into the box and sworn what is deliberately untrue – those three officers who on that night showed a devotion to duty for which they are entitled to the thanks of the community?'

In my view, the short and regrettable answer is that, on the balance of probabilities, the three officers in question – Fairfax, Harrison and McDonald – did lie, although by this time they may well have deluded themselves into thinking that they truly had heard those words spoken (they had to believe it to maintain their self-respect) and there was no likelihood of the jury doubting them. Perhaps if Goddard had also said to the jury something like, 'But the two defendants both deny the words were said, one of them, Craig, quite emphatically you may think, and you have got to bear that in mind', as he should have done, it could have made a difference. But I doubt it. As the barrister H. Montgomery Hyde, editor of the authorised account of the trial,[5] wrote, 'In those days no jury could be persuaded to believe that responsible officers and especially those facing death, would deliberately fabricate evidence in a capital trial.'

The jury returned the only verdicts they felt they could: both boys guilty of murder, although with a recommendation of mercy for Bentley. Then Goddard sentenced Bentley to death and for Craig to be detained at Her Majesty's pleasure.

At the appeal hearing Bentley's counsel made two good points in his favour: Bentley's denial of police evidence that, in the car going to the police station, he had said, 'I knew he had a gun but I didn't think he'd use it'; and his further denial that in a statement he had said, 'I didn't know he was going to use the gun'. Counsel complained that Goddard had not put these denials to the jury. Counsel for the Crown riposted that on one point or another Bentley was asserting that three police officers had lied, which was probably truer than he knew. But not to the three judges of the Appeal Court: the appeal was dismissed.

Bentley's only hope now of avoiding execution lay with the Home Secretary, Sir David Maxwell Fyfe, a Scot whose arrogance matched his ignorance. Before Timothy Evans, who was hanged in 1950 for the murder of his wife and baby daughter (see chapter 2) was finally cleared and granted a posthumous free pardon, Maxwell Fyfe told the House of Commons, 'There is no possibility of an innocent man being hanged in this country and anyone who thinks there is is living in a world of fantasy.' Another time he said of High Court judges that, so long as they refrained from giving their views from the Bench on anything other than legal matters, their reputation for wisdom and impartiality would

---

5   *Trial of Christopher Craig and Derek William Bentley* (Notable British Trials
     series, London: William Hodge, 1954).

remain unsullied – which some thought was pushing it a bit. The Bar had a jingle about him: 'The nearest thing to death in life/Is David Patrick Maxwell Fyfe.'

It was not, however, Maxwell Fyfe who was near to death, but the wretched Bentley; and two days before the day scheduled for his execution, the Home Secretary announced there would be no reprieve. Without 'Let him have it' there almost certainly would have been. To many people in the country the news came as a shock. Public opinion, which had been horrified and angered by the murder of PC Miles, now felt that it was against natural justice that, while the principal offender would escape the full rigours of the law, his much less guilty accomplice, recommended by the jury to mercy, would have to pay with his life. There were petitions to the Queen and the Prime Minister, marches in the streets and an outcry in Parliament. Frustrated by the Speaker on a point of order that the forthcoming execution could not be debated until after it had taken place, many MPs found their views voiced by a Labour member and QC, Reginald Paget. 'A three-quarter-witted boy is to be hung for a murder which he did not commit and which was committed fifteen minutes after he was arrested. Can we be made to keep silence when a thing as horrible and shocking as this is happening?' Even Goddard was said to have expressed surprise that the jury's recommendation to mercy had not been exercised; while my wife and I were so disturbed that we sent a telegram to Maxwell Fyfe (as I found out later thousands of others had done), begging him to reconsider. But he was immune to all pleas; and at eight in the morning two days later, on 28 January 1953 at Wandsworth prison, Bentley was pinioned, hooded and placed on the trap. Did those brave men Fairfax, Harrison and McDonald have any qualms when they heard the news, one wonders? I doubt it. They, in their own way, had become immune, too – victims of massive self-delusion.

In due course the body of Bentley was cut down from the rope that had broken his neck and buried in quicklime in the prison's precincts. But the case did not end there. Too many of us felt with passion that Bentley had suffered a grave injustice, and that something must still be done by way of protest against it. I wrote a play called *Murder Story*, in which the principal character was loosely based on Bentley. Its object was to show that such a youth, immature and illiterate, was yet capable of redemption. In several scenes in the condemned cell, with the help of the prison chaplain and prison officers, he learns the rudiments of reading and writing and discovers his potential as a human being; yet at that moment of self-discovery and self-awareness his life is ended. The play ran briefly in the West End, had a successful provincial tour, and was later adapted for television. Later still, in 1991, an admirable feature film (called, what else? *Let Him Have It*) was made on the case and well reviewed.

But the most tireless and in the end most effective campaigner to have the case reconsidered was Bentley's sister, Iris. As a result of her efforts, supported by many, the case was seldom out of the news, and she achieved a partial victory in 1992 when, after a successful petition for a judicial review, three Appeal Court judges ruled that another Home Secretary, Kenneth Clarke, had been wrong in law not to grant Iris's solicitor, Benedict Birnberg, a request either for a free pardon or a public inquiry: 'There is a compelling argument that even by the standards of 1953, the then Home Secretary's decision to allow the hanging to go ahead was clearly wrong ... It should now be possible to devise some formula which would amount to a clear acknowledgement that an injustice was done'; and they invited the new Home Secretary, Michael Howard, to consider the possibility of a Royal Pardon. Howard, known for his right-wing views, could not bring himself to recommend a full Royal Pardon, but a limited one based on sentence and not on the verdict, which he believed in law had been correct. This was not good enough for Iris and Mr Birnberg, who sent all the papers on the case to the newly established Criminal Cases Review Commission.[6] Sadly, Iris Bentley died of cancer before the commission could

---

6   A body long and unsuccessfully campaigned for by Labour MPs, but finally
    established on the recommendation of the Runciman Commission on Criminal
    Justice.

announce its findings, but her daughter, Maria, Bentley's niece, took her place as petitioner, and a final victory for the family came when Lord Bingham, the new Lord Chief Justice, announced in July 1998 what many of us already believed, that Goddard's summing-up had denied Bentley a fair trial and therefore his conviction of forty-five years must be quashed. So far as is known, this was the only case where a court presided over by one Lord Chief Justice had overturned the verdict of a court presided over by another.[7]

---

7   Craig served 10 years in prison, had no further convictions, and subsequently became a plumber.

2

EVANS AND CHRISTIE
1949–66

The year after my play *Murder Story* appeared in the West End, a slim volume with the title *The Man on Your Conscience* written by Michael Eddowes, a London solicitor, arrived on the desk of George Scott, editor of the weekly magazine *Truth*. George and I had shared David Cecil's English literature tutorials at Oxford after the war and he had also been a member of a dining club I had founded, the Oxford University Writers Club. The theme of Eddowes's book was that another illiterate young man, Timothy Evans, had been wrongly hanged for the murder of his baby daughter Geraldine at an address in the Notting Hill area of London, 10 Rillington Place. Casting round for someone to notice the book, George Scott thought of *Murder Story* and sent it to me. Although the book was only some hundred pages long, Eddowes was not a natural writer, and I had to read it three times to understand it fully. My review, which appeared in the *Spectator*, ended with these words: 'I believe – and will continue to believe until I die – that on March 9th 1950 we hanged an innocent man'; and I resolved then to put aside time to write a definitive book on the case.

Now the story is so well known that there is no need to relate it in detail, but the main facts are these. Ten Rillington Place was the last in a double row of run-down houses in a Notting Hill cul-de-sac which no longer exists. They were quite small, almost miniature houses, yet built on three floors. At the material time the ground floor flat consisted of a front sitting-room, back bedroom, kitchen, outside lavatory (shared by all three tenants) and adjoining wash-house. Its occupants were John Reginald Halliday Christie and his wife Ethel. The middle floor flat was temporarily empty, its tenant, a retired railwayman named Kitchener, having gone into hospital; and in 1948 Timothy Evans, a 24-year-old illiterate Roman Catholic Welsh van driver, moved into the top floor flat with his pregnant wife Beryl.

If it was police corruption of one sort – telling lies in their depositions and in the witness box – that had led to the execution of Derek Bentley, it was that of another sort – browbeating suspects into agreeing to sign bogus 'confessions' – that was directly responsible for the execution of Timothy Evans. On the night of 2 December 1949 Evans, already a suspect in the murder of his wife and daughter, arrived from Wales at Notting Hill police station to be interrogated by Detective Inspector Jennings and Inspector Black. The interrogation, which began soon after his arrival at about 10 p.m., went on for most of the night. A *News Chronicle* reporter rang the station at 3 a.m. to get an update and was told that questioning was still going on; a headline in the following day's *Evening Standard* read MAN ALL NIGHT WITH POLICE and Evans later told his mother that the interrogation did not finish until after 5 a.m. By that time he was ready to put his signature (the only words he knew how to write) to two 'confessions' dictated to him by the policemen.

Today we know that Evans did not murder his wife and child and that his fellow lodger Christie did. At that time Christie was forty years old, bald and bespectacled, a man whose life so far had been something of a failure. He had earned a living mostly as a clerk, but had also acquired a minor criminal record: stealing postal orders when employed by the Post Office and a car from a Roman Catholic priest who had befriended him; hitting a prostitute with whom he had been living over the head with her son's cricket bat, which earned him six months' hard labour. His only moment of glory had come when in 1939, despite his record, he had managed to con the Metropolitan Police into accepting him as a War Reserve Special Constable as which – a nice touch – he had received two commendations for work on crime. He and his wife Ethel, by all accounts a docile, colourless creature, had lived at 10 Rillington Place since 1938.

Christie was also a sexual inadequate, having suffered all his life from impotence (as a young man, according to the evidence of a girl he had failed to satisfy, his contemporaries had taunted him with cries of 'Reggie-no-dick'); in the summer of 1943, the frustrations and resentments of his need for women, coupled with his inability to satisfy either himself or them reached a sort of climacteric. On the beat as a Special Constable he met a pretty 21-year-old Austrian girl, Ruth Fuerst, a part-time prostitute; he invited her to Rillington Place while his wife was away in Sheffield, attempted to have intercourse with her (and probably failed) and, in the course of it, strangled her. Later he dumped her body temporarily in his wash-house, then buried her at night in the piece of wilderness outside the back door that he euphemistically called the garden. The following year Christie gave a repeat performance with a 31-year-old work colleague, by the name of Muriel Eady, described as short and stout, whose body he also dumped temporarily in the wash-house, then buried alongside that of Fuerst. On both occasions, he said, just looking at their dead, naked bodies gave him a strange, peaceful thrill. Months later, the skull of one of them worked loose from the soil and Christie dumped it in the ruins of a house destroyed in the Blitz where it was found and judged by the local coroner to have belonged to a casualty of war.

The arrival in 1948 of attractive 19-year-old Beryl Evans again aroused in Christie his old murderous sexual yearnings, and he waited for an opportunity to satisfy them. He had to wait a long time, for first

Beryl had to go into hospital to give birth to her daughter, Geraldine. A couple of months later, she found she was pregnant again, and told her husband in no uncertain terms that to look after another baby in their cramped, two-room flat was not on. She began douching herself and taking pills in order to bring about a miscarriage. She talked about her situation to Mrs Christie, who in turn told her husband, who must have realised with mounting excitement that his long-awaited opportunity had finally come. Christie tackled Evans head on, showed him his St John's Ambulance book with its pictures of parts of the body, told him he had trained as a doctor before the war but had had to give it up because of an accident, said he had helped to abort a number of women in the past, and if only Evans had come to him in the first place there would have been no problem. There was not a word of truth in any of it, but poor gullible little Evans believed him and so did Beryl; an assignation was made for Christie to abort her one morning after Evans had gone to work. Anticipating what he knew to be the inevitable, Christie warned Evans that with the stuff he used one out of ten would die of it. Evans asked Christie how exactly he did an abortion, but Christie, having no idea, 'would not say'.

When Evans came home that evening, he was greeted by Christie with the statement, 'It's bad news. It didn't work.' Evans asked Christie where Beryl's body was, and Christie said in the bedroom. 'So I went in the bedroom. I looked at my wife and saw that she was covered over with the eiderdown. I pulled the eiderdown back to have a look at her. I could see that she was dead and that she had been bleeding from the mouth and nose and that she had been bleeding from the bottom part.'

In admitting to the crime three years later, this is one of several statements that Christie made about it:

She brought the quilt from the front room and put it down in front of the fireplace (in the kitchen). She lay on the quilt, she was fully dressed. I got on my knees and found I was not physically capable of having intercourse. I turned the gas tap on, and as near as I can

make out I held it close to her face. When she became unconscious,
I turned the tap off. I was going to try again to have intercourse
with her but it was impossible. I think that's when I strangled her
… I then left her where she was and went downstairs.

In the interval between killing Beryl and writing the above Christie seems to have quite forgotten the reason for his visiting her – the promised abortion. Nor does he mention the matter of the blood on her face or on the 'bottom part', or the piece of tubing he must have attached to the gas tap. Everything must be speculation now, but my guess is that to convey verisimilitude he probably inserted some blunt instrument like the end of a spoon into Beryl's vagina.[1] Then, having attached a piece of rubber tubing (which he had already used on Muriel Eady), he turned on the gas ('Just a whiff to make you comfortable, my dear') so that Beryl became panic-stricken and struggled, but Christie, not to be denied another victim, began hitting her savagely about the face, drawing blood which he may even have smeared blood on to her bottom part to convince Evans that he had at least attempted an abortion.

What to do now? What was to happen to Beryl's body and who would look after little Geraldine? Christie told Evans he would dispose of Beryl's body down one of the drains. When Evans said he thought that a foolish idea, Christie replied that it was the only thing to do to avoid getting into trouble with the police: Evans would be in trouble, too, he added, as he had given his consent. As for the baby, he said, he knew of a couple in East Acton who would be happy to adopt her. A day or two later, when Evans returned from work, Christie told him that the couple from East Acton had collected Geraldine that morning, and that he had put Beryl's body down one of the drains.

---

1   Dr Teare, the pathologist, found bruising in the wall of Beryl's vagina. In my book I said that if he had taken a swab from there, he would probably have found traces of Christie's sperm. I now think this unlikely.

The following day Evans went to his employers to collect his week's wages; they gave him the money but also, in view of his slackness and lateness, the sack. This suited Christie admirably. 'Now the best thing you can do is to sell your furniture and get out of London,' he told Evans. And soon after that Christie's friend, Mr Hookway, took his van to Rillington Place to collect Evans's furniture and give him £40 for it. Then Evans, having cut up Beryl's clothes and given them to a ragman, caught the overnight train to Cardiff, and from there made his way to Merthyr Tydfil, to the home of his uncle and aunt, Jack and Violet Lynch.

For Evans to have fallen in so readily with Christie's suggestions may seem strange, but one has to remember that Christie was old enough to be Evans's father, was educated where Evans was illiterate, and for the younger man carried all the authority of a former policeman. No wonder that Christie once said, 'I could make Evans do or say anything I wanted.' And what he wanted, and was granted, was that Evans should be convicted and punished for the crimes that he himself had committed.

Before leaving London, Evans had told his mother and sisters that Beryl and Geraldine had gone to stay with her father in Brighton, but to the Lynches he spun two different tales: first, that they had gone to Bristol; later that his wife was going to have a baby by another man and he never wished to see her again. But for most of the time in Merthyr Tydfil his thoughts were centred more on the living than on the dead. He spoke often to the Lynches about Geraldine, what a smasher she was and how much he loved her, and that when they saw her, they would, too. Yet to himself he worried about her, how she was faring with the people in East Acton and whether they were giving her the right things to eat. There was only one way to find out – return to London and ask Christie. At Rillington Place Christie answered the bell and, in reply to Evans's inquiries, said gruffly that Geraldine was all right but needed time to settle in, which wouldn't be for another two or three weeks. Evans returned to Merthyr Tydfil.

Here he was confronted by his aunt, who had received a letter from his mother and another from his sister Maureen saying that he had been telling lies about the whereabouts of Beryl and Geraldine. To this Evans said it was his mother and Maureen who were telling lies, which he knew in his heart could not be true. But he also knew he had reached the end of the road and must seek help elsewhere. So he took himself to the local police station and made a foolish statement: that a man in a transport café had given him some pills to bring about an abortion, that Beryl had taken them when he went to work, and that when he had returned in the evening he had found her dead. Asked what then happened to her, and remembering what Christie had told him, he said that he had put her body down a drain.

The statement is remarkable in that Evans makes no mention at all of Christie (of whom he stood in great fear), in the vain hope that he would not incriminate him. The Merthyr police telephoned the Notting Hill police, who searched the Rillington Place drain but found nothing. To the Merthyr police officer's remark that he doubted if Beryl's body had ever been in the drain, Evans replied, 'No, I said that to protect a man called Christie. I'll tell you the truth now.' Then Evans made a second statement recounting the events as they have been recounted here and which formed the basis for the defence at his trial.

Meanwhile, the Notting Hill police did three things: they sent two officers to Merthyr to bring Evans back to London; they made a thorough search of 10 Rillington Place; and they interrogated Christie at the police station. This last gave Christie the opportunity to tie another noose round Evans's neck. For he lost no time in telling the officers interrogating him of his own police service (no doubt including his two commendations), so that from the start he was one of them, psychologically committed to believing him:

'At no time have I assisted or attempted to abort Mrs Evans or any other woman ... I cannot understand why Evans should make any accusations against me, as I have been very good to him in lots of ways.'

And how did Evans and his wife get on?

'Very badly. They were always rowing. Mrs Evans has told my wife on more than one occasion that he assaulted her and grabbed hold of her throat. She said he had a violent temper and one time would do her in.'

Anything else?

'It is very well known locally that he is a liar and my wife and I have expressed the opinion that he is a bit mental.'

The damning words were taken down, and Christie must have walked home with a lighter step. At the outset he had succeeded in putting himself among the hunters and not, as he had feared, the hunted.

On his arrival at Notting Hill police station Evans was taken to the charge room, where Detective Inspector Jennings and Inspector Black were waiting for him. Beside Evans's chair were two piles of clothing. One pile he recognised as Beryl's; on top of it was a blanket, a tablecloth and a length of rope. The other pile, which Evans looked at with horror, belonged to Geraldine, on top of which lay a tie, tightly knotted. While Evans was taking in what he saw, appalled, he heard the voice of Jennings say to him:

'At 11.50 today I found the dead body of your wife Beryl Evans, concealed in a wash-house at 10 Rillington Place, Notting Hill, also the body of your daughter Geraldine, concealed behind some timber in the same outbuilding, and this clothing was found on them.'

Until then Evans had shown no reaction to what was being said, but now the tears came into his eyes and he picked up the tie, quite unable to believe what he had heard and seen. The voice of Jennings droned on:

'Later today I was at Kensington mortuary when it was established that the cause of death was strangulation in both cases.'

Then came the final body blow.

'I have reason to believe that you were responsible for their deaths.'

As I wrote in the original edition of the book I was to write on the case, *10 Rillington Place*, in that moment it must have seemed to Evans that the whole world was conspiring against him, and that he himself was going off his head. Who? Why? Where? Why on earth should anyone want to strangle Beryl and Geraldine? The only person who *could have done* was Christie but *why should he want to?* For nearly two years Evans had thought of Christie as a respectable former police officer and for the last three weeks as a man who had tried to help his wife out of a difficulty but had failed. Now he was being asked to throw out this image for one of a madman who pointlessly strangled people. However, it was not Christie who was being charged with murder, but himself – and not only with the murder of his wife but also that of his baby daughter, whom he loved more than anyone else in the world. In a flash he must have realised the madness of his actions of the past three weeks – the selling of his furniture and shredding of his wife's clothes, the lies to his mother, sisters and Mrs Christie about Beryl's whereabouts, the running-away to Wales and further lies to the Lynches and the Merthyr police. Even if he stuck to the truth now, who would believe him?

Certainly not Detective Inspector Jennings and Inspector Black, who had not the smallest doubt in their minds that they had found the man they were looking for. Yet, before the night was out, they were to prove themselves in their own authoritarian way as fluent liars as Christie. They knew, as every police officer knows and is trained to know, that however obvious a defendant's guilt is to them, it must be equally obvious to the jury; and that however strong the factual evidence may be, the strongest evidence of all is the defendant's own confession. As one of the greatest judges of the twentieth century, the late Lord Devlin, put it: 'The high degree of proof which the English law requires often could not be achieved without the assistance of the accused's own statement.'

No one knew of the importance of this more than Jennings and Black. According to them Evans made two statements in the course of the night. The first, which they claimed gushed out of Evans within minutes of his arrival, was quite brief:

*She was incurring one debt after another and I could not stand it
any longer, so I strangled her with a piece of rope and took her
down to the flat below the same night whilst the old man*

[Kitchener] was in hospital. I waited till the Christies downstairs had gone to bed, then I took her to the wash-house after midnight. This was on Tuesday the 8th November. On Thursday evening after I came home from work, I strangled my baby in our bedroom with my tie and later that night I took her down into the wash-house after the Christies had gone to bed. (Signed T. J. Evans, 9.55 p.m., 2.12.49)

On any level this reads unconvincingly: the *non sequitur* of the open-ing sentence ('she was incurring one debt after another … so I stran-gled her', the words 'incurring' and 'whilst', which smack of police phraseology and were almost certainly outside Evans's vocabulary; the hard fact that he could not have put any bodies in the wash-house on 8 or 10 November because, as I proved in the original edition of my book, there were workmen in and out of the wash-house every day of that week until 11 November (the time sheet of one of the workmen that would prove it, the police conveniently 'lost' – the only one missing in a five-year period from the firm's files). Furthermore, although Evans's signature and the time and date at the end of the statement were in Evans's own hand, his family said he had only the haziest notion about numbers (for instance, he thought that eighteen hundred was *less* than a thousand) and to have written '9.55 p.m., 2.12.49' without help would have been beyond him. It was not, however, beyond Mr Black, who had recorded in his notebook the same arrangement of numbers and fig-ures to denote the time the statement was started: '9.45 p.m., 2.12.49.' The conclusion therefore must be that Evans wrote down the time and date at the end of the statement with Mr Black's help and at his dicta-tion.

Yet, apart from the proven falsity of the details, the statement is unbelievable on other grounds. Black and Jennings declared that it was made within a few minutes of Evans's arrival – that is, immediately after he had heard for the first time that his wife, whom he thought had died from a botched abortion, had been strangled and that his much-loved daughter, whom he thought was alive and well in East Acton, had been strangled, too; which told him that the murderer must have been Christie. With all this on his mind, it is inconceivable that at that moment he would have volunteered responsibility for Beryl's and Geraldine's deaths.

Yet when doubts were raised about the two statements in the House of Commons, that prize ass Maxwell Fyfe, still Home Secretary, assured members that they had been made *voluntarily, spontaneously and without any preliminary questioning.* In those days people were prepared to believe such lies, but after the string of miscarriages of justice that have occurred since, it is now generally accepted that pretty well all statements given to the police (even those concerning minor matters like car accidents and thefts – and especially those of admissions of wrongdoing) are the result of questions and answers; without them, most suspects being uneducated and inarticulate, meaningful statements would rarely get made at all.

The same criticisms as I made of the first statement can be made of the much longer second statement. For instance, phraseology such as 'No fixed abode', 'under false pretences', 'squandering the money', 'signed for in a receipt book', 'which I counted in his presence', 'made my way' must have been outwith Evans's vocabulary and also smack of police jargon. Twice in this statement he claims that he locked the wash-house door to give the impression that he was concealing something, unaware that the wash-house door did not lock. It is also astonishing that in his admission to the death of Geraldine Evans says, 'I then went home, picked up my baby from her cot in the bedroom, picked up my tie and strangled her with it' – he gives no reason for his actions, not even that the presence of the baby might lead to questions about the whereabouts of her mother. Presumably neither he nor Jennings and Black could think of an explanation for anything so implausible.

But the fundamental falsity of the statement lies with the time Jennings and Black said it had taken. Evans's second, truthful, statement to the Merthyr police took two hours and forty minutes to record. The second Notting Hill statement was longer, yet Jennings and Black would have us believe that it took only seventy-five minutes – which is plainly an impossibility.

In the original edition of my book I said there had never been any suggestion that Jennings and Black had done anything improper, and that there was none now. Today (2002) I wish to withdraw that remark. I wrote that then because at the time there was a general belief in police incorruptibility and, had I challenged it openly, I would have been served, probably successfully, with a writ for libel – my word against that of Jennings and Black (at least until Christie himself was arraigned for murder three years later). Also, false confessions being then such a novelty to the public, I felt the need to devote eleven pages to explaining how they came to be made by referring to the brainwashing techniques used by the Chinese Communists. There would be no need for that today.

What I believe happened in the course of that long night at Notting Hill police station is that the police gradually wore Evans down into a state of submission. There is no evidence that he was offered any refreshment during the five-hour train journey from Cardiff to Paddington, nor during the seven hours of interrogation that followed, and by the time his ordeal ended at 5 a.m. with him saying, in the classic false confessional mode, 'It's a great relief to get it off my chest. I feel better already', he must have been totally exhausted. As to why Evans eventually caved in, he said at his trial that he believed the police would beat him up if he did not confess – which he would have had no reason to say unless Jennings, whom he greatly feared, had threatened him with it. He also said, when told that his daughter was dead, that he felt he had nothing left to live for.

Having obtained at around 5 a.m. the admissions they had been seeking all night (why else would they have prolonged the questioning?) the two officers, in order to prove that Evans could hardly wait to admit his guilt, backdated both the first statement, recording that it started at 9.45 p.m. and ended at 9.55 p.m., and the second, saying that it started at 10 p.m. and ended at 11.15 p.m.

In condemning Jennings and Black unreservedly for these malpractices, I think it only fair to allow them mitigating circumstances. Let us not forget that only that morning they had seen with their own eyes the dead bodies of both Beryl, corded up in a tablecloth and blanket, and poor little Geraldine, the tie that had strangled her still around her neck. It must have been a sickening sight, and they would have been less than human if they had not felt not only disgust and anger towards the perpetrator of such a double crime but also a burning desire to bring him to justice. And in their view, which I submit would have been the same as most of us, it was as clear as crystal that the only credible perpetrator was Timothy John Evans.

To quote Devlin again: 'The fault to be looked for today is not the frame-up but the tendency to press too hard against a man believed to be guilty.' 'It is', he wrote, 'a very understandable fault' – and he goes on to say that it is not corruption or the desire to pervert justice that makes the police less fair and dispassionate than they ought to be, but 'honest indignation such as the ordinary citizen himself experiences if he is brought into contact with some pestilential crime in which the inno-cent child or the poor man is maltreated or defrauded'.

Yet the fact remains that Jennings and Black did pervert the course of justice, and in a just world they should have been held to account for it. Evans's counsel at his trial, Malcolm Morris, put up a brilliant defence, but not even he could wipe from the jury's mind the ever-present stain of the two 'confessions'. The jury took only forty-five min-utes to find Evans guilty. Mr Morris might have had more success had he analysed the two confessions, as I have done, shown them to be false in detail, cross-examined Black and Jennings on the contradiction between the interrogation going on all night yet the confessions allegedly ending by 11.15 p.m. and asked them to square the fact that while the second Notting Hill confession was 150 words longer than the second, truthful, Merthyr one, it had taken less than half the time to record. But, as I have already said and before long will have to say again, in those days it was considered not only bad form but counterproduc-tive to question the integrity of the police; they were seen to be, as they still largely are, our guardians and protectors against crime, revolution and anarchy. That could be one reason why Mr Morris did not raise the matter. Another could be that it simply never occurred to him.

Leaving aside the confessions, how would Evans have otherwise fared? Mr Morris was in no doubt. Without the confessions, he told the jury in his closing speech, 'you would not convict Evans, you would not dream of it'. My own view is that a hung jury would have been more likely than an acquittal, but even that might not have resulted in renewed police inquiries about Christie.

So what is the protection against false confessions? In my view, all police investigations and interviews must be overseen by a qualified legal officer, similar to the examining magistrate used in many countries on the Continent. Lawyers have their faults but they are generally better educated and more neutrally inclined than police officers, and less vulnerable to corruption.

In the condemned cell at Pentonville prison Evans maintained his innocence until the very end. 'Says he hasn't done it', commented Father Francis, the Roman Catholic chaplain, adding, 'Seems to have convinced himself it was another man.' The resident physician, Dr Coates, reported, 'He sticks to the story of Christie. Does not tell clumsy lies otherwise.' When Evans was interviewed by the Statutory Medical Board to see if he was fit to hang and asked if there was anything further he wished to say, he replied, 'The police caught me for a statement when I was upset. The one thing that sticks in my mind is that I am in for something I haven't done.' As he left the room, he spoke with vehemence and emotion: 'I say Christie done it.'

When Evans's mother and sisters paid him their last visit, they seemed far more upset then he was. He repeated to them what he had already told a dozen other people, both at his trial and afterwards. His sister Eileen stayed behind a moment after his mother and other sister Maureen had left. 'Look, Tim,' she said, 'you've got nothing to lose now. Tell me the truth so that I can know. Did you do it?' Evans, who had never lied to Eileen, looked her straight in the eyes and said, 'No, Eileen,

I didn't do it. Christie done it.' Such was the force of the 'confession', even on her, that until that moment Eileen had not been sure whether he had done it or not. Now for the first time, as she told me, she knew with absolute certainty that he was innocent.

Christie, meanwhile, was finding his murderous desires were consuming him once again. But there was one stumbling block to his inviting any more women to his flat – his wife Ethel, who, like his teenage contemporaries long ago, had begun to taunt him about his impotence, and complained endlessly about the numbers of black people now inhabiting the other two flats. So early one morning in December 1952 Christie strangled his wife with one of her stockings and buried her beneath the front-room floorboards where he had once put Fuerst. Then, in quick succession, he lured three local prostitutes to the flat, strangled all three, hid their bodies in an alcove at the back of the kitchen and papered over the opening. After that Christie left the house and wandered about London for a week until a passing policeman spotted him leaning over Putney Bridge, unshaven, hungry and penniless. Meanwhile, the new tenant of Christie's flat had discovered the bodies in the alcove and another chapter in the history of 10 Rillington Place was revealed to an astonished world.

After Christie had been tried and convicted in July 1953, a question mark arose in the minds of many. Was it possible that there had been *two* stranglers of women living at 10 Rillington Place? The clamour was such that the Home Secretary (still Maxwell Fyfe) announced that he had appointed the Recorder of Portsmouth, John Scott Henderson, QC, to conduct a private inquiry into the matter and report his findings before the date set for Christie's execution, only nine days away – a virtually impossible task. However, Scott Henderson completed his inquiry in the time allotted and, being one of those lawyers to whom the very idea of British justice miscarrying is anathema, concluded both in his main report and a supplementary one that there *were* two stranglers living in Rillington Place.

In the House of Commons Sidney Silverman, MP, called the report not just mistaken but dishonest. Even more effective was the ridicule that another Member, Geoffrey Byng, QC, heaped upon it. If Evans was guilty, he said, his guilt depended on not one but two quite fantastic coincidences: that in this one small house in London the only two male occupants were both murdering women in almost exactly the same way, and each was doing so without the knowledge of the other. He might have added that both murdered only women, both murdered by strangling with a ligature, both murdered women without knickers on, both murdered women who were found wrapped in dark blankets, both had attempted intercourse with their victims around the time of death, both doubled up the bodies of their victims, both put the bodies of their victims (Fuerst, Eady, Beryl, Geraldine) in Christie's washhouse, both moved the bodies of their victims around the house, both sold their furniture to the same dealer before leaving, both kept newspaper cuttings of murder cases, both sold their dead wives' wedding rings. Furthermore, it was pure chance that Evans, unaware of Fuerst's and Eady's graves in the back garden, happened to cast the blame for the deaths of his wife and child on the one man in London who was murdering women in the same way he was.

Mr Byng's logic led him to one final, remorseless conclusion. If the remains of Fuerst and Eady had been found at the same time as those of Beryl and Geraldine – that is, after Evans had made his second, truthful Merthyr statement, but before the two Notting Hill 'confessions' – then Christie not Evans would have been arrested, tried and most probably hanged three years earlier and (he could have added) the lives of Ethel Christie and the three prostitutes in the alcove would have been saved. And if Christie had been apprehended in 1949, said Mr Byng, then the gospel according to Scott Henderson meant that Evans going free would have been a grave miscarriage of justice. But one doubts if Mr Scott Henderson had the imagination to see that.

My book on the case, which took me four years to research and write, was published in 1961. In it I included a letter to the then Conservative Home Secretary, R. A. Butler, in which I quoted the views of a number of eminent people who had all rejected Scott Henderson's findings and believed in Evans's innocence: among them, Lord Altrincham (the late John Grigg) and Ian Gilmour, MP, who had jointly written a pamphlet on the case; Michael Eddowes, author of *The Man on Your Conscience*; Dr William Sargant, author of *Battle for the Mind*, a definitive book on brainwashing; Dr J. A. Hobson, the psychiatrist who had examined Evans for the defence; Harry Proctor, the journalist who had helped Christie compile his memoirs for a Sunday paper; and last but not least, Chuter Ede, the Labour MP who as Home Secretary had written on Evans's papers, 'The Law must take its course' and now regretted it. I also mentioned new items of evidence favourable to Evans that had come to light and suggested that more might be found if another inquiry could be set up free of the time constraints imposed on Scott Henderson. 'Although,' I concluded, 'I myself am wholly convinced of Evans's innocence, I am not asking you to go as far as that: what I am asking is whether you are prepared to say *there can be no doubt of his guilt.* If you conclude, as I think you will, that there is doubt, consider-able doubt, reasonable doubt, will you please set the machinery in motion to set up a fresh inquiry to clear the matter up once and for all?'

I never received a reply to my letter or even an acknowledgement, but happily demands for a review of the case were already under way in Parliament. In June 1961, after my book was published, three former Labour ministers, Patrick Gordon Walker, Sir Frank Soskice, QC, and Chuter Ede, made passionate and powerful speeches demanding a new inquiry, the granting of a free pardon to Evans and the handing-over of his remains to his family for reburial in consecrated ground.

I had always thought R. A. Butler a rather flabby individual, and in his reply for the government he was at his flabbiest. He could not authorise the transfer of Evans's body, he said, because an Act of Parliament forbade it; he could not recommend a free pardon because there was no certainty of Evans's innocence; and he would not order a new inquiry because memories had become dimmed and no fresh evidence was likely to emerge. It was a contemptible performance.

The case remained dormant until 1964, when Labour again came to power and Frank Soskice became Home Secretary. Sincere though he had seemed to be in asking for a fresh inquiry in 1961, he was no less sincere than Butler in refusing one now. 'I really do not think that an inquiry would serve any useful purpose,' he said. 'Even if the innocence of Evans were established, I have no power to make an official declaration of it.' In 1961 he had called the case a nightmare, but what had troubled his mind in opposition had ceased to trouble it in office. His was an even more craven performance than Butler's.

But by now most people had taken about as much whitewash as they could stand, among them two men of courage and conviction who were living in Darlington. One was Herbert Wolfe, a German Jewish refugee who had come to this country in 1933, and the other his friend Harold Evans, editor of a local paper, the *Northern Echo*, and later editor of both *The Times* and the *Sunday Times*. Herbert Wolfe had read my book, believed passionately in Timothy Evans's innocence, and was outraged that nothing had been done to correct it. For him, a fugitive from German injustice, the integrity (as he believed) of British justice, which the natives seemed to take for granted, was infinitely precious, and Soskice's refusal to re-open the case was the last straw.

So he persuaded Harold Evans to publish an article on the case and, because Harold felt as passionately about it as he did, the *Northern Echo* mounted a campaign, publishing articles in the paper every week, getting them reprinted as broadsheets and sending them to every member of the House of Commons and to many of the Lords. That summer of 1962 all who had ever campaigned for Evans joined forces and formed the Timothy Evans Committee, and a group of us visited Rillington Place, inspected number 10 from top to bottom and were photographed on the pavement outside it. By July, 113 MPs had signed a motion asking for a new inquiry. Sir Frank, realising what he was up against, announced that there would be a fresh inquiry under the direction of a High Court judge, Sir Daniel Brabin.

Sir Daniel's inquiry sat for more than two months, accumulating a million words of evidence. Jennings and Black were among those who attended but at this remove I cannot recall their being asked to explain all the contradictions and discrepancies in the 'confessions'. My impression is that once again they went away without a stain on their characters.

In January 1966 Sir Daniel took away the million words to mull over and in October delivered his findings. These showed that, like Scott Henderson, he was a lawyer to whom the whole idea of British justice miscarrying was incomprehensible. For if Scott Henderson's findings had astonished by their effrontery, the Brabin report stunned by its absurdity. Whereas all those previously concerned with the case – the prosecution, the defence and the trial judge, the Court of Appeal, Scott Henderson, Michael Eddowes, F. Tennyson Jesse[2] and myself – were agreed that whoever had done one of the murders had done both, Brabin produced the novel idea that while Evans had probably *not* murdered the baby (for which he was hanged), he probably *had* murdered his wife (for which he had not even been tried!). This certainly was an arresting theory, especially as there was hardly a scrap of evidence to support it, and as good a rejoinder as I have seen to those who wish to substitute judges (who are often shaky on the facts) for juries. Having seen the pit that yawned in front of him, Sir Daniel had backed away. Perhaps he thought his findings would please everybody. Yes, we had done Tim Evans wrong, he appeared to say, but only on a legal technicality: the law could breathe again.

There were many lawyers and diehards who believed that such an inconclusive conclusion would obviate the need for anything further and that the whole affair would now be conveniently forgotten. On television Frank Soskice, now Lord Stow Hill, and Lord Dilhorne, a former

---

2   Editor, *Trials of Timothy John Evans and John Reginald Halliday Christie* (London: William Hodge, 1957).

Conservative Lord Chancellor (and in thickness of observation and judgement another Maxwell Fyfe), pooh-poohed the idea of anything else. Happily, the new Labour Home Secretary was made of grittier stuff. What Butler and Soskice said they were not empowered to do, Roy Jenkins did in an afternoon – what was quaintly called a posthumous free pardon, which the Queen immediately granted.

So at long last ended this sorry tale which was not only about a shocking miscarriage of justice but about the pusillanimity of those to whom a belief in the infallibility of the law is more important than a belief in its integrity, a tale about those who think that when a mistake is made, it is better to pretend it never happened than to have the strength of character to admit that the law, created by humans, is human, too.

3

TWO IMMORAL EARNINGS –
THE TRIAL OF STEPHEN WARD
1963

My book *The Trial of Stephen Ward* was originally published in 1964. It was republished in paperback in 1987, when the distinguished lawyer Lord Goodman said of it:

> *Ludovic Kennedy's powerful account of courtroom proceedings is even more shocking than when it first appeared in 1964. As the cast of motley characters parades before us, Kennedy's on-the-spot reactions show just how it was that the British legal system created in Stephen Ward an historic victim of an historic injustice.*

And Ward's junior counsel, David Tudor-Price, later a High Court judge, said that it had left him with a burning sense of injustice. This chapter, written nearly forty years after the conclusion of the trial, attempts to explain how that injustice came about, and why I, sensing something in the wind, applied for and was granted a press ticket to attend the proceedings.

Stephen Ward, a man of fifty at the time of the trial, was an artist and osteopath, whose patients included many rich and famous people. The son of an Anglican canon, he liked the company of peers and prostitutes, singly and together. He had been married briefly once, but his sex life had never been satisfactory and the older he grew the more dissolute he became. He was said to be very kind but rather mean. He had a plausible manner and great charm.

The story that eventually led to Ward's trial may be said to have started in 1956 when Lord Astor, a patient and friend since 1950, gave him the lease of a cottage in the grounds of his estate at Cliveden on the Thames. In July 1961 Lord Astor was entertaining a houseparty which included John Profumo, the Conservative MP and Minister for War, and his wife Valerie Hobson, the actress. Ward also had guests that weekend, among them Christine Keeler, aged 19, a night club hostess at the Cabaret Club who was now living (though not sleeping) with Ward at his flat in Wimpole Mews. That evening, Profumo met Keeler at the swimming pool, was attracted to her, telephoned her when he returned to London and began an affair with her. It was a brief liaison and not, one imagines, a particularly enriching one, yet it was to cost Profumo his career and Ward his life.

Christine told several people about the affair (it was, after all, quite a feather in her cap), which eventually came to the ears of press and Parliament; with the result that on 21 March 1963 an MP called George Wigg rose in the House to ask the Home Secretary either to deny the rumours circulating about a member of the government or else appoint a select committee to investigate them. Although Profumo had already assured the Attorney-General and Chief Whip that he had done nothing wrong, he made a personal statement to the House the next day to deny any impropriety between Keeler and himself, and threatened to issue writs if the rumours were repeated publicly.

His brazenness almost paid off. Two foreign magazines did print the rumours and Profumo successfully sued both. Ward and Keeler also publicly supported his statement to the House. And there the matter might have rested had not the government, irritated by the damage being done to it by the rumours and counter rumours coming so soon after the Vassall affair (in which a homosexual naval clerk at the British embassy in Moscow had been blackmailed by the Russians into revealing security secrets), decided to investigate the man they believed to be the cause of their discomfort. Was there, the Home Secretary inquired of the Metropolitan Commissioner of Police, any police interest in Ward? The Commissioner replied that there was not, although there might be if they could get the whole story, which he doubted. But he was happy to look into it, and on 1 April the police began to investigate Ward. From that moment, ironically, Profumo was doomed.

In the general run of criminal cases the investigations that led to Ward's trial were highly unusual, if not unique. In most cases a crime is committed, the police are informed of it and then, working backwards, seek to discover the criminal. In this case police proceedings had been activated not from below but from above, their investigations starting not after but before they were aware of any crime. Their efforts, therefore, were not directed towards finding out *whether* Ward had done something but *what* Ward had done; and to dish the dirt on him if at all possible.

The names of the investigators in the Ward case were Detective Chief Inspector Samuel Herbert and Detective Sergeant John Burrows. Their diligence knew no bounds; on their own admissions they interrogated *between 125 and 140 witnesses*, some more than once – Christine Keeler *no less than twenty-four times* – in their desperate efforts to find something that would stick. They interviewed Ward on many occasions, too, which put him under a great strain. Ward also felt, no doubt a little naively, that as he had done his best to protect the government's War Minister, the least the government could do would be to call their dogs off him. This not happening, he sent letters to the Home Secretary, his MP and the leader of the Labour Opposition, Harold Wilson, with copies to various newspapers. To Wilson he wrote,

> *Obviously my efforts to conceal the fact that Mr Profumo had not told the truth to Parliament had made it look as if I myself had*

something to hide. It is quite clear now that they must wish the facts to be known and I shall see that they are.

This was the final curtain for Profumo, who, pursued by the press, issued a statement admitting that he had lied to the House about Keeler and resigned both as a minister and MP.[1]

The questioning of Ward, his friends, patients and acquaintances went on unabated, and the strain on him increased. Because whatever misdemeanours the police were brewing up he knew to be trivial, he felt understandably that there must be some malice behind the inquiries (there was, the government's – which had let loose a runaway horse that was now out of control and could not be stopped). Ward begged Commander Townsend at Scotland Yard to expose the malice. Meanwhile, believing he had nothing to hide, he gave Herbert permission to search his flat if he wanted to, adding that, if it would help, he would authorise his secretary and solicitor to make available to the police his bank statements and records of income and expenditure. And because by now he had some idea of the direction the wind was taking, he wrote to Herbert:

It is ridiculous to say I have received money for introducing girls to men. Of course I always had pretty girls around me and took them to parties, but if this was followed up by the men giving them presents, surely there is no complaint against me, and in any case I don't see anything wrong in it.

This, in essence, was the case for the defence, and a view with which few would disagree. By the beginning of June 1963 Herbert and Burrows had at last completed their inquiries, and around noon on 8 June on a

---

1   He later made a second admirable career for himself working with some of the poorest people in the capital running the Toc H organisation at Toynbee Hall in the East End of London. He has steadfastly declined all requests to be interviewed on what has since become known as the Profumo Affair.

doorstep in Watford of all places, Ward was arrested by Herbert, with Burrows in tow, and charged with living *wholly or in part* on the immoral earnings of prostitution.

Here was a man who had a steady income from a well-established osteopathy practice and was also known to be a commercially success-ful artist. His combined income, he was to say in evidence, amounted to between £5,000 and £6,000 a year (the equivalent today of about £64,500 and nearly £77,400). How could the possibility of his living *wholly* on the earnings of prostitution be entertained? Perhaps in part? We would see.

It is practice in English (though not Scottish) criminal courts for prosecuting counsel to kick-start the proceedings by outlining to judge and jury the details of the charges against the accused. The disadvan-tages of this system, says the eminent QC Sir Louis Blom-Cooper, is that at the end of the trial the jury may have difficulties in distinguishing between what prosecuting counsel said he would prove and what even-tually he did prove. As we sat in No. 1 Court at the Old Bailey (where previous defendants had included Evans and Christie), I am sure it did not occur to any of us how wide that gulf would be.

There were five counts on the indictment against Ward. The first three concerned his living on the immoral earnings of Christine Keeler, Mandy Rice-Davies and two prostitutes named Ronna Ricardo and Vickie Barrett. Count four was his inciting Christine Keeler to procure a girl under twenty-one to have intercourse with a third person and count five was his *attempting* to procure a girl under twenty-one to have intercourse with a third person – both then (though not now) criminal offences. As these last two charges represented Herbert's and Burrows's scraping of what was left at the bottom of the barrel and as the jury found him not guilty on both, I am not going to waste time discussing them: they were charges that should never have been brought.

On counts one, two and three the law was this: that if it were proved that the women concerned were all prostitutes and that if the jury were satisfied that Ward was living with them or habitually in their company or exercising influence on them in any way, then the onus was on him to prove that he was *not* living on their immoral earnings, either wholly or in part. When I heard this I reflected that the chief prosecuting counsel, Mervyn Griffith-Jones, QC, was going to have an uphill task. Only that morning a new exhibition of Ward's drawings had opened at a West End gallery, with top prices of £500.

Mervyn Griffith-Jones's background was Eton and the Brigade of Guards, and his attitudes and general bearing reflected that. Good-looking in a chiselled, square sort of way, his dapper figure was often to be seen entering and leaving the building, wearing a neat double-breasted suit and bowler and carrying a rolled umbrella like any City gent. He had already won notoriety, not to say ridicule, when, as prosecuting counsel at the Lady Chatterley trial in 1960, he had solemnly asked the jury if it was a book they would wish their wives or servants to read.

Griffith-Jones's opening speech lasted an hour and a half. It reads moderately sensibly but it sounded totally unreal. He managed to make everything sound very much worse that it was, so that one was forced to conclude that, however badly Ward had behaved, it could not have been as badly as this. I recalled what Ward's counsel, James Burge, had said of him at the magistrate's court: that he could make even a honeymoon sound obscene. He gave the strong impression that he thought sexual intercourse shocking.

There were times, too, when Griffith-Jones's use of language wandered perilously close to Wonderland. Instead of 'although' he said 'albeit', a word which I did not think anyone wrote any more, let alone said; for 'it doesn't matter' he said 'it matters not', for 'with each other' he said 'the one with the other', for 'if in a mind to' he said 'if so minded'. When he wanted to tell us that Mandy Rice-Davies had gone off with a young Persian boy, he said that she 'went to live with a Persian boyfriend whose acquaintance she had made'. It was this weird blending of the archaic with the colloquial that made Mr Griffith-Jones to us on the press benches such a bizarre figure.

As he droned on, I occasionally shifted my gaze to others in the court to see how they were faring. On the Bench, in the company of a tall sheriff and lean alderman, sat the judge, Sir Archie Pellow Marshall, 64, in robes of grey, scarlet and black, Cornish Congregationalist and Nonconformist Liberal. On a recent visit to Washington he was reported to have said, 'Christian virtues, abstinence, discipline, unselfishness, patience and humility are at a discount in England now.' Abstinence and discipline, I reflected, were not among Ward's strong points. When Marshall interjected with a comment or additional question, his speech was orthodox; only a short 'a' in 'example' and long 'e' in 'period' hinted at the incubator in which he had first been hatched.

And facing him across the well of the court, the sole occupant of a dock big enough to hold a dozen defendants at a time (before shipping them off to Botany Bay, said Wayland Young) was the accused, the old roué himself. Ward may have been fifty but he looked thirty-five, his boyish hair swept back along both sides of his head to meet at the back like the wings of a partridge. He was wearing a sober heather mixture suit and one's first impression was that he was a man of intelligence and dignity. He had brought his pencil and drawing pad into court with him and for much of Griffith-Jones's opening speech he was busy sketching some of the participants in his trial – though quite who was his current model, the judge or Griffith-Jones, it was hard to say.

Between Ward and the judge sat counsel, bewigged and robed, among them Ward's leading counsel, James Burge. Burge was not a QC, as might have been expected in a case of such moment, but that was because Ward had been so pleased with his services at the magistrate's court that he had decided to retain him for the trial. I described Burge at the time as a jovial, sunshiny sort of a man, urbane and witty – in contrast to the pompous and plodding Griffith-Jones – but also rather a lightweight.

Let us now look at the details of the charges against Ward in relation to the four principal prosecution witnesses, Christine Keeler, Mandy Rice-Davies, Ronna Ricardo and Vickie Barrett, and see how far

Griffith-Jones's assertions were proved when they and others came to give evidence in the witness box.

First, his main allegation against Ward:

Whatever the extent of his earnings for this period may have been, from the evidence you will hear and indeed from what he has told the police, they were quite obviously insufficient for what he was spending.

No evidence had been brought to show this. Indeed, the police admitted that they had been unable to ascertain what his earnings were.

He introduced Christine Keeler to one Peter Rachman, of whom you have read in the newspapers. [This was said twice.]

Peter Rachman was an unsavoury Pole who had made a fortune developing slum property. He had kept Keeler at his flat in Bryanston Mews, Marylebone, and after her Mandy Rice-Davies, to whom he had given an allowance of £100 a week. But it was untrue that Ward had introduced Keeler to Rachman. 'We met by chance,' she said.

At one time Christine and Mandy had shared a flat in Comeragh Road, Barons Court, and, Griffith-Jones told us,

There they were frequently visited by the defendant, he bringing with him on a number of occasions his men friends to see them.

According to the evidence, the only named person who had been taken once to Comeragh Road by Ward was Lord Astor – and even then, according to Mandy, the girls had been out. There was no other evidence that Ward had brought men friends to see them.

Keeler was being used by him not only to make a little money from

intercourse she was having from time to time with the men who visited the flat, but also to procure girls for his own satisfaction.

No evidence was offered that Christine was being used by Ward in this way. There had been evidence that two men, and two only, had given Christine money for intercourse while she was staying at Ward's flat in Wimpole Mews. One was a Mr Eylan, who said in the witness box that it had happened three times, and the other was Mr Profumo, who, Christine said, had once given her a present for her mother.

She has said that over a period, roughly speaking, she must have paid to the defendant about half of what her earnings were from that particular exercise [i.e. sexual intercourse].

Christine's evidence was that she usually owed Ward more than she ever made, and that she had *only paid back half of that.*

Sometimes Ward would be hard up, short of cash, and he would tell the girl to telephone one of the gentlemen who was seeing her fairly regularly and who was paying her £20 a time. He would ask her to ring one of them up and go round to see him, earn her money and then bring it back.

Apart from a reference to a man called Charles, later said to be the financier Charles Clore, whom Griffith-Jones had mentioned separately, there was no evidence to support this claim at all.

Sometimes the man would go to the flat and Ward would be there throughout.

Christine offered no evidence of this.

The Indian doctor[2] was paying Mandy between £15 and £25 each time, out of which she said she paid Ward £2 or £3 a time.

We heard no evidence to support this allegation.

When Ward's counsel, James Burge, was cross-examining Christine, he elicited that when she was living in Ward's flat in Wimpole Mews she paid no rent and also had free use of the telephone, electricity and hot water. She admitted to Mr Burge that when Ward was hard up, she used to give him what she called 'small payments of money', but almost in the same breath added that Ward used to give her 'quite a lot of spending money', which he claimed in evidence to be between £70 and £80 in total. At the end of her cross-examination Christine repeated what she had already told Mr Griffith-Jones about owing Ward more than she ever made. 'You never returned to the accused,' asked Mr Burge, 'as much as you got from him?'

'No.'

How could anybody continue to assert, unless the English language had lost all meaning, that Ward was living on Christine Keeler's earnings?

Many of the assertions made in Griffith-Jones's opening speech failed for one of two reasons: either they went very much further than the subsequent evidence or, contrarily, they were completely let down by it. The sources of these assertions were the depositions – statements taken from witnesses by Herbert and Burrows and put into court as evidence. The fact that there were so many occasions when the spoken word failed to match the written word meant that one began to doubt their veracity. Time and again Griffith-Jones made assertions which no amount of questioning could confirm; time and again his witnesses gave quite different, sometimes contradictory, answers to what he

---

2   Dr Emil Savundra, later sentenced to eight years' imprisonment and fined £50,000 for offences connected with his Fire, Auto and Marine Insurance Company.

expected, so that often he seemed to be stuck in a mire of his own making without any means of extrication. What was the reason? Was it simply that the witnesses became nervous under examination and did not know what Griffith-Jones was driving at? Or was there a simpler explanation? Long ago and far away in the springtime of the year, had they been pressurised into making false statements to Herbert and Burrows, but now had forgotten what those falsehoods were? To many of us, this seemed the more likely.

But what of the jury? Had they even noticed the discrepancies between the written and the spoken words? I doubted it.

Although friends, in appearance the two principal prosecution witnesses, Christine and Mandy, could hardly have been more different. With her shoulder-length copper hair, tiny waist and long, slim legs on high-heeled shoes, Christine was a real little doll of a girl; many of the men in court must have found it hard to contemplate her without a stirring of the loins. When she spoke, though, her voice let her down; it was not just the voice of any little Eliza Doolittle, but as if a Professor Higgins or somebody had tried to improve it. The result gave an impression of a sort of forced gentility, as though Christine was anxious to convince the court that she was better than we thought.

Whereas Christine was ill at ease when faced with a world not of her choosing, Mandy was more self-assured. Still only eighteen, even after two years as Rachman's mistress she retained the bloom of youth. She came into court wearing a little rose-petalled hat such as debutantes used to wear at garden parties. Her shoes, unlike Christine's, were quite ladylike. Her simple grey sleeveless dress accentuated the impression of modesty – until one saw that the slit down the front was only loosely held together and that, when she walked, one could see quite a long way up her leg. At the proceedings at the magistrate's court she had used a phrase which has since passed into folklore. Told by counsel that Lord Astor had denied her claim of his having slept with her, she replied, 'Well, he would, wouldn't he?'

And now here she was in the witness box confronting Mr Griffith-

Jones, who asked her if those she had had intercourse with while she was staying in Ward's flat in Wimpole Mews had paid her any money?

'Oh no, sir.' She sounded quite shocked.

'Lord Astor?'

'Oh, no.'

'Did the defendant ever ask you to introduce girls to him?'

'No, sir.'

'Did you?'

'No, sir'.

'While you were there, did other girls visit the flat?'

'Yes, sir.'

'Were you ever in the flat with any other people who used either your room or his bedroom for sexual intercourse?'

'No, only Stephen.'

'Were you there when Stephen used his own room for intercourse?'

'Yes, sir.'

'How many girls did he go to bed with when you were in the Mews?'

'Two.'

'Do you know who they were?'

'No, sir. They haven't been in this case.'

'Did you see other men than Ward having intercourse in the flat?'

'No, sir.'

'Did you introduce anybody to the defendant yourself, girls I mean?'

'No, I don't think so, as far as I can remember.'

The dialogue turned to modelling and Mr Griffith-Jones asked, 'Whose suggestion was it that you should take up modelling?'

Here was an echo of an earlier suggestion to Christine that she had taken up modelling to bring back pretty young girls for Ward.

'It was my suggestion.'

'Did you meet other girls there?'

'Yes, sir.'

'Did you bring them back to the flat?'

'No, sir.'

So much for Griffith-Jones's promise in his opening speech that not only was Ward living off Mandy's and Christine's immoral earnings but they were also bringing back to the flat other girls off whose immoral earnings he was also living.

After Griffith-Jones had got Mandy to admit that in the six-week period she had stayed at Wimpole Mews, she had had intercourse with the Indian doctor on five occasions, for which he had paid her £15 or £25 a time, she was asked if she had any other monies coming in? 'What Stephen gave me,' she said, which was as good for the defence as the evidence about the Indian doctor had been bad. Yet when Ward came to give evidence, he denied any knowledge of the Indian doctor coming to Wimpole Mews. He was aware that Savundra had slept with Mandy at another flat in Great Cumberland Place, to which she and Christine later moved, and I began to wonder if the police had not pressurised Mandy to shift the venue of Savundra's visits to Wimpole Mews for obvious reasons.

Also, leaving aside the undisclosed weekly allowance from Rachman, the case against Ward on Mandy's evidence was hardly sustainable. Asked by the judge how much she had given Ward apart from the £6 a week rent they had agreed on, she replied about £25 in all, but that she had paid for food as well. There had also been a whole raft of telephone calls – Ward remembered one bill for £54, towards which Mandy said she had contributed only £5 or £6.

As I wrote at the time, 'Subtract from the £25 that Mandy said she gave Ward whatever monies he gave her, and there could not have been much in it either way.' Was this the reason for us all being here? For a £5 note and a packet of cornflakes? It seemed like it.

Confirmation of my view that Herbert and Burrows had overreached themselves in their attempts to get something to stick came in the cross-examination of Mandy by James Burge.

'Is it right you were going abroad on the night of 16 June?'

'Yes, sir.'

'Were you stopped at the airport by police officers in charge of this case?'

'The second time.'

'They'd stopped you before?'

'Yes, on a motoring offence, and they said they'd issue a warrant for my arrest.'

'Were you taken to Marylebone Lane police station by Chief Inspector Herbert and Detective Sergeant Burrows, the officers in this case?'

'Yes, sir.'

'Was it suggested there might be a charge of stealing against you in relation to a television set?'

'Yes, sir.'

'Were you allowed to go when you had entered into bail?'

'Yes, sir.'

'How much was the bail for?'

'A thousand pounds.'

'Did they give you any reason why the date 28 June had been selected for you to answer your bail?'

'No, sir. It was quite obvious.'

'That was the day on which you gave evidence at the magistrate's court?'

'Yes, sir.'

'And you gave evidence under the pressure that you had this possible charge being made against you?'

'Yes, sir. I had already seen the television company and told them I was settling the question of the television set.'

'Did you point that out to the police officers on 16 June?'

'Yes, sir.'

Here the judge intervened to give a helping hand to the prosecution, as judges often do.

'Whatever happened then, have you told the truth in the witness box?'

'Yes, sir.'

'Anything you said about the Indian doctor you still hold out as being true?'

'Yes, sir,' Mandy said. But then she would, wouldn't she?

At this point the judge, believing Mandy's answers to be Holy Writ, asked Mr Burge if in view of her last two responses it was really worth his while going on asking them. Mr Burge replied that '*whatever the atmosphere of this trial*' he had been instructed to present Ward's defence, and would continue to do so.

'Is it correct that on 28 June you went into the witness box at Marylebone and gave evidence about the Indian doctor?'

'Yes, sir.'

'While still under oath in the witness box, were you seen in a room at Marylebone police station by Chief Inspector Herbert and Detective Sergeant Burrows?'

'Yes, sir.'

'What happened then?'

'A man arrived from the television company, and I paid him some money.'

Burge returned to the Indian doctor.

'I am suggesting,' he said, 'that you are not telling the truth. You do understand that, don't you?'

'Yes, sir.'

'Has anybody in a position of authority ever said to you you are a liar?'

'Yes.'

'Is it right that on 1 May 1963 you appeared at West London magistrate's court?'

'Yes, sir.'

'And did the learned magistrate say to you that if you wanted to get something and get it by a lie, you would lie?'

'Yes.'

'Was it true?'

'He was talking about the motoring offence.'

'I don't want to embarrass you, but the motoring offences were not just parking offences. They were making a false statement, obtaining an insurance certificate and possessing a forged licence, and making a false entry in the registration book?'

'Yes, sir.'

'When the police [i.e. Herbert and Burrows] interviewed you, you knew that you had already been convicted on a criminal offence?'

'Yes, sir.'

'Was it clear they were out to gain criminal evidence against the accused, Stephen Ward?'

'Yes, sir.'

'Was pressure placed upon you that these matters which I have mentioned might make it difficult for you unless you gave evidence against Stephen Ward?'

'Yes, sir.'

In further questioning Mr Burge referred to a time when Herbert and Burrows had interviewed Mandy in Holloway prison where she had been taken after her conviction for the motoring offences.

'You didn't want to go back there, did you?'

'No.'

'In those circumstances, you have given this account of the Indian doctor?'

'Yes, sir.'

If this was not a clear indication that under police pressure Mandy had been persuaded to alter the place and time when she had had intercourse with Savundra (and been paid for it) from Great Cumberland Place to when she had been staying with Ward at Wimpole Mews, then I don't know what else it could have been. And the slim volume of memoirs, *The Mandy Report*, she published a year after the trial more or less confirmed it. Although granted bail during the hearing at Marylebone magistrate's court, the police advised her not to accept it.

A detective [Herbert Burrows?] told me, 'As soon as you are released, we're going to arrest you on another charge. In fact, we've got two warrants for your arrest. One is a bench warrant for parking in a wrong street and not turning up at court … Take my advice and stay inside for another week. It'll cause you less trouble in the long run.

On two previous occasions the police had been to see me about making a statement on my relations with Stephen Ward. Each time I had refused. Clearly these proceedings were related to my refusal to co-operate and this was why I had to be kept behind bars. Well, back to jail I went. Holloway prison must be one of the last places God ever made on this earth. The conditions I thought were absolutely vile. I was turned out of my bunk every morning at 6 a.m., and locked up for bed again at 9 p.m. Compared to what I had been accustomed to, the food was like pigswill and tasted every bit as vile as it looked.

After a day or two of this, I was ready to do anything to get out. I am sure that this was the way the police had planned it. They came to see me and asked if I would like to reconsider my refusal to make a statement about Dr Ward. The prospects of perhaps having to spend another spell in Holloway over the motoring offence was enough to convince me that I had better keep on the right side of the police. I felt like a cornered animal. I told them all they wanted to know … and slowly the noose began tightening around Stephen's neck.

In court Mandy also said that she hoped Ward would be acquitted, and that he did not deserve it, adding, 'Why, you might as well arrest every bachelor in London' – which resulted in quite a titter in court. Yet at the end of her memoirs she went even further: 'He most certainly never influenced me to sleep with anyone nor ever asked me to do so.'

From the evidence of the next witness it was clear that Herbert and Burrows had been up to their tricks again. Her name was Ronna Ricardo, and she made no pretensions about not being a tart, though obviously unhappy about having to admit to it. She was a large, homely looking woman with red hair and a pink jumper, totally lacking finesse, which, after the genteel caperings of Mandy and Christine, was welcome.

Soon after her entry into the witness box, Griffith-Jones asked the judge's permission to treat Ronna as a hostile witness. This was because at the magistrate's court she had stated that on several occasions she had visited Ward's flat to have intercourse with a variety of men whom he had invited there, for which she had been paid £10 or £20 a time, but that she now wished to retract this; and Griffith-Jones read out a statement of retraction she had made at Scotland Yard a few days earlier:

> I have come here this evening to make a statement about the Ward case. I want to say that most of the evidence I gave at the magistrate's court was untrue. I want to say I never met a man in Stephen Ward's flat except my friend Silky Hawkins. He is the only man I ever had intercourse with in Ward's flat.
>
> It is true that I never paid Ward any money received from men with whom I have had intercourse … the statements which I have made to the police were untrue.
>
> I made them because I did not want my young sister to go to a remand home or my baby taken away from me. Mr Herbert told me they would take my sister away and take my baby if I didn't make the statements.

Between them Griffith-Jones and the judge badgered away at her to admit that her original statement – that she had been to Ward's flat on several occasions – was true, but courageously she stood firm. Then Griffith-Jones held up her original statement:

'The jury will want to know how it ever came about that you were able to see that in writing, read it through and sign it as true, when it is all invention put in by the police?'

Her reply was one familiar to witnesses pressurised by police officers:

'I think at the police station I was kept so long I was ready to sign anything.' (The police said that her interview lasted from 10 p.m. to 2 a.m.).

'You read the statement before you signed it, didn't you?'

'No, I didn't. It was read out to me.'

'Why did you sign it?'

'Because I wanted the police to leave me alone.'

'At some stage you were told you would have to give evidence?'

'No,' she replied sharply, 'I was told I would *not* have to give evidence.'

Before the court rose for the day the judge addressed Ricardo: 'I would advise you very seriously to consider your position overnight.' If that did not mean that he disbelieved her retraction today and was inviting her to go back to what she had said at the magistrate's court, it was difficult to know what he did mean. The harsh fact was that he and Griffith-Jones were too reliant on Herbert and Burrows to see that Ricardo had been an impressive and courageous – if somewhat nervous – witness. To most of us observers it appeared far more probable that under police pressure, she had made a false statement at the magistrate's court and was telling the truth now, and, that being so, the prosecution was doing its case more harm that good in not dropping Ricardo as a witness. Yet the proof of the pudding was in the ending. The jury shared our view that Ricardo was lying in the magistrate's court but was telling the truth in this one, and found Ward not guilty of living on her immoral earnings.

We were still on count three, which involved another prostitute, named Vickie Barrett. She had not appeared at the magistrate's court, having been a last-minute addition to Griffith-Jones's list. But we were all electrified by what he had had to say about her in his opening speech:

Vickie Barrett was picked up by Ward on a night in January 1963, as she was walking in Oxford Street. Ward, driving a white Jaguar, pulled up by the kerbside and asked her if she would like to go to a party.

Miss Barrett got into the car and was driven to Bryanston Mews. Ward told her that he would get her clients and look after her interests, take the money and keep it for her so that she would then be able to save a little, buy new clothes and a more luxurious apartment, and therefore charge higher fees.

On that occasion when they got back to the flat there was no one there. There was no party but Ward told her that there was a man already in the bedroom. He gave her a contraceptive and sent her into the bedroom where she had intercourse with the man.

Afterwards they came out and Ward was still there. Ward gave them coffee and, when she asked for payment, said he would save the money for her. He took her back to Oxford Street and arranged to meet her two days later at the tube station there.

This time Ward again brought her back to his flat and again a man was already waiting in bed for her. Thereafter, for the next two and a half months (according to the girl, some two or three times a week), the same thing would happen. That is in ordinary language just brothel-keeping. Finally the girl left, but she never received a penny of the money she had earned, which Ward had taken to save for her.

This brought an entirely new dimension to the case. Until now we had all known Ward as a lover of low life and company but had never imagined him in the role in which Griffith-Jones was now depicting him – as a professional ponce. Apart from anything else, one would have thought, it would have unutterably bored him; the odd piece of the jigsaw that did not fit. But was it true?

Vickie Barrett came into the witness box, a mousy little whey-faced blonde wearing a green raincoat with a white scarf tied round her neck. While she was taking the oath, one's first impression was one of shock, that Ward who, one had come to believe, was a man of some discernment, should have sunk so low. For of all the whores the prosecution had paraded before us, she was the bottom of the barrel. Christine and

Mandy, even Ronna Ricardo, had a certain style, a kind of robustness, but this little waif had nothing: she looked, as Rebecca West put it later, like an advertisement for a famine relief fund, or, in army mess parlance, a ten bob knock in the Bayswater Road.

Yet she was word perfect, confirmed everything that Griffith-Jones had said in his opening speech, never hesitated for an answer. And she sprung some new evidence on us, too. On returning to Ward's flat on another occasion, she was asked by Griffith-Jones, 'was there a man there?'

'Yes.'

'Was he in bed or in the sitting-room?'

'He was in the bedroom in bed.'

'Were you given a contraceptive?'

'No.'

'Did you go into the bedroom?'

'Yes, and there was a cane on the bed.'

'Did you use it?'

'Yes.'

'Was there anything said about money on that occasion?'

'Yes, Ward said he had received the money from the man.'

'Were you asked to whip other men?'

'Yes.'

'Was it always with the cane?'

'Not always.'

'On one occasion you used a whip?'

'A horse whip.'

'Did you whip only one man with the horse whip, or more?'

'Two or three men with the horse whip.'

'Was it the same horse whip each time?'

'No.'

'There were two different men with the same horse whip?'

'Yes.'

'Did you beat other men with the cane?'

'Yes.'

'Did you ever ask Ward how the savings were getting on?'

'He said he had nearly enough.'

'Did he say anything about clothes?'

'He bought me some clothes.'

'What sort of clothes did he buy?'

'Well, there was a dress and a costume and two pairs of high-heeled shoes.'

We now know there was not a word of truth in any of this, that from beginning to end the entire story was a fabrication of Herbert and Burrows. The truth, however, would only unfold gradually.

The first chink in Vickie Barrett's armour appeared during Mr Burge's cross-examination, when she admitted that she had been arrested for soliciting on 3 July, the very day that Ward had been committed for trial by the Marylebone magistrate. A diary had been found on her containing Ward's telephone number, and the police had taken her into custody to find out what they could about their relationship.

'And all this story you've told at the last moment on 4 July,' said Mr Burge, 'is absolutely untrue?'

'That's not true.'

'Did they say to you what a godsend you were?'

'No.'

'Sent at the last moment to give copy-book evidence about a man living on immoral earnings?'

'No.'

The next prosecution witness was Vickie Barrett's flatmate and fellow prostitute Brenda O'Neill. Physically she looked as unappealing as Vickie, with dullish hair scooped into a kind of beehive and a tattoo engraved on her right arm. She also admitted to having done business with Ward once at his flat, and it seemed that she and Vickie had sometimes discussed him. Presumably Griffith-Jones had called her to confirm what Vickie had said about her sexual activities with strangers in Ward's flat, but if under police pressure she had made a deposition to that effect she had by now forgotten it; her replies left Griffith-Jones floundering. Twice he asked her if Vickie had ever mentioned that Ward had proposed that Vickie should perform a service (eg. caning, sex, etc.) and both times she replied flatly, 'No'. Twice she also stated that Vickie had told her that she had only been to Ward's flat once.

When it came to presenting Ward's defence, Mr Burge, believing that the prosecution had failed to prove that Ward was living on Christine's and Mandy's immoral earnings, concentrated on witnesses who would refute Vickie Barrett's evidence, which he still saw as the most damaging to his case. Ward himself, shaking with anger, called it 'a tissue of disgusting lies from beginning to end'. To Griffith-Jones he said, '*She is lying, sir.*' And later, 'If this girl is telling the truth, then I am guilty. My case must depend on saying that this girl is lying, and why she is lying we must find out.' When Griffith-Jones asked him if it was not true about the cane and the horse whip, he said, 'May I appeal to your reason? Even with the somewhat disreputable pattern of my life, does it seem probable or possible?' This brought an intervention from the judge that the defendant would do his case no good by not answering the questions straightforwardly; in fact, he had done his case much good, for his answers were not those of a guilty man. He also did his case good when, goaded by Griffith-Jones beyond endurance, he banged the side of the witness box with his hand and almost shouted at his accuser, 'Any little tart from the streets can come forward in this court and say I am lying. Apart from this case I am considered a truthful person.' It was an impressive rejoinder because it was spontaneous.

Other defence witnesses testified that Ward could not have been in his Bryanston Mews flat orchestrating Vickie Barrett's whipping, caning and copulating when she said he was because they themselves were there at the material times. A Mr Edward Warwick was one – a sad, bald man in a green suit who had visited Ward with his wife at the flat several nights a week, sometimes staying into the early morning. Vickie Barrett was led into court like a prize ewe and he said he had never seen her before. A *Daily Telegraph* journalist, R. Barry O'Brien, also stated that he had been at the flat on many nights, and so did a tall, willowy redhead called Sylvia Parker, who had *actually stayed in the flat for five or six weeks* as a guest and was clearly keen to be well thought of. She described Vickie Barrett's evidence as a 'complete load of rubbish'. To cap it all, a painter called Vasco who, Vickie had claimed, was one of the men waiting for her in Ward's bed, was called to deny it. He was a square, burly man in a double-breasted blue suit with a carefully pressed blue handkerchief sticking out of his breast pocket like a tiny tent. He said he had been in Ward's flat only once, and that was at 9.30 in the morning to take him to his surgery for an appointment.

That concluded the case for the defence. There followed Burge's closing speech, then Griffith-Jones's, which was even more disgusting and damaging than his opening one. At one point he said something which led Ward, knowing it to be untrue, to shout out an objection from the dock. When the judge admonished him, Ward said, 'I'm sorry, my lord. It's a great strain' – which Griffith-Jones saw as an opportunity for a further twist of the knife. 'Of course it's a great strain,' he drawled, 'for a guilty man to hear the truth at last.' He spoke the words very slowly and deliberately, and I felt quite sick that one man should wish to humiliate another one so.

There followed the judge's summing-up, which most of us thought to be a 'hanging' one. Ward certainly thought so, for that evening, when he went home, believing that all that lay ahead of him was disgrace and a prison sentence, he wrote several suicide notes, then swallowed the contents of a bottle of sleeping pills. One of the notes was addressed to Ronna Ricardo. He thanked her for telling the truth at the Old Bailey and left instructions for her to receive £500 from his estate. Another note was for Vickie Barrett:

> *I don't know what it was or who it was that made you do what you did. But if you have any decency left, you should tell the truth like Ronna Ricardo. You owe this not to me but to everyone one who may be treated like you or like me in future.*

In No. 1 Court the judge concluded his summing-up. The dock was empty. Ward had been rushed to hospital following his overdose. 'Am I misrepresenting Barrett,' he asked the jury, 'when I say she answered her questions quietly and straightforwardly?' Of course not; it was this that had fooled us in the first place. But not to have added that her evidence had been discredited by half a dozen other witnesses was one of the more regrettable deficiencies in the summing-up. No wonder that Ward had written in one of his suicide notes, 'After Marshall's summing-up, I've given up hope.'

Although many had thought that the judge would postpone resumption of the trial until after Ward had recovered, he announced that after concluding his summing-up, he would ask the jury for its verdicts but postpone any sentencing until Ward's return.[3]

In the event, Ward was cleared on all charges except counts one and two, those of living on the immoral earnings of Christine and Mandy. To many of us in court this came as something of a shock, for in their evidence both girls had emphasised that they had owed Ward more than they had ever paid back.

Why, then, did the jury bring in perverse verdicts on these counts? I think for several reasons. Firstly, in those days police officers still enjoyed a high reputation for probity, and juries were always reluctant to accept allegations of police malpractice. Secondly the prejudicial effects of the committal proceedings at the magistrate's court, which in those days were reported in full in all the papers and which included Ronna Ricardo's original false evidence, may all have influenced them. Thirdly, there was the extreme partisanship of Griffith-Jones's conduct throughout the trial, deplorable in a senior Treasury counsel, in particular the many allegations he made against Ward in his opening speech which he promised to prove later but never did. 'Whatever other impressions juries may have when they first take their

---

3   Ward would never know the jury's verdicts, for he never regained consciousness. He died in St Stephen's hospital, Fulham, three days later.

seats', Blom-Cooper has written, 'the first words of the trial are likely to make the most lasting impression.' In addition, Ward's jury may well have felt that they had not been assembled for nothing and that, having cleared Ward on all the other charges, they had to produce something to show for it.

It was left to the journalist R. Barry O'Brien to discover what had made Vickie do what she did; the answer, predictably, was Herbert and Burrows. Half an hour after Ward had died, O'Brien had called at the house where Vickie was staying, taking with him a copy of Ward's suicide note to her. He wrote later:

She was greatly shocked at learning Ward was dead. She sat down and read the letter and remained for some moments silently crying. She looked at me and said, 'It was not lies.'

Later the landlady brought each of them a cup of tea.

After another silence Vickie Barrett began sobbing violently. She suddenly looked up at me and said, 'It was all lies. But I never thought he would die. I didn't want him to die.' At this point her whole body was shaking and convulsed with sobbing. She then said: 'It was not all lies. I did go to the flat but it was only to do business with Stephen Ward.' I reminded her that she had said that she had whipped men there and that Dr Ward had been handing out contraceptives. She said that it was not true that he had done this. I asked her why she had given evidence that was untrue. She said that she had told one of the police officers, when he had asked her what she had known about Dr Ward, that she was a friend of his and had visited the flat to do business with him. She said, 'I told him that I had whipped Dr Ward at the flat.' He said, 'Wouldn't it be better if you said you whipped other men at the flat?' I said, 'Why should I say that?' He told me if I didn't say that, I will never be able to show my face in Notting Hill again. He said that girls could get very heavy sentences for soliciting.' I asked her if the police officer had mentioned how long a sentence. 'He said I could get nine months or more.' After another silence, I asked her if she was telling me the truth. She said that she was. I repeated this question several times and each time she said she was telling the truth. I told her that if she was now telling me the truth, it was a very wicked thing to have done. She said, 'Yes, and I did it.' I told her that what she had just told me was a very serious accusation against two police officers. She said that she knew that, but that she had told the truth.

Stephen Ward's trial took place nearly forty years ago. What is there today about it that most sticks in my mind? The fact that Griffith-Jones appeared to accept uncritically the evidence as put forward by Herbert and Burrows, especially that concerning Vickie Barrett. Did it not occur to Griffith-Jones that her story showing Ward to be a professional pimp was out of keeping with everything then known about him and was therefore highly suspect? And should not he, or his junior Michael Corkery, have questioned Herbert and Burrows as to how these bizarre allegations came about? Perhaps they did, and perhaps Herbert and Burrows dissembled even to them, denying as they were to deny in the witness box that any pressure had been put on Barrett – or Ricardo – to tell the lies they did.

The lesson to be learned, it seems to me, is that it was vital then, and is even more so today, to have some extra judicial figure, such as is well established in some European countries, to oversee all police interrogations. To leave them as they are now, solely under police control, is a permanent temptation for detectives to pervert the course of justice. Had a judicial overseer been in place in 1963, it is virtually certain that there would have been no case for Ward to answer. And had he lived, there is a fair chance that his convictions on counts one and two would have been quashed on appeal.

4

THE CASE OF IAIN HAY GORDON
1952–2000

I have mentioned earlier the Statutory Medical Board, whose duty it was in the days of capital punishment to decide whether a condemned man was physically and mentally fit to be hanged. Being a medical, not a legal, tribunal, it had to ignore Timothy Evans's repeated affirmations of innocence and conclude that physically and mentally there was no impediment to his execution.

One of the members of that board was Dr Desmond Curran, an eminent psychiatrist who, after *10 Rillington Place* was published in 1961, wrote to me enclosing a copy of a report he had written about the conviction of a young Scottish National Service aircraftman named Iain Hay Gordon. Gordon had been found insane but guilty of the murder of Patricia Curran (no relation), daughter of a Northern Ireland High Court judge at an assizes there some eight years earlier. Dr Curran had examined Gordon at the request of his parents in Holywell mental institution, to which he had been committed after trial, and had also studied the papers on the case. Among these was a 'confession' Gordon had made to the murder after a lengthy police interrogation. This is what Curran's report said:

I am disturbed by the circumstances in which the confession was obtained. The sequence of events in this case corresponds closely with the sequence of events known to favour 'brain-washing', in which false ideas may be implanted and false statements made. The form of the confession is certainly consistent with its having been obtained in response to questioning and suggestion.

I think it only proper to add that in my experience of fifty or more murderers seen for the Director of Public Prosecutions I have never before experienced grave doubt about the prisoner's guilt. I have very serious doubt in this case and after serious consideration, my personal opinion is that the patient is not guilty. I could find no evidence that this patient is now suffering or has ever suffered from any mental disorder or disease.

As an appendix to his report, Dr Curran quoted from Dr William Sargant's brilliant book on brainwashing, *Battle for the Mind* (from which I quoted extensively in *10 Rillington Place*), outlining the psychological pressures which lead to successful brainwashing: the introduction of feelings of anxiety and guilt into the prisoner's mind; a greater willingness to admit to guilt if promises are given that the prisoner will be treated lightly if he does confess; the allegation that everything is known and that the prisoner would be wise to confess; concentration on some incident in the prisoner's life about which he feels particularly sensitive or guilty; and the development of a feeling of gratitude to the interrogator which frequently precedes or follows the final breakdown and confession.

In Gordon's case, wrote Dr Curran, 'the sequence of events appears to bear a strikingly close parallel with what has been outlined above, and from the accounts given by the various witnesses and my own impression of his personality, he is a very suggestible, gullible subject'. In an accompanying letter to me he said, 'Even more than Timothy Evans, this is a case you might well think it worth your while to investigate.'

It has never been my intention, having completed one investigation, to take up others (I could have spent my entire life, not just a part of it, doing nothing else). But I have always found it difficult to say no to an attractive proposition; and believing I had the capability, although self-taught, to correct a miscarriage of justice after it had occurred, I felt the Gordon case was a challenge it would be wrong to resist.

One of my first inquiries was to Dr G. M. Smith, the superintendent of the Holywell mental institution in which Gordon had been detained from 1953 to his release in 1960. He sent me a copy of a report he had made on Gordon:

> *During this period I examined him on numerous occasions and had ample opportunity of personally observing him in the social life of the hospital. I was constantly informed by my medical and nursing staff of his general attitude and behaviour. I never found any evidence of insanity while he was under my care.*
>
> *Mr Gordon's behaviour under very trying circumstances was excellent. He took an active part in the social life of the hospital and got on well with both patients and staff. He was a keen, active and willing worker in the Occupational Therapy Department; at all times was friendly and cheerful in his manner, always anxious to help others. I found him honest and trustworthy.*
>
> *I can recommend him for employment suitable to his ability and wish him happiness and success in the future.*

Did Mr Smith also believe, as Dr Curran did, that Gordon was not guilty of murder? He may have felt that to express a view on this was not his business, but it seemed to me the whole tone of his report, in particular the last sentence, was incompatible with a belief in his guilt. Had he not thought so, his duty would have been to have informed the legal authorities that Gordon, no longer insane but still a murderer, should be transferred to prison. But why had the Attorney-General who had prosecuted Gordon at his trial, now also knowing him to be sane, himself not applied for Gordon's transfer to prison? And why did the terms of his release specify that there was to be no publicity about it? This was the first indication of many that both Bar and Bench in Northern Ireland were half-hearted in their beliefs in Gordon's guilt.

The murder of Patricia Curran, a 19-year-old first year student at Queen's University, Belfast, had been particularly brutal. She had lived at home with her mother and father and brothers Desmond (another strange coincidence), aged 26, a practising barrister, and Michael, 24, an estate agent. Their house, Glen House, lay in grounds known as the Glen, and was approached by a long drive from the main road in Whiteabbey, a coastal town north of Belfast. On 12 November 1952 Patricia had been expected back from the university in the early evening and when, according to her father, she did not arrive on the last bus of the night, he and her brother Desmond say they began searching for her. When a Whiteabbey policeman, alerted by the judge that Patricia was missing, arrived at about 2 a.m., to be followed a little later by the Curran family solicitor, a Mr Davison, also alerted by the judge, they found Desmond kneeling beside the body of his dead sister under a tree in the grounds of Glen House. Her jumper was saturated with blood from thirty-nine stab wounds, evidence of a frenzied attack. So was Desmond's jacket – but there were only a few spots of blood on the surrounding undergrowth, indicating that she had been killed elsewhere.

Because Desmond said he thought she was still breathing, it was decided, despite legal injunctions against moving the bodies of victims of crime until after forensic examination (of which Desmond, the policeman, Mr Davison and the judge himself must all have been fully aware), to take the body at once to the house of the Curran family's GP in Whiteabbey. He pronounced Patricia dead on arrival and at 5 a.m. her body was examined by a pathologist, Dr Wells, who estimated time of death as probably about 6 p.m. but almost any time up to 10 p.m. There was no evidence of a struggle or sexual interference, and the money in her handbag did not seem to have been touched.

Over the forty feet of ground that separated the body from the drive were scattered some of her belongings: shoes, handbag, yellow beret and a portfolio holding books and papers. This suggested that her body had been dragged or carried from the drive to where it was discovered. Yet although a light rain had been falling all night these items were all found to be dry – another sign that she had been killed elsewhere.

With no obvious clues to lead them to a credible suspect, yet under pressure from the community to find and arrest the murderer of a judge's daughter, the Royal Ulster Constabulary (RUC) were at a loss to know where to start. As part of their routine inquiries they interviewed all twenty-two of the young National Service aircraftmen then resident at the Edenmore RAF camp half a mile away, among them Iain Hay Gordon, then twenty years old and living away from home for the first time.

The elder son of a Scottish engineer working for Burmah Oil, Iain was born in February 1932 in Rangoon then moved to Tharawaddy, seventy-six miles away, where the family lived in a comfortable house staffed by native servants. His mother Brenda testified at his trial that as a little boy he had been highly strung, difficult to understand and extremely sensitive. When he was six the family returned briefly to Scotland, where Iain was enrolled at Dollar Academy, first as a day boy, later as a boarder. In 1940, when he was eight, he and his mother boarded a ship returning to Burma. It being wartime, the ship was part of a convoy which was attacked by U-boats. One set of alarm bells had been outside Iain's cabin, and the whole experience had left him very nervous.

In 1942 the Japanese invasion of Burma had forced his mother to flee to India with her two sons, leaving his father temporarily behind to help destroy the oil installation. From India they had managed to get a passage to Colombo and thence in convoy through the now re-opened Mediterranean to England.

Back in Scotland, Iain first went to Rutherglen Academy, where he was very happy, but without consulting him his mother, daughter of a headmaster and herself a former teacher, had him transferred back to the more prestigious Dollar Academy, where she hoped he might succeed scholastically. Later, again without seeking his views, his mother enlisted him at a tutorial college to be coached for the London University entrance examination. ('My mother's attitude to me,' he wrote to me recently, 'was as if I didn't exist'). But despite two years of coaching at the tutorial college, he twice failed the university entrance exam. This greatly disappointed his mother and depressed him, and it was about this time he saw his doctor for a nervous condition. By now Iain was beginning to show signs of being a bit of a misfit: lacking in self-esteem, hopelessly impractical, finding it difficult to form relationships, especially with women, and being unnecessarily apologetic and anxious to please. In 1951, he was called up to do his National Service in the RAF.

At Edenmore camp Iain found himself attached to the central registry. His duties included delivering and collecting the camp mail, which necessitated twice-daily bicycle trips to the Whiteabbey post office. It did not take long for staff and fellow recruits to notice his shortcomings. Squadron Leader O'Toole said of him, 'He didn't seem able to do anything right. He put the wrong letters in the wrong files and minuted them to the wrong people, and after that he took the wrong files to the wrong offices. And he couldn't take a telling-off. He became terribly depressed and on several occasions bordered on tears.' His fellow aircraftmen found him an oddball. When they told him that he needed L plates for his bike, he dutifully put them on. 'He wasn't very social,' according to O'Toole, 'and had few friends to go out with.'

Like all his colleagues, Iain was interviewed by the RUC on several occasions in November and December, and once by Detective Superintendent Capstick of Scotland Yard, a ruthless but successful investigator who, with his assistant Detective Sergeant Hawkins, had been seconded to the RUC to help their inquiries. After his first interview by the RUC, Iain returned to tell his questioners he felt he ought to add that he had once met Patricia Curran when her brother Desmond had invited him to lunch one Sunday. They were both worshippers at a local Presbyterian church where the minister and camp chaplain was a Bible-thumping evangelical called the Reverend Wylie. Iain had made a confession to Wylie about a solitary sexual encounter he had had with Wesley Courtney, a well-known local homosexual, of which he felt ashamed, and which Wylie had passed on to the police. It seemed that Desmond had taken quite a liking to Iain and one day, in conversation after church, had told him of his commitment to the Moral Rearmament movement and how he had to write down his innermost thoughts in accordance with MRA practices. He told Iain that God had a plan for him, and if he were to put himself in his (Desmond's) hands, he would be able to lead a much more satisfying life. Iain told the police that he had been to lunch at Glen House on three further occasions. Then, apparently, Patricia had told Desmond she had taken a dislike to Iain and asked him not to invite him there again, though today Iain remembers her as being quite friendly. To the RUC, however, desperate for clues, a link between Iain and Patricia had been established.

Iain went home to Scotland on Christmas leave, thinking the RUC had no further interest in him. But when he returned to Edenmore in early January, he was in for a shock. The RUC detective branch, despite having conducted some 9,000 interviews and taken 5,000 statements, had made no further progress, and had come to be regarded as a bunch of hillbillies. Capstick and Hawkins were back in town, and Iain was told he would be required for further interrogation. To his colleagues the very idea of poor, timid, gullible Gordon as a murder suspect was so ludicrous that they teased him about it mercilessly.

For Iain, though, it was no laughing matter. On 13 January 1953 he was interviewed by two RUC officers for four hours, when they asked him about his relationship with Desmond Curran, and on 14 January he was interviewed for more than six hours, when he admitted to having lied to them previously in saying that for the crucial time of 5–6pm on 12 November he was in the company of an aircraftman named Connor. The importance to the police of the time was twofold: it fitted in with when Patricia got off the bus at 5.20; and also with when a paper boy going up the drive with the judge's evening paper had heard sounds of rustling in the leaves near where Patricia's body had been found (he had been able to fix the time of this as 5.45 p.m. which was when the local factory sounded its routine hooter).

When Capstick learned what Iain had said, he pricked up his ears. Here was the only airman in the camp who had admitted to meeting Patricia now saying that he had lied about his whereabouts at the time of the murder. This surely must be the man they were looking for – or, failing that, a scapegoat which, for his purposes and after all the weeks of fruitless inquiries, would suit equally well? So the next day, 15 January, without any other police officer, RAF officer (offered to but foolishly declined by Iain) or solicitor present, and without cautioning his suspect, Capstick hammered away at Iain for nine hours. In the morning he browbeat Iain into admitting his homosexual encounter with Courtney and, having thus weakened his resistance, persuaded him later to sign his name to a confession to having murdered Patricia Curran.

Gordon met her, his statement reads, at the entrance to the Glen on the evening of 12 November:

She said to me, 'Hello, Iain' or something like that. I said, 'Hello, Patricia'. We had a short general conversation. I forget what we talked about but she asked me to escort her to her home up the Glen …

After we had walked a few yards, I either held her left hand or arm as we walked along. She did not object and was quite cheerful. We carried on walking up the Glen until we came to the spot where the street lamps light does not reach. It was quite dark there and I said to Patricia, 'Do you mind if I kiss you'? or words to that effect. We stopped walking and stood on the grass verge on the left hand side of the drive. She laid her things on the grass and

I think she laid her hat there as well. Before she did this, she was not keen on me giving her a kiss but consented in the end. I kissed her once or twice to begin with and she did not object. She then asked me to continue escorting her up the drive. I did not do so as I found I could not stop kissing her. As I was kissing her, I let my hand slip down her body between her coat and her clothes. Her coat was open and my hand may have touched her breast but I am not sure. She struggled and said, 'Don't, don't, you beast' or something like that. So I struggled with her and she said to me, 'Let me go or I will tell my father.' I then lost control of myself and Patricia fell down on the grass sobbing. She appeared to have fainted because she went limp. I am a bit hazy about what happened next, but I probably pulled the body of Patricia through the bushes to hide it. I dragged her by her arms or hands, but I cannot remember. Even before this happened, I do not think I was capable of knowing what I was doing. I was confused at the time and believe I stabbed her once or twice with my service knife. I may have caught her by the throat to stop her shouting. It is all very hazy to me but I think I was disturbed, either by seeing a light or hearing footsteps in the drive. I must have remained hidden and later walked out of the Glen at the gate lodge on to the main road. As far as I know, I crossed the main road and threw the knife into the sea. I felt that something awful must have happened, and quickly walked back to the camp.

In the rest of the statement he says he saw 'some small patches of Patricia's blood' on his flannels and had taken a nail brush, soap and water to scrub them off. It will not have escaped the reader's notice that nowhere in the statement does he actually claim to have killed Patricia, only that she fainted and went limp and he dragged her body through the bushes to hide it *before* stabbing her 'once or twice' with a service knife (which, in any case, he didn't possess). To rectify this omission and no doubt prompted by Capstick, he added a post script:

I am very sorry for having killed Patricia Curran. I had no intention whatever of killing the girl. It was solely due to a black-out. God knows as well as anybody else that the furthest thing in my mind was to kill the girl and I ask his forgiveness. I throw myself on to the mercy of the law and I ask you to do your best for me so that I can make a complete restart to life. I should like to say how sorry I am for all the distress that I have caused the Curran family. I have felt run down for quite some time and the black-out may have been the result of over-studying and worry generally. I am also sorry for the worry I have caused my dear father and mother. I ask my parents forgiveness and if I am spared I shall redeem my past life.

The reader will also have noticed how unconvincingly the main statement reads, and the vagueness and uncertainty of much of it: 'I forget what we talked about'; 'I am a bit hazy about what happened next'; 'I do not think I was capable of knowing what I was doing'; 'I was confused at the time'; 'I may have caught her by the throat'; 'all very hazy to me ... I think I was disturbed'; 'I must have remained hidden'; 'As far as I know, I crossed the main road', etc. The most glaring omission (as with Timothy Evans and his daughter) was that he gave no motive for the crime at all.

Yet, however flawed the confession, it was enough – a confession is always enough – for Iain to be formally charged with Patricia's murder and to be remanded in custody until he could be tried (he spent his twenty-first birthday in prison). On his way to jail he said to the RUC officer escorting him, 'I'm glad I took your advice. I feel happier now I have told the truth' – the classic expression of relief (see chapter 1 and Dr Curran's notes on page 69) of those who have just made false confessions. What in fact was making him happier was an end at last to Capstick's bloody questioning.

The rest of the evidence against Iain Hay Gordon was insubstantial. A woman walking past the entrance to the Glen that evening at around

6 p.m. said she had seen a figure emerging from it and picked out Iain at an identity parade. But she and Iain had arrived at the same time, his photograph had already been in the papers, he was dressed differently from the rest of the line-up, and it cannot be ruled out that the police had tipped her off. A Mrs Jackson, wife of the camp commandant, also claimed to have passed Iain on the Edenmore drive soon after 5 p.m. as she was returning to the camp and he was leaving it, but it was dark and she could not say whether he was in uniform or civvies. There was also evidence that, at the request of the police, Iain had asked other colleagues whether they had seen him between 5 and 6 p.m. in the camp, but none had. However, he and Corporal Connor had agreed to say that they were together, even though they had not been. Here is Corporal Connor's account of the atmosphere prevailing when the police interviewed him:

The police questioned me about Gordon and me being together having tea in Edenmore on 12 November 1952. I maintained my story of the false alibi with Gordon until about 8.30 p.m. By this time Head Constable Russell was thumping the table and shouting at me, 'You and Gordon did the murder. Didn't you, didn't you, didn't you?' He used both his fists to thump the table.

I was very frightened by the menacing attitude of the police and HC Russell finally said to me, 'If you don't tell the truth, we will send you to prison.' When he said that, I was very scared, and I said that I had told a lie over the Gordon alibi, but still denied that I knew anything about the murder or was with Gordon during the time of the murder.

During the interrogation, Hawkins, I believe, wrote out a four-page foolscap statement which I signed. I don't remember being cautioned when I was accused of the murder. When I left the room, Superintendent Capstick told me that if I told anyone what had happened during the interrogation … it would be too bad for me. He swore me to secrecy and I left the Temp Barracks.

Then comes this revealing paragraph:

I am very glad to have this opportunity of telling about the
treatment I received from the police. I have told no one about this
until today. I did not even tell my wife or my father. In my opinion
Gordon was innocent of the murder of Patricia Curran. Gordon
was a weak character and if he had received the same treatment as
I had for a much longer period, I can quite understand him
making a false confession in order to stop the questioning. It is not
an experience I would like to repeat in my lifetime.

Iain's trial for the murder of Patricia Curran opened at the County
Antrim Spring Assizes on 3 March 1953, with Northern Ireland's Lord
Chief Justice, Lord MacDermott, as presiding judge. There was only
one issue on which Iain's fate stood or fell, and that was the admissibility in evidence or not of the confession. In the absence of the jury (what
lawyers call the *voir dire*) defence counsel argued strongly that it should
not be admitted on the grounds that it was obtained through induce-
ment, fear and pressure. It would have been interesting to have heard
Iain's version of how he came to sign the confession, but on the advice
of his counsel he declined to be a witness on the grounds that as he had
argued himself into making a confession and getting himself arrested,
he might equally well argue himself into a hanging (the death penalty
then still being in force).

Capstick took the stand and gave evidence about the various interviews he had had with Iain, including the one on 15 January. He produced his notebook, which read:

10.20 a.m., 15/1/53, saw Gordon at office. District Inspector Nelson
left him, and I questioned him at length re masturbation, gross
indecency, sodomy.

Iain's counsel, Bertie McVeigh, QC, rose and asked, 'How far do you think it is legitimate to go on questioning an accused about sexual matters outside the scope of a case?'

CAPSTICK: Question him about sexual matters to see if he speaks the truth. If he won't speak the truth about sexual matters, he won't speak the truth on the murder. That is my attitude.

COUNSEL: He had already broken down on one incident, the day before, on the Connor incident?

CAPSTICK: Yes.

COUNSEL: And I put it to you that you were trying to break him down on the 15th about the rest of the matter?

CAPSTICK: He was broken down on masturbation; he later admitted a gross indecency with another individual and sodomy. He denied the lot and eventually admitted them and quoted them to me.

LORD MACDERMOTT: These were matters the prisoner naturally would not wish to be given publicity.

CAPSTICK: Yes, my lord.

LORD MACDERMOTT: Were you doing that for the purpose of getting any hold on him, relative in any way to this?

CAPSTICK: No.

LORD MACDERMOTT: Are you quite clear about that?

CAPSTICK: Quite clear. My purpose was absolutely to find out what type of boy this was and what he was doing, and if he could tell me the truth about matters like that, I could depend on him to tell me other things and eventually he did tell me the things he had been committing, and he was speaking to me quite openly and freely and not keeping things back.

By now it must have been obvious to the meanest intelligence that Capstick, through a mixture of threats and bullying, had been putting intense pressure on the hapless Gordon to fall in with what he wanted, and that being so, MacDermott should have ruled the confession inadmissible. Why did he not? Perhaps it would have been too great a slap in the face of the RUC, on whose support and co-operation the Northern Ireland judiciary depended. Perhaps also, if Gordon was convicted, a deeply troubling case would be cleared up, the community would be satisfied and his friends Lancelot and Doris Curran would be spared further suffering.

If the dubiety of police behaviour had been one reason for not accepting the confession evidence, there was another, even stronger one. It is a fact known to all criminal lawyers that confession evidence is routinely obtained by question and answer, in spite of which Mac-Dermott went through the charade of pretending otherwise. 'Mr Capstick, did you at any time ask the prisoner questions during the course of his statement?'

'No, my lord,' replied Capstick, once again confirming Lord Devlin's observation that it is the habit of the police never to admit to the slightest departure from correctness.

For the prosecution, the Attorney-General asked the same question of County Inspector Albert Kennedy, the RUC officer in charge of the case who had assisted Capstick in taking the confession.

KENNEDY: No, the only question I remember … Mr Capstick asked him how he spelt 'Queries' when he spoke about being at the newspaper shop. I actually spelt it out for him.

Later Kennedy was reminded that he had said that Capstick was taking down what Gordon was dictating.

COUNSEL: Was there a long paragraph, and then that written down; or was the sentence written down, do you remember? Was it taken sentence by sentence or paragraph by paragraph?

Kennedy proved himself as glib a witness as Capstick: 'Just sentence by sentence. At times the sentences were longer than others, because he spoke rather quickly, and I asked him to take his time and watch Mr Capstick's hand, so that he could get down what he was saying.'

LORD MACDERMOTT: Well, during the taking of this statement, Mr Kennedy, are you quite certain that with the exception of the question as to how one spelt the word 'Queries', that no questions were put to the accused at all?

KENNEDY: I am quite positive, my lord.

LORD MACDERMOTT: And this statement represents what he dictated to Mr Capstick?

KENNEDY: Yes.

LORD MACDERMOTT: Now, are you quite clear – I don't want any doubt later – are you quite clear as to there being no other questions?

KENNEDY: I am quite clear, my lord.

Having gone through the motions the law demanded, the way was then clear for MacDermott to rule not what Gordon's counsel and common sense demanded but what he had foolishly and wrongly decided: that the confession statement was not procured by interrogation, and that it was not unfair that Iain did not have either an RAF officer or solicitor present. He also rejected the allegation that Capstick had brought up homosexual admissions so that if Gordon also admitted to the murder then his homosexual indiscretion with Wesley Courtney would not have to be made public. 'I therefore think that the confession statement is admissible as a voluntary statement, and I see no reason to think that it was taken unfairly or in a manner which … would justify me in excluding it.'

This injudicious ruling made one thing certain, that a guilty verdict was now inevitable. Without the admissibility of the confession, there would have been no case to answer. So at the end of the trial would the court and public see and hear MacDermott sentence Iain to death by hanging?

Fortunately for Iain, there was a way out. By this time in my researches I was gaining the strong impression that the Northern Ireland legal authorities (save for MacDermott) knew in their hearts that there was something deeply worrying about the case, and that to allow Iain to hang might result in a miscarriage of justice which would haunt the Northern Ireland judiciary for years.

No one knew this better than the defence, and so they engaged as their star witness a psychiatrist named Dr Rossiter Lewis, known to an aunt of Iain apparently, who was prepared to declare that at the time of the attack Iain was suffering from hypoglycemia (shortage of blood sugar) and schizophrenia, did not know either the nature and quality of the act he had committed or that it was wrong, and was therefore insane at the time of the attack as the result of a diseased mind.

Two other medical experts went along with this. In rebuttal the Crown called another psychiatrist, a Dr Mulligan, who did not so much rebut as concur, being reluctant to say anything that would help propel Iain towards the gallows; and instead of demolishing Lewis's findings, as had been expected, for the nonsense that they were, gave other psychological reasons why Iain could have acted as he did: he was, he said, an inadequate psychopath who had succumbed to what he called 'a frenzy attack'. Pilot Officer Popple and a fellow officer from Edenmore who attended the trial could see little difference in the effect of the evidence of Mulligan and Lewis. 'What I remember most,' says Popple, 'was my astonishment when the two psychiatrists gave virtually the same evidence. I said to my brother officer in court, "Hey, they're reading off the same script." I'm not saying there was any collusion, but it did seem very strange that the two psychiatrists who were going for opposite results should come up with the same evidence.'

For these reasons the jury had little alternative but to bring in a verdict of guilty but insane, though in my view there was another. From Iain's parents, and from Popple and O'Toole at Edenmore, they had been given a portrait of Iain that highlighted his inadequacies: highly strung, nervous, keen to please, over-apologetic, emotionally immature, gullible, naïve, a loner, the odd man out –or, as his fellow aircraftmen described him, 'an utter clot'. I guess that for the jury the idea of being responsible for sending such a character to the hangman revolted them. If he had really done what the prosecution claimed – and his confession proved it – he had to be insane, there could be no other explanation.

Poor Iain! Having suffered one injustice of being convicted for a murder he had not committed, he now had to undergo seven years in Holywell as a criminal lunatic, yet receive no treatment for his condition because, as Dr Smith observed, since he was sane, there was none to give. As knowledge of his sanity became more wide-spread, Iain's supporters petitioned the Northern Ireland government for his early release. This put it in a fix. The Home Affairs Minister, a Colonel Topping, although suspecting that Iain might be both sane and innocent, said that it was far too early to consider releasing a man who had recently been convicted of a particularly foul murder, in which opinion he was fully supported by Lord MacDermott.

In England, however, others had begun to interest themselves in Iain's case. A young barrister named Hugh Pierce was commissioned by the organisation Justice to submit a report on the case, which he eventually did in a document entitled *Regina v. Iain Hay Gordon*. The *People*, a Sunday newspaper, commissioned its crime reporter, Duncan Webb, to write a series of articles about the case for Iain's innocence and in October 1968 James Fox also wrote a critical piece for the *Sunday Times*. I followed it up with a letter to the paper linking Iain's case with that of Timothy Evans. Both convictions, I said, rested on so-called 'confessions' obtained by the police in the most dubious circumstances. I added that I had shown Iain's 'confession' to my friend and neighbour Lord (Norman) Birkett, the famous advocate and judge, who had found it as unconvincing as I had. I concluded by asking for an inquiry leading to a free pardon (the means by which miscarriages were recognised in those days) for a man who was quite clearly neither guilty nor insane.

Then came Dr Curran's report and findings which were duly forwarded to Stormont. But the government there continued to drag its feet, and it was not until an English QC, Frederick Lawton (later a Lord Justice of Appeal), came to Belfast on Justice's behalf to have talks with the Minister for Home Affairs that things at last got moving. A year later the new Home Affairs Minister (and future Prime Minister) Brian Faulkner signed the papers for Iain's release, with the proviso that there was to be no publicity about it, and Iain was at last allowed to go home.

I myself had it in mind to write a book on the case, but was advised not to as it would have involved criticising the police and judiciary who in those days were held in high esteem, their integrity rarely questioned.

A little later I experienced that climate of opinion for myself. Still working as a television presenter and reporter, I was invited to write and present a documentary film on the police, with Alasdair Milne (the future Director-General of the BBC) as producer, for the independent television network. In the end we made two films, in one of which I said, knowing it to be true from experience, that in their efforts to secure convictions against those they believed to be guilty, the police were sometimes apt to bend the rules.

This criticism, mild by today's standards, reaped a whirlwind of controversy, mostly in the correspondence columns of *The Times*. 'Bending the rules,' boomed the arch Conservative and future Attorney-General, Lord Dilhorne (whom Lord Devlin once described as not having a grain of judicial sense), 'seldom occurs.' The Commissioner of the Metropolitan Police, a man called Simpson, described my assertion as arrant nonsense; while the well-known lawyer Lord Shawcross said that my claiming that bending the rules led to many innocent people being sent to prison had no foundation whatsoever. Sir Lionel Heald, another right-wing Conservative and former Attorney-General, was rash enough to call the programme 'faked'. I consulted my solicitors as to whether to sue Sir Lionel for libel. They agreed that in their view it was a libel, but the costs of suing would be extensive, and even then I might not win. Reluctantly I put aside the idea of a book on the case, in the hope that some other opportunity for expressing my views on it would surface later.

Iain, meanwhile, was having a frustrating time in Glasgow. He had managed to obtain employment as a porter in the warehouse of William Collins the publishers, with a proviso that he change his name to John Gordon and did not discuss the case with any of the firm's other employees. Mentally, though, he could aspire to more satisfying work, and he began to take evening classes in business studies, eventually achieving credits in seven subjects, failing in none.

Regrettably, they were of no practical use, for when a job interview came up and he had to tell the truth about his past, no offers were made. His mother wrote to thank me for my letter to the *Sunday Times* supporting James Fox, but she shared Iain's sense of despair. 'He finds it impossible to get more congenial work. He returns home exhausted each evening and I sometimes wonder if he should not throw it all up and concentrate on trying to clear himself.' She ended, 'We feel so encouraged by your understanding of the injustice of it and your determination to speak out.'

However, it was not until 1970, some eighteen years after the murder, that an opportunity arose for me to set the record straight. BBC Television were running a series called *Personal Choice*, in which they invited well-known presenters to interview some man or woman they admired or believed had something interesting to say. When asked, I suggested Iain Gordon and told them why; and they gave me the green light to go ahead.

So I went up to Scotland, met Iain, now 38, for dinner at Edinburgh's North British Hotel and sketched out for him what I believed to be the right structure for the interview; and on 9 September 1970, in the BBC studios in Lime Grove, the interview took place. I began by asking how he had found life at Edenmore:

GORDON: Found it pretty dull and boring, as most did who were doing their National Service. I was also quite lonely at times. I just looked on it as a chore that had to be done.

L.K.: Your contemporaries described you then as being shy, diffident, naïve, easily offended, a compulsive talker and almost falling over yourself in your desire to please. Would that be a fair description?

GORDON: Yes, I think so.

L.K.: Had anyone up to this time questioned your sanity?

GORDON: Certainly not.

I moved on to the day when Desmond Curran had approached him after church.

GORDON: He came over to me and shook hands by the left hand which

I thought rather odd, and invited me up to lunch at his house, explaining that he was the son of Mr Justice Curran.

L.K.: Were you surprised at this invitation?

GORDON: Looking back on it, it is surprising, but at the time I was just so lonely I was glad of someone taking an interest in me.

Iain told me that the whole family had been at the lunch, including Patricia, and I asked him what he thought of her.

GORDON: I never thought about her.

L.K.: Were you at all attracted to her?

GORDON: Certainly not.

L.K.: And you were never alone with her.

GORDON: Never.

I asked him what he was doing between the hours of 5 p.m. and 6 p.m., according to the police the time of the murder, and he said that for most of the time he was alone in the central registry practising his typing for an RAF exam.

Since he had been alone, he had found it difficult to arrange an alibi, as his officers had suggested, and so eventually he and Connor (who had also been alone) had agreed to give each other false alibis.

L.K.: Did the other airmen in the camp rag you about not being able to establish an alibi and say that you must be the murderer?

GORDON: Yes, they did this quite frequently.

L.K.: How did you take that?

GORDON: Well, sometimes in good part, sometimes not so good part. It depended how the police interrogations were going.

L.K.: I presume they ragged you because the idea of you being the murderer was to them preposterous?

GORDON: I think so.

We moved on to his first interview with Capstick on 10 December 1952. He said that initially it had been about the affair with Wesley Courtney, of which Capstick had been informed by Wylie.

GORDON: He asked me a lot of questions about my private sexual life. He said the truth's the thing, it's a crime to tell lies to the police. We don't mind the first time but the second time we take a dim view. He suggested I might perhaps have been lying in bed thinking about a woman, wanting a woman, had gone out to meet one and met Patricia Curran. He said things like, 'Did you not perhaps go behind The Glen to pass your water?' or '… into the grounds to gather sticks for firewood?' and I said certainly not because I never left the camp.

L.K.: Now, were you worried about this interview and the possibility about your parents finding out about your sexual life?

GORDON: Yes, sir, I felt quite guilty about it.

L.K.: And as a result of your worry, did you go and see anybody, like the Reverend Wylie?

Iain said he had seen Wylie and told him about the Courtney affair but that Wylie had said he had nothing to worry about and there was no need to tell his parents. He also told me that he had asked Wylie if it would be all right for him to confide in Desmond Curran and that Wylie had said it would be.

L.K.: And did you see Desmond Curran?

GORDON: Yes, I did see him subsequently.

L.K.: Why?

GORDON: I was a bit worried about this incident with Courtney, and I knew he was a barrister and I knew he had a policeman friend in the MRA, and I wanted to talk it over with him.

L.K.: Is there evidence to show that Desmond Curran made notes of your conversation with him, and passed these on to the police?

GORDON: Oh yes, every evidence. He produced them at my trial.

We then moved on to the events of 13, 14 and 15 January 1953; I read out the words of his confession, ending with 'I'm very sorry for having killed Patricia Curran. It was solely due to a black-out.'

L.K.: Have you ever in your life had a black-out?

GORDON: Certainly not.

I asked if he would like to comment on the facts in the confession.

GORDON: Yes, certainly. There was no blood on my clothes whatsoever.

L.K.: I think the police had proposed that whoever had killed her would have been covered with blood.

GORDON: … where the body was found, there was only two or three drops of blood, so she was obviously murdered elsewhere.

L.K.: What about the service knife?

GORDON: We never carried any. I never had one in my possession at any time.

L.K.: Even if the facts are wrong, it remains that you did put your signature to a document in which you admitted murder and many people would like to know how you ever came to do that?

On 13 January, said Iain, Detective Sergeant Hawkins of Scotland Yard and Head Constable Russell of the RUC had asked him to write out a statement about his past life from the day he had been born and the schools he had been to, ending up with what he had been doing the night of the murder. So he had started to write down all this and in the middle of it, the two officers 'secretly went away, without any warning'. 'I think this was to unnerve me because I remember feeling a bit nervous and I whistled a popular tune to get a grip on myself.'

L.K.: And what happened on the second day?

GORDON: In the morning they began questioning more, particularly Russell. Russell kept shouting and he waved his arms about. Sometimes his voice was soft, and he'd say, 'You've been a sick boy for a long time, Iain', and I looked at him vacantly, I didn't know what he was talking about. Other times he stood by me and shouted, waved his hands all over the place, clenched his fist and said, 'I wonder what two or three of you boys do together when you go out?' He suggested that Connor and myself went out quite often looking for an easy pick-up and that if we didn't find one, we forced ourselves on someone we didn't want … He kept shouting at me that I wasn't telling the truth, I'd been telling lies all along. I said, 'I don't know what you're talking about, I'm telling you the truth and you're not listening to me.'

They wouldn't let me away, even for dinner. If I went to the toilet, one of them went with me. They took me to Belfast for my dinner and then they came back and started shouting at me. They said, 'You've lied about your past sexual life, you've told us nothing but lies.' It didn't matter what I said to them, they just said, 'Lies, all lies, you're telling us lies, you'll have to do better than this.' It got so bad that in the end I felt, well, if I admit the truth about the alibi with Corporal Connor, perhaps it will help. Russell lost his temper completely and said, 'All right, we'll find out about this from Connor', and they left me alone again. They left me alone on the second day, you know, quite frequently.

And then about forty-five minutes later they came back and Russell shouted in my face, standing next me, 'Lies, all lies. Connor said you suggested it.' I'd always maintained that Connor suggested it. 'You're telling lies, you've lied to us all along', and it went on like this intermittently. Then about half-past four they took me to an upstairs room, about the size of an ordinary kitchen with a table and chair. Russell, Capstick, Hawkins, Kennedy and myself were there till about seven. They shouted questions at me non-stop, they never let up for a single second, I just never got a break and in the end my head was spinning. Their voices seemed to boomerang off the wall and it didn't matter what I said to them, they all shouted, 'Lies, all lies, you're telling us lies.'

L.K.: And then you went back, pretty exhausted I think, in the evening and on the third day you were with them for nine hours. What happened that day?

GORDON: On the third day I was just completely and mentally fagged out as a result of my experiences. I saw this Inspector Nelson on the third day and he kept tapping my arm, I think for psychological effect, and said, 'I advise you to go upstairs and tell Superintendent Capstick the truth. If you tell the truth, we'll help you all we can, but if you don't tell the truth, you'll be left to your own devices and you won't have a chance.'

So I went up and saw Capstick and he said, 'You've been a sick boy, Gordon – that's how he referred to me – we know you can't help these things, we'll get you the best medical help. You're over sixteen, your name doesn't need to appear in the papers, your mother won't know anything about it. If you confess to this crime, we'll let you go and see a doctor', and he went on with this patter till in the end I was in such a state I actually believed him.

And he then came to talk about the events of the night and he would say, 'Suppose you went out again that night, would you walk down the road to the grounds of Glen House?', and I would say, 'Probably.' And he said, 'If you happened to meet Patricia Curran, would you offer to escort her up the drive?', and I would say, 'Probably' and he said, 'Would you walk up the pathway?', and I would say, 'Probably.'

L.K.: So this statement which I read of yours was not a spontaneous statement by you, it was a hypothetical question and answer from Capstick?

GORDON: Yes, and not only that, the entire wording was Capstick's, the whole statement from beginning to end was Capstick's, not one single word in it was mine.

L.K.: So when Capstick said that this was a spontaneous statement on your behalf, he was not telling the truth?

GORDON: Oh no, it was a pack of lies.

L.K.: Is it true that Capstick was also heard to say to a Miss Kitty Duncan, matron of the training school where your interrogation was taking place, 'We will get him off insane'?

GORDON: Yes, he was heard to say this, 'We'll get him off insane.'

L.K.: An odd thing to say about a man who's just confessed to a particularly brutal murder?

GORDON: Yes, it does seem very strange.

I took him to his entry to Holywell and asked whether he believed he might have committed the murder.

GORDON: When I went there first, I did think I might possibly have done it, but then as time wore on and the effects of the brainwashing wore off, I realised the whole thing didn't make sense. Up till then I'd been leading a normal life, nothing led up to a frenzied attack on a girl I didn't know – I'm shy about approaching girls – it seemed utterly inconceivable that I should approach a judge's daughter I hardly knew, and why should I want a sobbing, hysterical woman on my hands? ... The whole thing just didn't make sense. Then I realised not only that I couldn't have done it, but I didn't do it because I wasn't there.

Did he feel very bitter about all that had happened?

GORDON: No, surprisingly, I feel no bitterness at all. I think bitterness corrodes your own soul. It just destroys yourself, it doesn't take you one step further forward.

Lastly, I asked how the whole experience had affected his life, as he was living it today.

GORDON: It has affected it in every conceivable way. It's like an octopus with tentacles, it reaches out into every department. I'm doing semi-labouring work when I feel I could be doing something much better. If I go for another job, I've got the task of explaining those eight years. If I go out with a girl friend, I risk the chance, if it gets serious, I've got to tell her and risk the chance of losing her, and this has happened two or three times. I believe it's vital that this has to be cleared up and I intend to clear my name, come what may.

Within the BBC the initial reactions to the recorded programme had been good. My producer sent me a line saying, 'Congratulations on a fine job.' One or two friends in current affairs who had watched it liked it and, most important of all, Iain himself was happy with it. It was scheduled to be broadcast on 1 November and Iain believed that, when it was seen in Northern Ireland, it would provide the breakthrough he had been looking for. My own belief was that, whatever the response, they could hardly ignore it, and I looked forward to the date of transmission more eagerly than for any other of my programmes before or since.

And then a spanner landed in the works. At a series of separate meetings of the BBC Board of Governors, Board of Management and Current Affairs Group, it was decided that the programme was not suitable for transmission because, as one member pompously put it, 'It made grave charges against persons who had no immediate chance of reply, and made out a one-sided case in which reputations were impugned.' In other words, it lacked balance, in the BBC the cardinal sin against the Holy Ghost. Yet it would have been perfectly possible on the night of transmission for BBC Belfast to have mounted a discussion programme after it, as had been done – and is still done – on numerous similar occasions: it would have been good to hear what Kennedy, by then Inspector-General of the RUC and others had to say. In any case, the programme itself was a form of rebuttal of everything official that had gone before. I was also intrigued to learn that pressure on the BBC to cancel the programme had been brought by Northern Ireland's Prime Minister, a Major Chichester-Clark. The name rang a faint bell for me, and I recalled that he had been a junior boy when I had been a senior in my house at Eton, and that when fagging, long since discarded in the wheelie-bin of history, had been à la mode, he was one of the boys I had sometimes sent on errands to other houses or into the town. I did my utmost to remember anything about him, good or bad, but nothing came. Like many embryonic politicians, he was unmemorable; like them, too, an opponent of truths that made him feel embarrassed or uncomfortable.

Naturally, Iain was dreadfully disappointed with the decision, though I was temporarily able to keep his spirits up with a BBC promise to look into the possibilities of using the interview in a broader survey of the whole case – though in the end nothing came of it. His hopes of redemption dashed, he would have to wait another thirty years before he saw his name cleared and, at the end of a wasted life, a victory that was total.

It came about in this way. In 1995 there landed on the feature editor's desk of the *Glasgow Herald* a video tape of a programme about Gordon shown only in Northern Ireland called *More Sinned against than Sinning.* A journalist on the paper, John Linklater, was asked to view it and, when he did, was not only outraged by Iain's failure to get any redress for what had happened to him but became an instant recruit to the small band of us (Paul Foot, Bob Woffinden and Robert Kee are others) who feel an urge to try to correct miscarriages of justice when they occur.

So Linklater went to work, contacting Margot Harvey, the solicitor whom Iain had retained (without fee because he had no money and she also was appalled by what had happened to him), and under the Thirty Year Disclosure Act, he inspected the archives of past Northern Ireland criminal cases housed in a shed near Belfast. Among other things, he found evidence that it was not possible for Iain to have committed the crime because he was not where the confession said he was between 5 p.m. and 6 p.m.

A statement given to the police by an aircraftman called Spence said he had seen Iain at 5 p.m. in the camp and again before 6 p.m., although the police had bullied him into making a second statement saying that 'thinking it over' (a familiar phrase in many miscarriage of justice cases) he could have been mistaken. Neither of these statements seems to have been passed to the defence; nor indeed a whole series of statements by witnesses who had seen Patricia *but not seen Iain* near the entrance to the Glen around 5.20 when her bus from Belfast arrived. These could have done much to undermine the evidence of the two women who said they had seen him.

Another of Linklater's discoveries was that if the time of the murder was between 5 p.m. and 6 p.m., as stated in the confession, then the car drivers who had collectively made thirteen journeys up and down the drive from 5.30 p.m. on, as well as the paper boy, had failed to spot Patricia's bright yellow beret lying on the verge of the drive – a sure sign that it had been placed there much later.

There was also evidence that on the bus from Belfast, Patricia's books were not in a portfolio but held together by a strap. Here was a reason for thinking that, before her murder, Patricia had reached home and that while there she or someone else had put the books into the portfolio. Another deduction to arise from this was that if Patricia had dropped the portfolio, the books would have fallen out. As they had not, it meant that someone other than Patricia had placed it there.

But the most surprising and disturbing item brought to light for the first time was a report on the case in January 1953 by County Inspector Albert Kennedy, head of the Northern Ireland CID and the officer in charge of it. The report quoted statements made by Judge Curran and his wife Doris to their solicitor Malcolm Davison on 16 November 1952, i.e. long before Iain became a suspect. These showed that at about 1.35 a.m. on 13 November the judge had telephoned Davison's house: the call had been taken by his wife, Doreen, to whom Curran had said that Patricia had caught the 5 p.m. bus from Belfast but had not been seen since. Ten minutes later, at 1.45 a.m., the judge had called the Whiteabbey police and told them the same thing. Five minutes after that, Doris Curran had also telephoned the police, 'sounding quite agitated', and confirmed that Patricia had left the Belfast bus station at 5 p.m. *The only person who could have told the Currans this was Patricia herself* – further proof that she must have reached home safely some time between 5.20 p.m. and 5.45 p.m. Yet at approximately 2.10 a.m., ten minutes after he had seen the dead body of his daughter in the Glen, the judge had telephoned the Steel family, having learnt that fellow student John Steel had spent the afternoon with Patricia, to ask *what bus she had caught and where she might be now.*

Faced with this damning and contradictory evidence, and because the Curran family had been treated with kid gloves all along, Kennedy organised a police search of Glen House which revealed nothing, although Desmond, on his own initiative, handed them from a drawer in his bedroom the bloodstained jacket he had been wearing when he had been found kneeling beside his sister's body in the Glen. Soon after this the judge and his wife left for the George Hotel, Edinburgh, then to a house in Belfast and never set foot in Glen House again.

Of the Currans' statement Kennedy wrote, 'I decided to pursue every other line of inquiry before allowing our thoughts to concentrate on something which seemed too fantastic to believe, *namely that the Currans were covering up the murderer and telling a tissue of lies* [my italics]'. Alas, Kennedy's courage did not match his convictions and in the end he lamely concluded that when the judge said he was hazy about times, he was speaking the truth and that members of the Steel family had made a genuine mistake about the time – an allegation which all three Steels – father, mother and son – hotly denied, both then and on several subsequent occasions. Although the Attorney-General who prosecuted Iain at his trial was also aware and concerned about the discrepancies, neither the statements of the three Steels that the judge had telephoned them at 2.10 a.m. asking what bus Patricia had caught nor Kennedy's report were given to the defence as they should have been.

It is, however, doubtful what use they would have made of it, as Bertie McVeigh, QC, Iain's counsel, had only agreed to defend Iain on the understanding that he would not be required to cross-examine Judge Curran, his and Lord MacDermott's partner and companion in the Northern Ireland Bar Golfing Society. In the end, shamefully and to avoid exposing a can of worms, Judge Curran was never called. The Northern Ireland legal establishment was protecting its own.

So what happened that night at Glen House? Everything must be speculation now, but Linklater thinks the most likely explanation is that Patricia was killed in a frenzy by her mother, with whom she had never been on good terms, and who was later found to show signs of mental instability. He also has in his possession a letter from the Northern Ireland police archives written by Doris Curran within a day or two of arriving in Edinburgh to her sons Desmond and Michael. It is a strange letter, more in what it omits than in what it says. Neither her daughter Patricia nor her murder, only a week past, are mentioned at all, nor is there any word of interest or comfort for the welfare of sons Desmond and Michael, whom the Currans had, without warning, summarily abandoned. It concludes with a diatribe against Doris Curran's former employees and neighbours, whom she accuses of madness.

Linklater also believes that the body was moved to where (according to Desmond) it was found.

There is another point to be made here, which indicates Desmond's possible involvement as an accessory after the fact. It will be recalled that when in the early hours of 13 November 1952 Desmond was found kneeling by his sister's dead body under a tree in the Glen, he had said that he thought she was still breathing. This was incredible. Death having occurred between 6 and 10 p.m., her body would have been cold to the touch and in any case rigor mortis had already set in: when Desmond and the others lifted the body into the Davisons' car to lay it lengthwise on the back seat, they found her legs would not bend and had to be left sticking out of the half-open back door. Saying he thought Patricia was still breathing and therefore needed urgent medical attention enabled Desmond to get away from that place as quickly as possible and gave him time to consider his and the family's movements that night.

Yet when one considers Desmond's subsequent rather curious career, it does not seem unreasonable to suppose that he was seeking redemption, if not atonement. Born into an established Northern Ireland Protestant family and on the verge of carving out a successful career at the Bar, he gave it all up to train for the Roman Catholic priesthood. Having been ordained, he took up a post as resident priest in a poor South African township, thus renouncing the world he had been brought up in. Now in his mid seventies he still lives there.

For years Desmond clung to the belief, against all the weight of evidence, that Iain was guilty, perhaps feeling he had no alternative, but in the spring of 2001 he admitted to John Linklater that he did not now think this likely, although he did not offer an alternative explanation. Desmond Curran is the only man still alive who must know more about what happened in the Glen that night than he has ever let on.[1]

---

1   When he was near my home in Wiltshire in July 2001, Curran agreed to come over and see me to help tie up loose ends: but at the last moment, and without informing me, pulled out.

By now the Criminal Cases Review Commission (CCRC), a sort of tribune of last resort, was up and running, and Linklater, through solicitor Margot Harvey, prepared two submissions to it on Iain's behalf that, in the light of all the new evidence, the case should be referred back to the Northern Ireland Court of Appeal. In due course the evidence, supported by the written opinions of a whole battery of psycholgical experts who said that in the light of the pressures put on Iain to admit to a homosexual indiscretion and his fear of his parents getting to know about it, the confession should not have been admitted in evidence, was submitted to the court. On 20 December 2000 the appeal was heard in Belfast before the Lord Chief Justice, Lord Carswell, sitting with Lord Justice Campbell and Mr Justice Kerr. Concurring with what some of us had believed for decades, they quashed the conviction. They also said that if a solicitor had been present at the 'sex' interview on 15 January, it is doubtful if it would have been allowed to take the course it did; while a criticism of MacDermott was that he had not sufficiently emphasised to the jury the well-known perils of identification evidence.

The Appeal Court judges considered the discrepancies and contradictions in Judge Curran's account of telephone calls on the night of the murder which, they said, should have been handed to the defence (though they stopped short of drawing attention to Kennedy's damaging report). Instead, they brought up the evidence of a 12-year-old girl who had deposed on three occasions that she had seen Patricia in or near the Glen in the company of a scar-faced man of about thirty who had made her look frightened, and pronounced that this too should have been disclosed to the defence as it posited the possibility of a different suspect. This struck me as a red herring, one that deflected attention from brand new suspects in the shape of the Curran family, and I was sorry that the judges did not at least draw attention to that.

When the gaunt, haggard figure of Iain Hay Gordon, then aged 68, came down the steps of the High Court in Belfast that morning and told the press how pleased he was that his name had been cleared at last, the curtain fell on what had been the longest lasting – forty-eight years, even longer than Bentley's – and one of the most shocking miscarriages of justice in British criminal legal history.

5

A PRESUMPTION OF INNOCENCE – THE CASE OF PATRICK MEEHAN
1969–76

In 1966 my wife and I sold our beautiful Queen Anne house in Amersham, Buckinghamshire, and moved to a rented Georgian manse in the Scottish borders so that I might complete a book I had recently started about Americans abroad. The house was on the north side of the Tweed valley and from my study window above the front door I had a breathtaking view of the distant and, in winter, snow-capped Cheviot hills. There was a delightful small walled kitchen garden in which we grew raspberries and asparagus, and an orchard full of Victoria plums. It was an ideal place to write.

I also took part in a number of voluntary activities, one of them as a speaker in the Rectorial Debate of the Revd Lord McLeod of Fuinary in October 1969 at Glasgow University. One of my fellow debaters was Nicholas Fairbairn, QC, a sartorial dandy with a razor sharp mind, reputed to be the best criminal defence lawyer in Scotland and one whose skills in advocacy had on several occasions resulted in the accused, who in his view ought to have been convicted, being acquitted. We travelled back to Edinburgh on the last train, he to his miniature fairytale castle of Fordell across the Forth, I to pick up my car and return to the borders. On the way, Nicky said, 'This might interest you. Tomorrow morning in the High Court in Edinburgh, I have to make my closing speech on behalf of a man accused of murder *whom I know to be innocent* [my italics].' Two days later I read in the *Scotsman* that the man in question, Patrick Meehan, aged 42, had been convicted of murder by a majority verdict of a fifteen-man Scottish jury (nine to six, Nicky said) and sentenced to life imprisonment. After the verdict Meehan was asked by the judge if he wanted to say anything before sentencing. 'I want to say this, sir,' he replied. 'I am innocent of this crime and so is James Griffiths. You have made a terrible mistake.'

Meehan, said Nicky, was a well-known Glasgow 'Ned' or villain, an indifferently successful safe-blower who had spent most of his life in and out of approved schools, borstals and prisons; but there had never been anything of violence in his record, and the crime of which he stood accused had been an act of extreme violence. Nicky must have mentioned to Meehan that he had spoken to me about his case, for several weeks later I received a letter from him. 'Dear Mr Kennedy, I am serving life imprisonment for a horrible murder in which I was never involved.' I took my time answering, for in the wake of my publications on the Timothy Evans and Derek Bentley cases, protestations of innocence from convicted prisoners were reaching me every month.

Eventually, sheer curiosity led me to visit Meehan in Peterhead prison on Scotland's north-east coast, and I applied for a visiting order. He turned out to be short and stocky, with grey-blue eyes, reddish hair and a florid, rather patchy facial appearance. He was neatly turned out and had an unexpected and attractive sense of humour. In affirming his innocence he was rather more verbose that I had bargained for, but this could be explained by his having opted for solitary confinement as a protest against his conviction and sentence. The governor of the prison, Alexander Angus, had also come to believe in Meehan's innocence. 'First,' he told me, 'and as a general rule, guilty men when they come to prison don't go on asserting innocence, at least not for long. As for

Meehan, it was a crime which would have been totally out of character, and it was the way he spoke about it that convinced me.'

In my more limited experience, I have found the same. Guilty men trying to persuade you of their innocence are apt to be over-assertive: innocent men do not so much assert innocence as assume it, and also assume that you must be aware of it, too. It is a hard thing to explain but when you encounter it face to face, as solicitors and barristers often do but judges and juries rarely, it is instantly recognisable.

That is why, over the years, before taking up any new case, I have made it a routine practice to consult the convicted man's solicitors. If, as has happened, they express uncertainty about innocence, I do not follow things up. In the three years that Meehan had been in prison since his trial, he had had four solicitors, three in Glasgow and one in Aberdeen; all four were convinced of his innocence. After I had spoken to each in turn, they agreed to join me on the Patrick Meehan Committee, which I had set up with the object of quashing Meehan's conviction and getting his early release from prison. At that time we had no inkling of the length of time it would take to achieve our goals, nor of the bureaucratic bigotry and frustrations that would be put in our way.

The following is Meehan's story, the particulars of which are now generally accepted to be true. During one of his incarcerations in Parkhurst prison on the Isle of Wight, Meehan met another prisoner named Jim Griffiths, a Rochdale man with a pronounced Lancashire accent which he had tried to improve by overlaying it with standard English. Aged thirty-four at the time of the murder for which Meehan was convicted, he too had a long criminal past. But there was one striking difference between them: Griffiths was a man of violence, Meehan not. Once, when a BBC radio team visited Gartree prison to interview some of the inmates, they recorded Griffiths (who was there for another offence at the time) saying that when he was released he had no intention of going straight – 'though with my past record I know that if I'm caught, I'm going to face a big sentence, fifteen or maybe twenty-five years'.

He added, 'I don't go out with the intention of committing violence, but if in the course of my going on a job it means I either get caught and put in prison, or I whack somebody over the head and they die, that's their bad luck. So if a policeman charges at me shouting, "Stop, stop, stop" and I had a gun in my possession, I would use it.'

Before another year was out, Griffiths was to fulfil his prediction to the letter.

Yet although a mental nurse who had once met Griffiths described him as a psychopath and although both Griffiths and Meehan had in childhood felt themselves to have been rejected by their mothers, there was another side to each. Meehan was a regular blood donor and always eager to help anyone in trouble. Griffiths loved climbing and potholing and, perhaps surprisingly, classical music, especially Beethoven and Tchaikovsky – 'new horizons all the time'. Equally surprising were his good manners – opening doors for women, offering others his seat. He was a good-looking man, always nicely dressed, and Meehan's 18-year-old daughter Liz was bowled over by him. 'You couldn't meet a nicer man. He was really suave. I think my dad felt sorry for him – he always hates seeing people left out of things.' In fact, at Parkhurst and again in Glasgow, Meehan found Griffiths a crashing bore, droning on endlessly about how he was supposed to have got nine or ten 'O' Levels and to have flown with the Red Devils. All Meehan's family and friends knew him as Paddy but Griffiths, an outsider, liked to call him Pat.

Until recently Griffiths had operated in the Midlands and the south, but had come to Glasgow because he had heard from a fellow prisoner at Parkhurst of a trustworthy fence there who could take goods he had stolen. This arrangement worked so well that Griffiths fell into the habit of carrying out a robbery in England, then driving through the night to Scotland to exchange the booty for cash. At first he had nowhere to stay, so Meehan's wife Betty lent him an unoccupied flat she owned. Later he acquired a flat of his own in Holyrood Crescent, ensconcing in it his 17-year-old mistress, Irene Cameron, a punch-type operator at the electricity board described by Betty Meehan as 'a wee girl with spectacles and a blonde beehive wig'. To the naïve young Irene Griffiths fantasised that his father had been an army colonel, and that when he had been away from home his mother had had an affair with another man, the result of which had been Jim, but that when the colonel returned, he had beaten Jim with a stick and made him eat his meals with the servants.

Griffiths also leased a lock-up garage in which to hide the cars he was stealing with increasing regularity. Later he found in the Highlands an ideal place for dumping them, a stretch of deep water in Loch Awe.

Yet despite both Patrick and Betty Meehan's growing antipathy towards Griffiths – she would no longer allow him in the house – Meehan and Griffiths each wanted something from the other. Meehan wanted the tranport of which Griffiths seemingly had a limitless supply, to investigate suitable places for blowing safes, and Griffiths wanted to be at hand when Meehan blew one in order to share in the proceeds. He was also becoming fed up with his time-consuming trips to Loch Awe, where in any case his graveyard of stolen cars was now becoming a little crowded. So when Meehan suggested an evening drive down to Stranraer in Ayrshire to case the motor taxation office, Griffiths saw an opportunity to steal registration books so that he could sell stolen cars instead of dumping them.

On the evening of Saturday, 5 July 1969, Griffiths, driving a blue Triumph car which he had stolen from a hotel car park in Gretna Green a few days earlier, picked up Meehan outside his flat in Old Rutherglen Road, Glasgow. Meehan was wearing casual trousers, suede shoes and a cap; Griffiths wore dark glasses by way of disguise. It was a warm summer's evening, so neither took a coat.

The Triumph drove through Kilmarnock, by-passed Ayr, then headed south along the coast road. Loch Ryan, the big bay that gives access to Stranraer, came into sight and, as they passed the Lochryanhall Hotel, Griffiths remarked that on the way back they might stop and look over the cars parked there in case any cameras had been left in them.

Arriving in Stranraer between 7 and 7.30 p.m., Griffiths filled up with petrol at a garage (where Meehan noticed a second-hand Morris he fancied), then parked in the car park on the sea front. While Griffiths was repairing the offside traffic indicator, which had broken, Meehan went off to look at the motor taxation offices in the County building up the hill in Sun Street. Approaching it, he remembered he had been there once before, in 1955, and that the next year his friend John Harvey had blown the safe in the rent office. Observing that there were now several new houses adjoining the offices, he decided that breaking into it would be too risky.

He rejoined Griffiths in the car park and together they walked to Spencer's Hotel in Church Street for high tea. This was served by Mrs Harkness, sister of the proprietress, and her niece Janet. At the next table were an English family from Yorkshire – Griffiths told Meehan he could tell by their accents. At 8.30 p.m. it was time for Janet to dress for her weekly dance and she gave Meehan and Griffiths their bill. Back in the car park Griffiths had a final go at repairing the traffic indicator while Meehan went to a pub, had a couple of drinks and telephoned Betty to say he would be back late. Upon his return to the car, he and Griffiths had a swig of coffee from Griffiths's flask and, after Griffiths had had a catnap, they set off for the Lochryanhall Hotel, reaching it in time to hear the Saturday night band playing the National Anthem. It was 11.45 p.m.

For three-quarters of an hour the pair stood in the shadows of an abandoned Ministry of Defence camp the other side of the road while various people left the hotel, some in the staff bus, some on foot. One light stayed on in the hotel: it was in the sitting-room of the hotel's owner, Mr Stanyer, who was having a nightcap with the band. Some time between 1.30 a.m. and 2 a.m. Meehan, bored of waiting, bored by Griffiths and wanting his bed, said 'This is a waste of time. We're going to be here all night.' Griffiths replied that as they had already waited so long, they might as well wait a little longer. Soon after, the sitting-room light went out and the whole place was in darkness. Griffiths crossed the road to the car park, noticed a white minivan which he thought might contain a tourist's camera, forced the lock and searched it: unfortunately for him it belonged to Mr Stanyer and contained only empty cartons. 'We'd best go home,' said Meehan wearily, and reluctantly Griffiths agreed.

On the way back they stopped briefly at Ballantrae for Griffiths to look at a parked Jaguar. After that Meehan nodded off and the next thing he remembered was Griffiths saying, 'That's a lovely sight' and looked up to see the lights of Prestwick airport.

A few miles further on the Triumph's headlights picked up an unexpected sight – a very young girl standing in a lay-by on the left-hand side of the road. Good Samaritan Meehan said, 'That kiddy seems to be in some sort of trouble', and told Griffiths to stop. He let down the window and the girl, whom Meehan thought was about fifteen, said, 'Mister gonny help me?' She said that two men had dumped her from their car and driven off with her pal. 'How long ago?' asked Meehan, and the girl said, 'Just a couple of minutes.' He told her to get in the back seat and said to Griffiths, 'Let's catch them.' Griffiths put his foot down and, inviting the attention of any police cars that happened to be about, pushed the speedometer up to a hundred. 'What's your name?' Meehan asked the girl. 'Irene Burns,' she said, to which Meehan quipped, 'No relation of Rabbie', and laughed.

They caught up with the boyfriends' car, a white Anglia, on the outskirts of Kilmarnock and, having forced it to stop, transferred Irene's friend Isobel Smith to the Triumph and took the two girls to their nearby homes: the reason Irene had been dumped, it emerged, was that she had spurned the attempts of one of the boys to make a pass at her.

By the time Meehan and Griffiths left Kilmarnock for Glasgow, it was close to 4.30 a.m. and getting light. Having been dropped off at Old Rutherglen Road, Paddy woke Betty letting himself in ('He's that clumsy', said Betty, 'he'd wake the dead'). He said nothing about why he had gone to Stranraer, but then he never did. But he did mention the two girls and chasing the white Anglia. He said the girls were both teenagers and he could not get over their being allowed out so late at night. Later he told Liz about them and, although eighteen herself, she was quite shocked, for Betty never liked her to stay out late without ringing in or saying where she would be.

After a cup of tea Meehan went to bed. It had not been a very fruitful outing.

Two other Glasgow villains, however, were also operating in Ayrshire that night. Their names were William 'Tank' McGuinness, so called because his skills at safe-blowing were such that it was said he could even penetrate a tank, and Ian Waddell. McGuinness was then thirty-nine years old, a small, wiry man with auburn hair and a little, foxy face. The son of a shipyard worker on the Clyde, he was one of eight children but, as with Meehan's family, none of his siblings were ever in trouble. After National Service he never took a job, but lived on social security and the proceeds of crime. His offences included theft, housebreaking and assault with intent to rob.

He had a wife, Agnes, whom he married when on leave from the army. Like Betty Meehan's, Agnes's married life consisted of interludes between prison; yet she succeeded in bringing up four children. By contrast with her husband's vicious criminal life, she saw in him 'a good family man, never lost his temper with me or the children, always very quiet-spoken'. When at home he liked watching sport on television. He smoked a lot and rolled his own cigarettes. He did not like company, was always a bit of a loner.

Waddell was thirty years old, with reddish hair, of a cheerful disposition and indistinct speech. His father had killed sheep in a Glasgow abattoir: he himself went through a string of jobs, at a bakery, as a food porter in Manchester, as a storeman for tractors. He married when he was twenty-three and had a child, but separated from his wife five years later. In 1964 he drifted into crime and since then had had several convictions for theft, housebreaking and carrying an offensive weapon. At this time he bore two scars on his face, imprints from a fight with a broken bottle, and a missing front tooth caused by falling over when drunk. He walked with a pronounced stoop, had a clammy handshake and a ready smile (for one may smile and smile and be a villain).

These two villains left Glasgow in a hired Ford Cortina on the afternoon of this same 5 July. They were on their way to break into the bungalow near the seafront in Ayr of a bingo hall owner named Abraham Ross and his wife Rachel. Word had reached them that Mr Ross had a safe containing large amounts of bingo hall cash and they intended to persuade him, in the course of the night, to hand over the key of that safe; if he refused, they had ways of persuading him to change his mind. They were not fastidious people.

On arriving in Ayr they went to a betting shop for a couple of hours, where Waddell won some money on a horse. To fill in time they then drove to Girvan and had a cup of tea on the front, but did not look up McGuinness's daughter Elizabeth, who was on holiday there at the time. They then returned to Ayr and discovered that the address of the Rosses' bungalow was 2 Blackburn Place. They went to look at it and found it was situated on the corner of Blackburn Place, a cul-de-sac, and Blackburn Road, which runs westwards to the sea. They also noted that at the back of the bungalow was a telegraph pole which carried the telephone lines to it.

It was now early evening. The two men walked down to the front, had a meal in a café and killed yet more time sitting by the sea. Not until 11.30 p.m. when, according to Waddell, it was 'half dark, half night' did they feel it safe to approach Blackburn Place again, having first parked their car in an adjoining street. Stepping over a low garden wall, they crept across the lawn to where a chink of light showed through the curtains of the last room at the back. Through the window they saw the Rosses lying in twin beds, Mr Ross reading in the one nearest the window. They spotted a key in the bedroom door and wondered if it was locked. They then went to the other side of the house and inside the garage found a pair of garden steps. McGuinness used them to climb on to the roof of an adjoining garage from which he could reach the telegraph pole and cut the lines to the bungalow. He also cut a piece of rope from the clothes line on the drying green in order to tie the Rosses up.

Abraham Ross was then sixty-seven, a small man (5 feet 3 inches), who weighed under ten stone. His wife Rachel was seventy-two. They had been married for thirty-six years.

One of five children from a Glasgow Jewish family, after school Abe had joined his father in the rag trade and scrap metal business. When he was twenty-one, though, he emigrated to Canada and the US, where he worked as a dishwasher, bellboy and waiter. His happiest time was working for H. M. Stevens, the firm that did the catering for American horseracing tracks. Customers left him generous tips which, if he had saved, would have made him comfortably off, but he was a born gambler who was often broke until next pay day. In 1933 Abe returned to Glasgow and rejoined his father in the rag trade. He also re-married (his first wife having died in New York in childbirth). His new bride, Rachel Freedman, was from another Glasgow Jewish family and an old friend. They were saddened when told by a gynaecologist that Rachel would be unable to have children.

In 1941, when Glasgow experienced its first wave of enemy bombing, Abe and Rachel moved into rented rooms in Ayr, commuting to Glasgow daily. When his father died, Abe became the sole owner of the family business. Inevitably he got to know many Glasgow villains, a large proportion of what he was offered for sale having been stolen. He told me that in the rag trade the police come to inspect the books every seven days, and if you re-sell metal without first telling them, you are likely to lose your licence.

In 1952 Abe bought 2 Blackburn Place, Ayr, and continued to commute to Glasgow daily. Nine years later, he launched the business venture that was to make him prosperous: along with three friends, he purchased a cinema in Paisley and converted it into a bingo hall.

Abe's friends describe him then as a soft-spoken man, shrewd and extremely conservative. He still gambled modestly on the pools and horses and was also fond of cigars. He said generously of his wife that she was far above his own intelligence. 'She was a great reader and much interested in politics. She was very left-wing, anti-apartheid and didn't think the Queen did enough. This didn't make her popular with many of our friends in Ayr.' But their marriage was a happy one.

On this particular Saturday, 5 July, Abe and Rachel spent most of the day at home, then at 7 p.m. they drove to Prestwick airport for dinner. On their return they spent the rest of the evening watching television and around midnight prepared for bed. Before getting into bed, Abe drew the curtains, then, as was his custom, he 'pushed them apart a little before lying down to sleep'. In bed he read for about a quarter of an hour, unaware that through the gap in the curtains McGuinness and Waddell were watching him. Then he turned out the light.

Waddell and McGuinness, meanwhile, had been sitting quietly in the back garden, biding their time. They discussed what names to call each other should the need arise and decided on the two common Glasgow names of Jimmy and Pat: McGuinness was to be Jim or Jimmy and Waddell Pat. By about 1 a.m., when the light in the Rosses' bedroom had been out for some time, they took off their shoes and put on home-made masks. With an iron bar and a weeding tool they had taken from the garage, they crept to the window of the spare bedroom to the left of the front door. McGuinness levered the weeding tool and then the iron bar between the bottom of the window and the sill and pushed upwards. The latch gave without any noise, the window opened and the two men climbed in. Having shut the window behind them, they groped their way across the room and into the corridor, walked slowly down it, and came to the last door on the right, the Rosses' bedroom. One of them turned the handle quietly and pushed: the door was not locked.

The first thing Abe Ross remembered of that dreadful night was a figure leaping at him out of the darkness, which must have been terrifying. At first he thought he had woken from a nightmare, then, hearing his wife shouting and screaming, he realised it was the real thing. His assailant was McGuinness, who had slipped sideways on to the floor so that Abe fell on top of him. Despite the darkness he saw that McGuinness was wearing a hood with slits for eyes and some kind of one-piece nylon suiting.

Waddell, meanwhile, had thrown himself on top of Mrs Ross and was hitting her about the face. 'Get this cunt off me, Pat,' shouted McGuinness from the floor, so Waddell left off hitting Mrs Ross and struck Abe Ross several times with the iron bar. McGuinness hit him, too, with the weeding tool then, when he was quiet, they put him on the floor and covered his face with a blanket. Next they turned on the light. Whenever Abe tried to remove the blanket, they hit him again, although by now he was bleeding profusely from face and head. To prevent further movement they tied both his and Rachel's hands behind their backs. As the two men talked among themselves, Abe noted their distinctive Glasgow accents.

Rachel Ross, now also under a blanket, began moaning and asking for an ambulance; she was suffering from Waddell having sprayed her with ammonia. Waddell later recalled her saying, 'Are you all right, Abe?' and telling him and McGuinness to take what they wanted and leave. She said they would find money in the dressing-table drawer, where they did indeed find £200. McGuinness asked Abe where the wall safe was. He replied that he did not have a wall safe, but each time he said it, McGuinness hit him. Then Waddell heard Abe say, 'You can kill me if you like but I haven't got a wall safe.' Eventually he admitted to having an ordinary safe and told them where to find the keys.

McGuinness found several thousand pounds in the safe, mostly in new notes contained in a small case. The pair then ransacked the bungalow, pulling out drawers, breaking into cupboards, even ripping away the side of the bath to see if anything had been concealed there. In the bedroom they found some new £10 notes in Abe's trouser pocket and some travellers' cheques in a black plastic folder. When Wadell noticed a gold watch on Rachel Ross's wrist, he pulled it forcibly off her.

Exhausted by their activities and not wanting to leave the house until daylight to make their getaway less conspicuous, the two then repaired to the Rosses' kitchen to drink Abe's whisky and lemonade. They stayed there for about an hour, drinking and talking. At one point Abe thought that he heard one of them say, 'They're not here yet, Jim', but that he must have been mistaken as they had no accomplices.

Now the pair decided to tie up the Rosses even more securely so that after they had left, the old couple would not be able to give the alarm. They turned them on to their backs, bent their legs behind them and tied their ankles with rope: they then tied the rope binding Abe's legs to the one binding his hands. The Rosses now lay on their bedroom floor like trussed chickens. Mrs Ross again begged them to send for an ambulance, to which Waddell replied, 'Shut up, shut up, we'll send an ambulance', which he said he intended to do but never did.

At around 5.30 a.m., when it was quite light, McGuinness went to fetch the car which he had left a couple of streets away: at this hour on a Sunday morning one man in the street would look less suspicious than two; also, Waddell's jacket was covered in blood. But as McGuinness was going down Racecourse Road, a police panda car spotted him and drew alongside. This was a tense moment for McGuinness, as he had Abe's car keys and two of his rings in his pocket. In answer to questions McGuinness gave a false name, said he had walked from Girvan where he had been visiting his daughter and missed the last bus to Glasgow. They took pity on him, said they would take him to the bus station and so they rode there together, seekers of criminals assisting a criminal who had just come hotfoot from his latest crime.

The two officers, Inspector Hepburn and Sergeant McNeil, dropped

McGuinness off at the bus station, saying a Glasgow bus would be leaving shortly. When they had gone McGuinness, much shaken, started back on foot to retrieve the car and then drive to the bungalow to pick up Waddell. Waddell had had a scare, too, for peeping round the curtains to see if McGuinness had returned, he saw another (or the same) panda car cruising down Blackburn Road. 'I got a real fright,' he told friends later, 'I thought the game was up.' Waddell went out by the back door, leaving it open, put on his shoes and, holding the case containing the money, joined McGuinness in the car.

The route from Blackburn Place to Glasgow goes through the centre of Ayr but, not wanting to risk another encounter with the police, McGuinness drove south along Racecourse Road and made a long circuitous sweep through Cumnock and Douglas before joining the A74, the dual carriageway from Carlisle to Glasgow. Along the way the pair stopped at a lay-by to divide the loot. Waddell recalled all the blood lost by Abe Ross and wondered if he would die; but neither man telephoned for an ambulance. They arrived in Glasgow at around 8 a.m. Worried that the officers in the panda might have remembered his face from a mugshot, McGuinness told Agnes he was going away for a few days and left almost immediately for London by car.

Back in Blackburn Place, Abe Ross looked about him, saw through his left eye (the other was clotted with blood and badly damaged) the chaos of the room, his blood all round him, his wife lying helpless on the floor. He tried to move but found it impossible. Rachel's legs, however, were not tied to her hands, so he asked her to try and move to the telephone that lay on the table between the two beds. She did manage to crawl over and lift the receiver, only to find the line dead.

As the day wore on Abe made several attempts to loosen his bonds, but without success. From outside in Blackburn Road he heard cars and people passing at intervals, and shouted and screamed as loud as he could to attract attention. But his voice was not strong enough; nobody heard him. Evening came on and then night; by now the Rosses had been lying helpless on the floor for twenty-four hours without food or water. In the early hours of Monday morning, Abe heard Rachel make a gurgling noise in her throat. 'I knew then that she was going'.

Their dreadful ordeal finally ended at 9 a.m. with the arrival of their domestic help, Mrs Grant. She knew something was wrong, for Sunday's milk and papers were still on the step and the back door was open. She put the milk on the kitchen table, then heard Abe's voice calling feebly from the bedroom, 'Who's that?' She said it was her. 'Thank God,' she heard him say, 'call the police. We have been murdered.' Finding the line dead, Mrs Grant went over to a neighbour's house opposite to borrow the phone.

The police arrived almost immediately and, before the ambulance came to take the Rosses to hospital, a sergeant took a brief statement from Abe, Rachel by now being unconscious. All he could say about their attackers was that both had distinctive Glasgow voices and called each other Pat and Jim or Jimmy; this information was passed at once to all police stations in central and western Scotland.

The news of the vicious attack on the two pensioners left tied up on the floor over the weekend broke on the Monday evening, and was met everywhere with a sense of shock and revulsion. This changed to a mood of anger the next day, when it was learned that Rachel Ross had died of her injuries without regaining consciousness. Newspaper editorials expressed outrage and many people said they would like to kill the perpetrators themselves. The Meehan family were as shocked as anyone and Liz, remembering what her father had told her about the two boys in the white Anglia who had dumped Irene Burns by the roadside, urged him to telephone the police anonymously about them as possible suspects. At first Meehan declined, but when Mr Struthers, the police superintendent in charge of the case, appealed to the public for any information, if necessary anonymously, he agreed to do so and telephoned the duty officer at Ayr police station to tell him what he knew. An hour later he remembered his little joke about one of the girls being called Burns and rang back to give her name and to explain where they had dropped her in Kilmarnock.

In their search for those responsible for the murder the Ayr and Glasgow police had little to go on except that both men had Glasgow voices and called each other Pat and Jim or Jimmy, which at least narrowed the field. As a start they decided to interrogate the city's best-known villains. On 12 July, a week after the attack, two officers came to Old Rutherglen Road to get a statement of Meehan's movements on the night of 5 July. Had Meehan been one of the intruders, he would have undoubtedly insisted on a solicitor being present, as was his custom, but having committed no crime, he saw no need. Nor, at this time, did he know about the intruders calling each other Pat and Jim, for the police had only released one name, Pat, and people knew Meehan as Paddy.

Three days later, Griffiths and Meehan went on another of their jaunts in the blue Triumph, driving through the night to Scunthorpe for Griffiths to see a fence called Matthews. But Matthews was not there, so Griffiths took Meehan over to a local prison so that he could visit an old girlfriend called Lil. When he got back to Glasgow, Betty said that a Detective Constable Baxter, who was making routine inquiries about people's movements on the night of 5 July had called to see him. Meehan lost no time in telephoning Baxter, who said he would be round in the morning. He also told Griffiths that in any statement he made to Baxter, he would have to give an account of the trip to Stranraer in the stolen Triumph and advised him to dispose of it without delay. Griffiths lost no time in setting off in the Triumph for Loch Awe and in the dead of night pushing it over the edge to join the rest of his stolen cars.

For some reason Baxter cancelled the proposed meeting, but instead two other detectives named Smith and Lawrie came to Old Rutherglen Road to ask Meehan for a statement. This was a mixture of truth and falsehood. On 5 July, Paddy Meehan said, he and his friend Jim Griffiths had motored to Stranraer in Griffiths's blue Triumph (true) to look at a car which had been advertised for sale (false). He and Griffiths had had high tea and then Griffiths had returned to the Triumph to fix a broken traffic indicator while he had gone for a walk and a drink in a pub (true). They had left Stranraer to return home about midnight (true, but nothing about time spent at the Lochryanhall Hotel). There followed a long, detailed account of the incident with Irene Burns and the boys in the white Anglia and he admitted that it was he, to satisfy his daughter's pleading, who had anonymously informed the Ayr police about the incident. He concluded by stating (truthfully) that he and Jim had arrived back in Glasgow at around 5 a.m. but offered no explanation why, if they had left Stranraer at midnight, it had taken them five hours to reach Glasgow, a journey of eighty-six miles.

One can only imagine with what joy and incredulity senior police officers read this statement. It was like receiving an unexpected legacy. For the past week they had been under great pressure to produce results, well aware how passionately both public and press wanted Mrs Ross's killers brought to book, yet not having a clue who they might be. Now, out of the blue, their identity had been revealed. They had been looking for two criminals called Pat and Jim, and Pat and Jim had been handed to them on a plate: what is more, they had given no explanation of their movement during the unaccounted-for hours, because obviously they had spent this time assaulting the Rosses and taking the money from Mr Ross's safe. Finally, to remove suspicions from themselves and cast it on to others, they were suggesting that the two boys in the Anglia and not themselves were the Rosses' assailants. It all fitted together like a glove: there could be no doubt about it.

Labouring under these misapprehensions, the police applied for warrants for two things; a search of Meehan's flat, where they might find bloodstained clothing and cash from the safe; and for Meehan to take part in an identification parade where witnesses might recognise him.

Four detectives in plain clothes arrived at Old Rutherglen Road at eight in the morning, led by the Ayr police's Superintendent Struthers. 'The way they hammered at the door,' said Liz, 'put the fear of God into me.' They started searching at once; in the cupboards, under the carpets,

JUDICIAL PRONOUNCEMENTS
IT WOULD HAVE BEEN WISER
NOT TO HAVE MADE

1

Lord Goddard, Lord Chief Justice. Trial of Craig and Bentley. February 1953.
'Do you believe that those three officers have sworn what is
deliberately untrue – those three officers who showed devotion to
duty for which they are entitled to the thanks of the community?'

Mr Justice Lewis. Trial of Timothy John Evans. January 1950.
'Christie is a man who has told you he is a sick man. I am not going over again what I have already told you, that is under doctor's orders and still is, but in passing may I say ... he could not possibly have taken that woman [Beryl Evans] down the stairs ...'

2

Lord MacDermott, Lord Chief Justice of Northern Ireland. Trial of Iain Hay Gordon. March 1953.
'I therefore think the confession statement is admissible as a voluntary statement and I see no reason to think it was unfairly taken or in a manner which would justify me in excluding it.'

3

Lord Robertson. Trial of Ian Waddell. November 1976.

'There can be no legal justification whatever in saying that Meehan was wrongly convicted, and having heard the evidence in this case, you might well have come to the conclusion he was rightly convicted.'

4

Inquiry of Lord Hunter into the cases of Meehan and Waddell. 1977–82.

'It cannot be disproved that Meehan and Griffiths were not a follow-up team to deal with the safe or safes believed to be in the bungalow … Reliance is rightly placed on the integrity and competence of police officers.'

5

Lord Justice Roskill, sitting with Lord Justice Lawton and Mr Justice Wien. Failed appeal of McMahon and Cooper. July 1976. 'The conclusion that each of us has independently reached is that Mathews was clearly telling the truth ... we see no justification in disturbing the verdicts which in our view were entirely correct.'

6

Mr Justice Bridge. Trial of the Birmingham Six. June 1975. 'If the defendants were telling the truth, I would have to suppose that a team of fifteen officers conspired among themselves to use violence on the prisoners and fabricate evidence. ... All the officers who gave their evidence in the circumstances in which the statements were taken impressed me as straightforward and honest witnesses.'

7

Lord Denning, Master of the Rolls. Judgment in the Failed Appeal of the Birmingham Six for legal aid to sue the police for injuries received while in police custody. November 1977.

'Just consider the course of events if this action is allowed to proceed to trial. If the six men fail, it will mean that much time and money will have been expended by many people for no good purpose. If the six men win, it will mean that the police were guilty of perjury, that they were guilty of violence and threats, that the confessions were involuntary and were improperly admitted in evidence and that the convictions were erroneous. This would mean the Home Secretary would either have to recommend they be pardoned or he would have to remit the case to the Court of Appeal. This is such an appalling vista that every sensible person in the land would say, it cannot be right that these actions go any further.'

9   10

*Lord Lane (left), Lord Chief Justice, sitting with Lord Justice O'Connor
(right), and Lord Justice Stephen Brown. Judgment in the Failed Appeal
of the Birmingham Six. January 1988.*

'As has happened before in References by the Home Secretary to this
court, the longer this hearing has gone on, the more convinced the
court has become that the verdict of the jury was correct.'

Mr Justice Donaldson. Trial of Vincent Maguire. March 1976. 'Do you think he was beaten up? You have seen the police officers. It was put to them and they denied using any violence towards Vincent at all. You will no doubt consider whether, if he really was beaten up, he would not have complained to somebody at the time.'

11

Lord Justice Lawton, sitting with Lord Justice Roskill, and Mr Justice Boreham. Failed Appeal of the Guildford Four. October 1977. 'The new evidence gives rise to no lurking doubts whatsoever in our minds. We are sure there has been a cunning and skilful attempt to deceive the court by putting forward false evidence ... We are all of the clear opinion that there are no possible grounds for doubting the justice of any of these convictions or of ordering new trials.'

12

13

*Lord Justice Kelly. Trial of Guardsmen James Fisher and Mark Wright for
the murder of Peter McBride. February 1995.*

'I am quite satisfied that when Fisher and Wright realised what
adverse inference could be brought against them if they admitted to
having seen McBride searched in Trainfield Street, they lied about it.
They also lied when they said they first saw the bag being carried by
McBride when he began to run away from them.. There was no
reasonable possibility that Fisher could have held an honest belief that
McBride was carrying a coffee-jar bomb.'

beneath floorboards and mattresses, even in the bathroom and kitchen. Betty asked what they were searching for. Was it something large or small? But they wouldn't say. They asked Betty for two suitcases and she put into them all Meehan's clothes, tools and papers. For him, watching in silence and knowing there was nothing to find, the search must have had a sort of mad, surreal quality, like an early Chaplin two-reeler.

Before the search was completed, two officers took Meehan across the river to Glasgow Central police station for the identification parade, which was under the supervision of Detective Sergeant Inglis of the Ayr police. Certain they had targeted the right man, the police had no hesitation in rigging the parade to provide evidence that would stick. It was a scorching hot morning when the parade was assembled, consisting of Meehan and eight other men picked off the street who matched roughly Meehan's height and build; though, unlike them, he was wearing a blue pinstripe suit and a green tie. On the floor in front of each man on the parade were big printed numbers by which the witnesses could identify them.

There were to be six witnesses: a Mrs Mathieson, who the day before the break-in was asked by two men in Ayr for directions to Blackburn Road; a Mr Falconer, who on the afternoon of the break-in heard two men in a lane opposite the Rosses' bungalow saying something about the backs of houses (possibly McGuinness and Waddell); Mr Haxton, a petrol pump attendant at Stranraer; Irene Burns and Isobel Smith; and lastly, of course, Abe Ross.

They all assembled in the Detective Constable's room on the ground floor. Abe Ross, whose eye was still heavily bandaged, had a nurse in attendance. The police usher at the door called for the first witness. Ross and the nurse left the room and the others naturally assumed he would be the first to see the parade. Instead, he and the nurse were taken down a corridor to the interview room and told to wait.

The first witness to view the parade was Mr Falconer. He began with the man nearest to him as he entered, worked his way up to number one without indentifying anyone and was then shown to the interview room where he saw Mr Ross, whom he assumed had viewed the parade. The next witnesses were Mrs Mathieson and Mr Haxton. Like Mr Falconer they started at number eight and walked up to number one; but they, too, were unable to identify anyone and went to join Abe in the interview room. Then came the two girls, Irene Burns and Isobel Smith. Both identified Meehan as one of the two men who had rescued them and taken them home to Kilmarnock. Isobel was so hesitant in her identification that Meehan said to her sympathetically, 'Don't worry, pet. Everything will be all right.'

What happened in the interview room when these two joined the others was later described by Irene Burns. 'The old man asked me if I had picked out anyone. I told him I had … Isobel came in and we discussed the parade and I described Mr Meehan to Isobel. The old man was sitting near us as we were talking. Isobel and I both agreed we had picked out the same person.' Other witnesses confirmed this.

Now it was time for Mr Ross to view the parade and, well briefed by Irene and Isobel, come face to face with one of the men he believed had murdered his wife. It must have been a dreadful moment for him. The door was opened and he and the nurse went in. Meehan, who had changed position once or twice as he was entitled to, was now at number one, at the far end. He expected Mr Ross to start viewing the parade from the other end, as all the others had done, but instead Mr Ross was steered by a police officer (who may also have tipped him the wink) to where Meehan stood at number one.

Following instructions, Mr Ross then asked for the men to say, 'Shut up, shut up, we'll send an ambulance.' Had Paddy Meehan been the murderer of Mrs Ross he might have tried to disguise his voice. Having, as he thought, nothing to lose he spoke the words firmly and clearly.

The effect on Abe Ross was catastrophic. He staggered back, visibly shaken, and exclaimed, 'That's the voice. I know it. I know it. I don't have to go any further.' Meehan, appalled, said, 'You're mistaken, laddie.' 'Oh, that's him, that's him,' cried Abe, collapsing. 'Sir,' Meehan continued with some heat, 'you have got the wrong man, honest.'

The wretched Meehan was then taken up to the bar of the police station and charged with robbery and murder. On his way down to the cells he passed his wife Betty, who had brought him a packet of cigarettes, sitting on a bench. 'He was chalk white,' said Betty, 'and kept saying, "That old man *picked me out*." He couldn't understand it.'

One of Meehan's first visitors in the cells was the head of Glasgow's CID, Detective Chief Superintendent Goodall, whom Meehan knew from his past. 'We know the two men at Ayr had Glasgow accents,' Goodall told him, 'so Griffiths couldn't have been with you. Who was with you, then?' Meehan replied that he had been with Griffiths but that neither of them had been in Ayr. 'In that case,' replied Goodall, 'the sooner you can get Griffiths to come in and clear you, the better'.

When Griffiths rang the Meehans' flat later that morning, knowing nothing of Paddy's arrest for murder, Betty put him in the picture. She also told him what Goodall had said about both the intruders having Glasgow accents. 'Paddy says you must go down to the station and clear both of you,' she told him, to which he replied, 'If I go to the station, they'll release Paddy, and for all the things I'm wanted for I'll get ten years. What am I to do?'

He did the least, and the most, of what he felt he could do: three times that day he telephoned Goodall to say that neither he nor Meehan had been in Ayr, only Stranraer; three times Goodall told him that if that was so, he should come to the station and make a statement; three times Griffiths said he was unable to do so.

Until now Meehan had observed a certain honour among thieves by not disclosing to the police Griffiths's address. But now, if the charges were to be lifted from him, he had no alternative but give it. And when he did, orders went out to detectives to go to 14 Holyrood Crescent and bring Griffiths in.

That same day Meehan arrived at Ayr sheriff's court to answer the charges against him. A big, hostile crowd was waiting. As he got out of the police car with a blanket over his head, the crowd broke into a chant of hatred, believing, as crowds do, that a man charged with murder must be guilty of murder. There were cries of 'Hang him!', 'Shoot the sod!', 'Murdering bugger!' In the court Meehan's solicitor, Joseph Beltrami, one of the most brilliant and successful defence lawyers in Scotland, was waiting for him. In front of him, Meehan grabbed the lapel of one of the detectives escorting him and said, 'For fuck's sake, do your job. Go to Stranraer, check my alibi and get the bastards who did this.' Observing him, Mr Beltrami said, 'It was a completely spontaneous outburst and simply couldn't have been put on.' He added, 'He had the air of absolute innocence about his person. This is rare indeed, and what a burden it proved to be.'

After the hearing, which was brief and formal, there were more catcalls from the crowd and, before the police could stop him, a man ran out and kicked Meehan on the shin. Back in Glasgow, he was taken to the remand wing of Barlinnie prison, where he learned the astonishing news that Griffiths was dead.

It came about in the way that Griffiths had predicted it would in the interview he had given in Gartree prison. 'If a policeman charges at me shouting, "Stop, stop, stop" and I have a gun in my possession, I would use it.'

Knowing from his record of Griffiths' propensity for violence, the Glasgow police were taking no chances. A car containing five detectives stopped outside 14 Holyrood Crescent. They ran up the stairs to Griffiths' attic flat inside which they heard a radio playing music. They banged on the door. The radio was switched off. They banged again, saying who they were, then, getting no answer, they pushed the door in. There was a loud report and they saw Griffiths coming at them with a shotgun. Being unarmed they had no alternative but to beat a hasty retreat down the stairs, Griffiths firing as they retreated and hitting the last man of the squad with seventeen pellets.

The next hour and a half were almost unbelievable. It was as though Griffiths was determined to release in one great destructive flood the pent-up rage he felt at being hunted for a crime which, for once in his life, he had not committed. He was fulfilling another prediction, too.

'When I go,' he had told Wally Gow, a Scunthorpe friend, 'I'm going to take everyone with me that I hate. I won't go on my own.' So now from his attic window he began firing with shotgun and rifle not only at the police car but at anybody who moved, injuring several passers-by. While ambulance men were attending to them, Griffiths slipped down the stairs with his guns and ammunition, ran down the back road, spotted a Ford Anglia containing a commercial traveller, fired a shot at him through the passenger window, then ran round to the driver's door, pulled the man's bleeding body on to the pavement and drove off in it himself.

Next he crashed the Anglia at a place called the Round Toll and, although he seldom drank, strode into the Round Toll bar, like something out of a cowboy film, dangling guns and with ammunition round his waist. Perhaps that is how he saw himself – Big Jim Griffiths, toting gunman from the West. In true John Wayne style he fired two shots into the ceiling then marched up to the bar. 'Don't mess me about,' he shouted to the landlord, John Connolly, and his wife. 'I've shot some people already this morning. Nobody moves or they've had it.' He demanded a bottle of brandy and took a big swig from the neck. Then a man called Hughes, an elderly news vendor, reached for his glass. Griffiths, misinterpreting the move, shot him dead.

Police cars were nearing the Round Toll bar when Griffiths left as suddenly as he came, commandeered a stationary lorry and drove off. Presently he found himself in the derelict Springburn area, and, with the traffic lights against him, turned left into Kay Street, which, he found, to his horror, was a cul-de-sac. He jumped out of the lorry, ran up the stairs of a run-down two-storey house to the top flat and, finding it locked, shot away the lock and went in. The back window opened on to an open space and continuing to act out his fantasies, Griffiths took a few pot shots at people there.

But now the police were closing in fast. Two officers with revolvers went up the stairs to the top landing. One lifted the flap of the flat's letter-box and peered through. At this moment Griffiths happened to be moving across the entrance area. He saw the officer's eyes looking at him through the flap and made towards him. 'It was either him or me,' said the officer afterwards. He raised his arm and fired at Griffiths's shoulder. Griffiths fired at about the same time and missed. Then, hit in the body, he slumped to the floor. The officers grappled with him to remove the guns. Within minutes Griffiths was dead.

For Meehan it was shattering news. His only alibi had gone.

The Ayr and Glasgow police were not the only ones who had deluded themselves into believing that Meehan and Griffiths were responsible for the Ayr murder (there was nothing to connect Griffiths with it at all). In Edinburgh, the Crown Agent who authorises the prosecution of criminals under Scottish law, relying on the information supplied to him by the police, sanctioned the publication of the following statement:

> *With the death of Griffiths and the apprehension of Patrick*
> *Meehan, the police are no longer looking for any other person*
> *suspected of implication in the incident concerning Mr and Mrs*
> *Ross at Ayr.*

It would have been difficult to think of any statement more calculated to prejudice Meehan's case. When Mr Beltrami heard of it, he was outraged and at once issued a statement of rebuttal:

> *It will now be near impossible for my client to have a fair trial*
> *before an unbiased jury.*
> *   The Crown Office statement with regard to the finality of the*
> *police inquiries perturbs me. This would appear to mean that the*
> *police are satisfied that they can preclude any possibility of error or*
> *mistake.*

In my opinion, in the particular circumstance of this case, there might well be a possibility of a mistake. I am far from satisfied that this possibility can be excluded.

My client is entitled to a presumption of innocence. Following the Crown Office statement it might well appear to some that he is now required to prove his innocence, whereas Scots law requires the prosecution to prove his guilt.

I therefore feel that my client's case has been prejudiced.

This rather diffuse wording was all right as far as it went – but that was not very far. A more forthright statement, that there were good reasons to believe in Meehan's innocence, might have made more impact.

And as if the Crown Agent's statement were not enough to prejudice the case, the law authorities compounded it twice. First, they leaked Griffiths' criminal record to the press. Had he been only wounded and survived to stand trial, his record could not have been made public for fear of prejudicing the jury. For the same reason, Meehan's record would be barred from publication at his own trial. Yet his defence was that he was with Griffiths that night and, as the jury already knew that Griffiths had a long record, it would be fair to assume that Meehan had one, too. Secondly, because the police were anxious to trace the Triumph in which Meehan had stated that he and Griffiths had travelled to Stranraer, they inserted a paragraph in the *Police Gazette* that it was now *known* – not believed or thought, but *known* – that the car that had played a part in the Ayr break-in was a turquoise blue Triumph, registration number MAV 810G, and that any information as to its whereabouts should be given to police headquarters at Ayr.

By their actions the Crown Office and the police had committed themselves irrevocably to the case against Meehan and Griffiths. Griffiths, of course, was in no position to answer. But for Meehan, alive and as well as could be expected in Barlinnie jail, his case had been lost before it had even begun.

Another Glasgow villain the police wished to interview, however, was Ian Waddell. Although he was only a petty crook and had no record of violence, he had become a big mouth, blabbing to fellow crooks and others of the part he had played in the crime, and spending money, too. Informants passed this information on to the police and it became known in the Glasgow underworld that he was wanted for questioning.

Having no place of his own, Waddell was staying with a fellow crook named Dick, a fact of which the police were unaware, so they had been unable to track him down. Waddell took the initiative himself and hired a solicitor, Mr Carlin. He told the solicitor that he had heard the police were looking for him in connection with the Ayr murder, and that, although he had nothing to do with it, he would have no objection to giving the police a statement; also, if charged, he would like Mr Carlin to act for him. He handed the solicitor ten new £20 notes from Mr Ross's safe.

A day or two later, Carlin took Waddell along to Glasgow Central police station to be interviewed by Detective Chief Inspector Macalister. The questioning, which Carlin described as very thorough, lasted an hour. Waddell stuck closely to the false alibi: another crook named Carmichael would vouchsafe that on 5 July he had been in Glasgow all night, staying in Carmichael's house. In fact, he had been dropped off there by McGuinness in the early morning of 6 July, and the first thing he had done was burn his blood-stained jacket on Carmichael's rubbish tip. Later Carmichael was interviewed twice and confirmed Waddell's story; Waddell was not questioned again.

Free from danger, Waddell went on a spending spree. With what money that remained from his share of the loot, he gambled heavily on the horses, bought several new suits, spent a lot on drink and gave some to friends.

Within six weeks of the robbery, Waddell's share had gone. McGuinness, a family man, took his cut to the Shettleston branch of the Royal Bank of Scotland and had it credited to his account.

Happy in the knowledge that Mr Beltrami knew he was innocent, Meehan spent the three months leading up to his trial writing to his solicitor on a daily basis, sometimes twice daily, emphasising points that he felt might be helpful to his defence.

The first thing that troubled him was the Crown Office statement:

If the Crown really intend to take me to trial, I very much fear I can't be getting a clean trial … the police will be determined to get a conviction.

Talking to prisoners and staff I have come to grasp the extent of the damage done by the Crown Office statement. The prison doctor actually assumed from it that I had confessed. Can you not raise an action in the High Court before my trial date is set, and argue that the Crown Office have forfeited their right to put me on trial? It was a shocking statement to make when the case was sub judice.

But what he feared most was that, to be certain of a conviction, the police might commit perjury: 'The possibility that one of the policemen in the case might manufacture evidence is ever in my mind.' He remembered a conversation he had had with two detectives before his appearance at Ayr. One had said to him that Griffiths and he must have been guilty because Griffiths had tried to shoot his way out, to which he responded, again, that he was innocent. The other detective had said, 'We've got evidence you don't know about yet. You'd be surprised at what the boys in the backroom can do.' Meehan asked, 'What's that supposed to mean?' and he had replied, 'You'll soon find out.'

It was Mr Beltrami who first learned what the boys in the backroom had done when the police informed him that some pieces of paper found in the pocket of Griffiths's car coat matched pieces of paper, both brown and white, found in Mr Ross's safe.

Aside from the fact that 5 July was a very hot day, Griffiths had not been wearing a car coat and, in any case, was nowhere near the Ross bungalow, it was as devious a piece of police corruption as one could imagine in that Meehan could not answer for evidence found in the clothing of another.

Meehan was the first to see how cleverly and wrongly he had been trapped. 'The Crown are going to point to the paper in the pocket of Griffiths as evidence against me,' he wrote to Beltrami, 'the Crown case being that evidence against one is evidence against both. But Griffiths is not present to explain the paper in his pocket. Am I to sit in the dock with a ghost who can't communicate with court counsel or jury? Can we apply to the High Court to have a spiritualist medium in the dock, just in case Griffiths decides to get in touch?!!'

The bogus evidence about the pieces of paper came about in this way. On 7 and 8 July, immediately after the break-in, Detective Inspector Cook of the Glasgow police forensic department and Detective Superintendent Cowie of the Ayr police closely examined Mr Ross's safe, which had been taken to Ayr police headquarters, and found it completely empty. In the days that followed, other detectives made a careful search of Meehan's and Griffiths's clothing but found nothing incriminating. The rest of the month went by without any further progress and then, on the very last day of the month, 31 July, Griffiths's coat, which had already been examined once before, was re-examined by Mr Cook and this time, hey presto, contained little bits of brown and white paper which Cook described as very old and fragmented. Then, on 21 August, *seven weeks after the break-in,* Cook was asked to have another look at the safe and, hey presto, the safe which he had examined on 8 July and had found to be empty now contained little bits of brown and white paper which exactly matched those found in Griffiths's car coat pocket.

Depressing though this news was for Meehan, he was heartened by the arrival in Barlinnie of Ian Waddell who, having spent all his share of the money from Mr Ross's safe, was now broke and had been sent there on remand for house breaking; and, proud of the part he had played in the break-in, continued to blab about it to anyone who would listen.

From fellow prisoners Meehan learned for the first time not only that Waddell was one of the two perpetrators of the break-in but also, firstly, that he had given £200 to Mr Carlin, and secondly, that the police in the panda car had picked up McGuinness at 5.30 a.m. on 5 July. Later he managed to buttonhole Waddell, saying that it was important for his defence to know if it was daylight when they left. Waddell said that it was, which led Meehan to write to Mr Beltrami: 'If Counsel can get Mr Ross to agree that the attackers left at daylight, then it couldn't have been Griffiths and I because we were with the two girls at Prestwick when it was still dark.'

On 10 October Meehan was taken to Ayr to answer the indictment. He pleaded Not Guilty and – a speciality of Scottish law – put in two special defences, one of alibi, the other of impeachment against Ian Waddell. He was aware that a feeling of hostility towards Waddell was developing among the other prisoners at Barlinnie. 'Although prisoners normally stick together,' he wrote to Beltrami, 'they don't take kindly to men who beat people up and murder old ladies.' He added, 'If we brought everyone forward to whom Waddell had admitted guilt, then there would be a couple of hundred witnesses for the defence.'

A day or two later, Mr Beltrami went to London to ask Dr William Sargant, who had been an expert witness on the truth drug in the case of the Boston Strangler, if he would do the same for Meehan. He agreed to travel to Glasgow and administer the drug himself, without fee. But three High Court judges would not allow it. 'The Court has a duty,' pronounced Lord Cameron, 'to protect an accused person against the folly of his advisers.' Beltrami's response was succinct. 'Had I had the slightest doubts about Meehan's innocence it would indeed have been folly. As I had no doubts it wasn't.'

A week later, the trial of Patrick Connolly Meehan opened in No. 3 Court in the Old Parliament buildings in Edinburgh, transferred there from Ayr at Mr Beltrami's request to avoid local prejudice. Here had stood, in 1865, the notorious Dr Edward Pritchard, convicted of the double murder of his wife and mother-in-law, and subsequently hanged at the last public execution in Scotland. And here, too, in 1909 had come poor Oscar Slater who, like Meehan, had been found guilty as the result of wrongful identification, sentenced to death, reprieved and served nineteen years in Peterhead prison before the mistake was acknowledged and he was freed; considered until modern times the most famous (and to some, the only) case of a miscarriage of criminal justice in British legal history.

Apart from Nicky Fairbairn and Meehan, among the principal dramatis personae was the judge, Lord Grant, who was the Lord Justice Clerk, second most senior judge in Scotland. A tall man, in his red and cream silk robes adorned with big red crosses and small red diamonds, he was an imposing sight; and for the next five days his presence was to dominate the court.

In private Lord Grant was said to be a shy man. He had a clear, forceful mind and his opinions were always cogently expressed, though, because of a recent thyroid operation, in court he could sometimes be extremely testy: once during the course of Meehan's trial he told Nicky Fairbairn not to be stupider than he seemed. Like Mr Justice Marshall in the Ward case and later Mr Justice Bridge in the Birmingham Six case, he was to show an injudicious bias in favour of the prosecution.

Opposite Nicky Fairbairn stood counsel for the Crown, Ewan Stewart, QC, the Solicitor-General, a skilful and experienced advocate.

In Scottish law there are no opening speeches by prosecuting counsel, the Scots preferring to let the story unfold from the beginning through the mouths of witnesses; and the beginning in the Meehan case was the break-in and assault on the Rosses.

'Call Abraham Ross.'

Abraham Ross was ushered into the witness box, small and frail, the wound above his right eye still visible for all to see. The oath in Scotland is administered by the presiding judge, so Lord Grant rose to his fully robed six feet two, and faced the tiny man beneath him.

'Raise your right hand and say after me …'

Ross did so.

'I swear by Almighty God …'

'I swear by Almighty God …'

'And as I shall answer to God at the great day of judgement …'

'And as I shall answer to God at the great day of judgement …'

[This piece of nonsense has now been dropped and my guess is that the routine of swearing by Almighty God soon will be – indeed in a mostly secular society should be.]

'… that I shall tell the truth, the whole truth and nothing but the truth.'

Abe Ross swore to do so.

In evidence he was much less certain now that the voice saying, 'Shut up, shut up, we'll send an ambulance' he had heard at the ID parade was the same as the one he had heard in his bedroom. And when Waddell, whom Nicky had called under one of the special defences of incrimination, was led into court like a prize heifer and asked to say the same words, Mr Ross said that they *sounded* similar; also, when asked point blank if Waddell's voice could have belonged to one of the robbers, he admitted it was possible. However, Lord Grant gave the prosecution a helping hand by asking if his memory was as fresh now as it had been three months earlier, and of course Mr Ross agreed that it was not.

But on two other points Ross's evidence helped Meehan. First, as Meehan had requested, Nicky Fairbairn got him to admit that when the robbers left, it was daylight, 'quite full daylight' – when the two boys in the white Anglia gave their evidence, they agreed that when they had been overtaken by Griffiths and Meehan in the Triumph it was still dark. Then, when Mr Stewart, knowing the evidence Cowie and Cook would bring, asked Mr Ross if there was any shelving paper in the drawers of his safe, he expected him to say that there was. But Ross did not know what he was on about. 'I don't remember that,' he said.

'Do you know if there was *any* paper in the safe?' asked Mr Stewart, hopefully.

In Abe Ross's eyes safes were for holding cash and other valuables, not pieces of paper.

'I don't think so,' he replied.

Next Irene Burns and Isobel Smith took the stand. Nicky Fairbairn asked them if, when they were being taken home in the Triumph, they had noticed anything unusual about Meehan's and Griffiths' behaviour. No, the girls agreed, they seemed to be two perfectly ordinary, normal people, in no way agitated or frightened by the sight of policemen in Kilmarnock; the men did not behave in any way as if they had just carried out a robbery in which they had beaten and tied up old people.

If their evidence was a plus for Meehan, that of the three that followed was a minus. The witnesses were all police officers – Inglis, Struthers and Cowie – who, after they had gone through the great day of judgement routine and sworn to tell the whole truth, mostly told fibs.

The first was Detective Sergeant Inglis, in charge of the identification parade.

'I think,' Mr Stewart said to him, 'that certain witnesses viewed the parade and the first witness was Abraham Ross?'

'That is correct,' replied Inglis.

Meehan thought he had heard wrong: Ross was not the first witness, but the last.

Mr Stewart asked Inglis to look at Production No. 17, a schedule of the parade, written and signed by Inglis.

'And is that a correct account of the parade?'

'That is a correct account.'

'The accused elected to stand in position one for the first witness. Is that right?'

'He did.'

'For the first one, that is Abraham Ross?'

'Yes.'

Now Meehan realised his ears had not deceived him. He leaned over to Mr Beltrami and said, 'Ross wasn't *first*, he was *last*.' Beltrami passed a note containing that information on to Nicky Fairbairn, who did not think it of any importance. What did it matter if Ross had been first or last? He, no more than Beltrami or Meehan himself, knew of the circumstances in which Ross was *meant* and by the other witnesses *thought* to have gone first, but in fact was sent last so that he could hear Irene and Isobel describe Meehan's appearance.

Later Inglis compounded his lie. After telling the court how Ross had identified Meehan's voice as that of one of the criminals, he was asked by Stewart, 'And I think *after that* various other people viewed the parade?'

'*That is correct.*'

When Superintendent Struthers, who had also been at the parade, came to give evidence, he compounded Inglis's lie:

'And did you see *the first witness who viewed the parade*, Mr Abraham Ross?'

'I did.'

Then it was time for Detective Superintendent Cowie of the Ayr police to tell his porkies. His having told Mr Stewart that he had come back from leave on 18 August, he was asked, 'Did you hear when you came back about some fragments of old paper having been found in a car coat?'

He said he had heard about it from his colleague Mr Struthers.

'Now because you heard about this, did you recollect having seen something similar?'

Yes, he said, in the drawers of the safe in the house at 2 Blackburn Place. *But on 7 July he himself and on 8 July Mr Cook of the Glasgow police forensic department had examined the safe and declared it to be empty.* It was unfortunate that this could not have been pointed out at the time, for it would have flatly contradicted Cowie's next statement, that on 21 August, nearly seven weeks after the crime, he and Cook had examined (naturally he did not say re-examined) the safe at Ayr police headquarters, and on this occasion had both found some brown paper and a small piece of white paper, a page from a diary, in the safe. He also said that he and Mr Cook had found pieces of brown paper on the floor of the cupboard at Blackburn Place where the safe had stood.

Then Mr Cook took the stand to confirm and amplify Cowie's evidence. On 31 July, he said, he had examined the car coat sent to him from Holyrood Crescent and in the right-hand pocket had found fragments of paper, some brown and one white on which there was printing in a dark blue coloured ink. On 21 August, he said, he had examined the safe at Ayr police station; and agreed that it had a right-hand drawer.

'And on that day,' asked Mr Stewart, 'did you find something in that drawer?'

'Yes, I found paper in the drawer. Some brown paper in the drawer had been used as a lining for the drawer, and I also found a piece of paper which looked like a diary page.' In conclusion, Cook said that the bit of paper in the car coat and those found in or near the safe matched each other in every respect and in his view were of common origin.

Meehan listened to the evidence of Cowie and Cook, appalled. The message to the jury was that in robbing the safe Griffiths had inadvertently taken little bits of paper from it and its surrounds and at some later date had carefully transferred them to the pocket of his car coat which he was not wearing that night. It was a fantastic story and, as neither Meehan nor Griffiths had been anywhere near Blackburn Place, there was not a word of truth in it. But it made the Crown case unassailable, as the police knew it would; for Griffiths, being dead, could not contradict the story. For the same reason Nicky Fairbairn, when he came to cross-examine, hardly touched on it. 'There was nothing I could usefully say,' he told me, 'for I had no rebuttal to it.' He did not know, because the Ayr police had not disclosed to the defence as they should have done, that Cowie and Cook had first inspected the safe on 7 and 8 July and found it empty.

Nicky had always believed that his trump card in Meehan's defence was the fact that Griffiths was known to have a pronounced English accent. He desperately wanted to secure a copy of the Gartree prison interview tape, play it to Mr Ross in court and ask him if that was one of the voices he had heard. Application was made to the BBC, but unsuccessfully. However, in cross-examination, Ross declared emphatically that he was sure the two voices were Scottish and that both sounded Glaswegian. Nicky then asked of witnesses who had met Griffiths to describe his voice. His girlfriend, Irene Cameron, said that it was very English, that you could tell it was English whenever he opened his mouth and no one on earth could have thought he had a Scottish accent or a Glasgow one. A Mrs Murray, a friend of Meehan whom Griffiths had met on some of their trips south, endorsed this, saying that Griffiths did not have much of an accent but you could tell it was Lancashire, and that it was obvious when he and Meehan spoke that one was a Scotsman and the other an Englishman; while a Mrs Boyle, a stranger whom Good Samaritan Meehan had helped at a road accident and had spoken with Griffiths, called his voice 'definitely English'.

Nicky was more successful in his special defence of incrimination with Waddell. Among the prisoners at Barlinnie while Meehan and Waddell were there were two called Macintyre and Macafferty. Both sympathised with Meehan's predicament and were sickened by Waddell's boasting of having beaten up the old couple; and both wrote to Beltrami to say that they would be prepared to give evidence on Meehan's behalf. Macintyre's evidence was that some time previously a fellow crook named Dick had passed on to him an invitation from Waddell to join him in a tie-up job on two elderly people in Ayr which he had declined; and that some time after the break-in, when he had asked Waddell for a loan of £10, Waddell had said that if he had been on the Ayr job with him, he would have had no need to ask for a loan. Macafferty was more direct. Waddell, he told the court, had admitted to him that he had taken part in the Ayr break-in and murder.

When Waddell himself entered the witness box Lord Grant warned him that he was not bound to answer any questions that might incriminate him and that, as a defence witness, he had no immunity from prosecution. Nicky began by asking him to read out from a piece of paper the words 'Shut up, shut up, we'll send an ambulance'. Waddell did so.

'Have you ever said these words before, apart from in this court?'

For Waddell this was the crunch. If he said he had, in less than no time Meehan would be out of the dock and he in it.

'I refuse to answer that,' he said. Why, unless he had taken part in the crime? He also refused to answer any questions about staying with Dick before the break-in.

Then Nicky Fairburn took Waddell to the occasion when he had visited Mr Carlin the solicitor and given him £200 in new notes as an advance fee if he was charged for the Ayr murder. Waddell, realising that continued refusal to answer questions was wearing a bit thin, decided to lie outright. When asked if he had given Mr Carlin £200, he flatly denied it, and even when asked if he would be willing for Carlin to give evidence, continued to deny it. He also denied that he had invited Macintyre, through Dick, to join him in a tie-up job in Ayrshire and strongly denied having admitted to Macafferty that he had done the Ayr job.

Mr Stewart's cross-examination was quite simple. Having taken Waddell through all his past convictions, he asked, 'You have no violence whatever in your record?'

'No.'

'No robbery?'

'No.'

The jury were not to know that Meehan had no record of violence or robbery either.

Then Mr Carlin was called and, after Lord Grant had warned him that his position, unlike Waddell's, was not privileged and he was bound to answer questions put to him, described how Waddell had given him £200 in new notes (which he admitted had surprised him) in case he was charged with the Ayr murder. The upshot of this was that six months later Waddell pleaded guilty to committing perjury at Meehan's trial. Sentencing him to three years' imprisonment, Lord Cameron said, 'Supposing he had told the jury the truth, they might have taken a very different view of an unemployed labourer handing over a substantial sum of money …' In other words, the jury might well have found Meehan not guilty.

In his closing speech for the Crown Mr Stewart told the jury the four important points to remember: 1) Pat and Jim; 2) the voice indentification by Mr Ross; 3) the bits of paper in the safe and Griffiths's car coat pocket; and 4) the destruction of the stolen Triumph car. Mr Stewart was not to know that the first was coincidence; the second was false; the third was also false; and the fourth, while true, was to avoid charges of having stolen a car, not of having committed a murder in Ayr.

In his speech, Nicky Fairbairn said that when two villains embark on a joint criminal enterprise, they are not so foolish as to address each other by their own names, rather by pseudonyms, and those they had chosen were two of the commonest first names in Glasgow. As for Ross's voice identification, he reminded the jury that Ross, having just lost his wife by murder and having been savagely assaulted himself, would have been in a very emotive state of mind when he heard a Glasgow voice saying those eight words he had first heard while lying trussed on the floor. 'If Waddell had been number one in the parade,' Nicky asked the jury, 'would Ross have made the same identification?' It was as good an explanation as any; yet Nicky did not know, any more than Ewan Stewart, that the reason Ross had identified Meehan was because he had come to know what the suspect looked like. Nor could he say anything useful about the bits of paper because he knew nothing of the skulduggery that lay behind them.

Nicky made another good point when he submitted that the boys in the white Anglia had agreed that when they had been overtaken by the Triumph, it was still dark, yet when Mr Ross realised the intruders had gone, it was 'quite full daylight'. How, he asked the jury, was that conceivably possible? And he stressed once again the striking Englishness of Griffiths's voice.

Then came Lord Grant's charge to the jury, in which he made several errors of fact. He diminished the daylight at Ayr/darkness at Kilmarnock argument of Nicky by citing the evidence of a meteorological officer stationed at Prestwick airport who had said that it gradually became lighter after 1 a.m. and that by 4 o'clock he could see Brown Carrick hill eight miles away; also, by wrongly quoting Irene Burns as saying that it was light when they were overtaken by the Triumph and by not quoting the evidence of the two boys and Isobel that it was still very dark.

But his worst mistake concerned the amount of time that the intruders spent in the Rosses' bungalow. If the jury accepted Meehan's claim that they left Cairryan at 1.45 a.m. and picked up Irene at the lay-by at 3.30 a.m., he reckoned that, going fast, Meehan and Griffiths 'could have had half an hour or more at the Rosses' house'. This ignored several points of rebuttal. First, it was clear from Mr Ross's own evidence that the intruders had been in the house a considerable time; secondly, at a press conference on 8 July Superintendent Struthers had told the media that they had stayed there 'for several hours', as indeed they would have to have done to have performed all the tasks they had set themselves, from ransacking the rooms to tying up the Rosses to drinking whisky and lemonade while waiting for daylight. The idea of fitting all this into half an hour, then picking up Irene Burns all cool and collected fifteen minutes later was pure fantasy – but not one which the jury were invited to consider.

What made the jury bring in a majority verdict of guilty? I would say four things: Pat and Jim; Meehan admitting to being in the vicinity of Ayr; the bits of paper; and the voice identification – i.e. two coincidences and two pieces of false evidence. Yet there were still many who went away with doubts. One was Mr Stewart's junior counsel, John (now Lord) McCluskey, who thought the voice identification very unsatisfactory and had found Meehan's explanations of the evidence against him coherent and convincing. Another was Stanley Bowen, the Crown Agent who had initiated the case against him. He knew

Meehan's previous record as a racing tipster knows form; and never before had he been present at a trial where the accused had so persuasively asserted his innocence from its very start to its conclusion.

Was it conceivable, he asked himself, that Meehan was innocent? Had they all made a terrible mistake?

Less than a month later, Meehan's appeal was heard in the High Court before a panel of three judges, Lord Clyde as Lord Justice General, senior judge in Scotland, presiding with Lords Cameron and Guthrie. Nicky Fairbairn made several points in his submission, one being that Lord Grant had not put the defence case fairly by allowing the jury to think it was light when Meehan and Griffiths were in Kilmarnock. But he also had new evidence to offer the court in the form of the tape of Griffiths being interviewed in Gartree prison, which had now been made available. 'In my submission,' he told the court, 'Mr Ross should be given an opportunity to hear that voice in the witness box and if he says it is definitely not the voice of either Meehan or Griffiths, that would be critical new evidence. If Mr Ross says the man with that voice was not in his house that night, then Meehan too was not there.'

This was devastating and supremely relevant fresh evidence, the key that would unlock the truth of the case at last, so I could hardly believe it when I heard that Nicky's submission had been rejected – the more so having heard the tape myself and noted the marked difference between the Glaswegian accents of Waddell and Meehan, on the one hand, and Griffiths's unmistakably English enunciation on the other. I was convinced that if Abe Ross had been permitted to hear Griffiths's voice, it would have been impossible for him to have said beyond doubt that that was one of the voices he had heard.

As a judge Lord Clyde was a hardliner who regarded jury verdicts as sacrosanct. Whatever Mr Ross might say on hearing Griffiths speak, he said, the court could not conclude that Meehan's jury would have reached a different conclusion. Why not? My own conclusion is that judges of appeal in Scotland are invariably reluctant to upset the verdicts of trial courts, all High Court judges being members of a close-knit fraternity who alternate between conducting trials and hearing appeals and are invariably reluctant to make decisions which might reflect adversely on their friends and colleagues. Whatever the reason, it was a deplorable decision.

For the next six years, 1970 to 1976, Meehan did everything within the limited power available to him to get his case reviewed, in which he had the full support of the Patrick Meehan Committee, who all believed in his innocence. Time and again he issued Bills of Criminal Letters (a Scots law speciality) for perjury against Struthers and Inglis, or a private prosecution against them and Carmichael; time and again his solicitors sent dossiers on his case to the Crown Agent and/or Lord Advocate and/or Secretary of State for Scotland (William Ross when Labour was in power, Gordon Campbell for the Conservatives), only for them to be disallowed or rejected with depressing regularity. His family also gave him support. Realising there was something suspicious about the police saying that Mr Ross had viewed the ID parade first when he knew he had viewed it last, he persuaded his son Pat to interview as many of those who had taken part in the parade as he could find, as well as the girls Isobel and Irene, and so learned the truth of what had happened. Mr Beltrami sent Pat's findings to the Lord Advocate, with the same negative results.

I have sometimes wondered why the authorities were so obdurate in their repeated refusals to review the case over so long a period, and have concluded that, to them as to the Meehan jury, the Pat and Jim thing was proof positive that Meehan and Griffiths were the two intruders; that it might conceivably be a coincidence was beyond the bounds of possibility; and the false evidence about the bits of paper made Meehan's guilt, as was Struthers's and Cowie's intention, certain. All the same, the presentation of persistent and cogent submissions for reviewing the case from one eminent QC, four respected solicitors and myself (who by now had gained a respectable track record in exposing miscarriages of justice) might have given them pause for thought; sheer curiosity might have tempted them to explore further.

Yet to some degree I understood their views about Pat and Jim, for at one point in my researches I was – to my subsequent shame – a victim of it myself, and so indeed was Meehan. For some reason, the defence had not been able to obtain a copy of the Ayr police telex of 7 July 1969 which contained the information that the intruders had called each other Pat and Jim. Mr Ross Harper[1] applied for it in May 1971 but it did not arrive until December. For Meehan, who until then thought that Pat and Jim must have been another police fabrication, it was shattering news; I, too, was shaken by it, and wrote to Meehan to point out that the police were looking for a Pat and a Jim long before they knew that he and Griffiths were in Ayrshire that night. I described this new evidence to him as 'devastating' and asked, 'Did you know anything about the possibility of Mr and Mrs Ross being robbed and was your trip to Stranraer in any way connected with this? I do not know if I can be of help in your case but I do know that I only can be if I am told exactly what happened.'

In reply Meehan emphatically denied any knowledge of the break-in and concluded that Pat and Jim must be no more than an astonishing and unfortunate coincidence. I also began getting letters from Betty Meehan begging me to intervene.

As I say again Paddy or Jim had never heard of Mr Ross until after the crime and I know if not this week or this year, he will clear himself some day. Meanwhile it's a living hell for all of us and I need all the help we can get to shorten the time he will be in prison!

Such an appeal was not to be resisted, although I had to tell her that with an already busy television and writing life I could not commit

---

1   One of Meehan's four solicitors and a member of the Patrick Meehan Committee.

myself to a book, only an article in the *Scotsman*. But first I felt it necessary to get an assurance from her husband. If I did write an article, I
said, it would have to be on the condition that I would be free to come
to whatever conclusions my investigations led me, whether of guilt or
innocence.

Meehan's reply was unequivocal.

*I am certainly willing to give you a free hand … and to express
whatever conclusions you come to as to guilt or innocence. If there
are any questions you wish to put to me, please do not hesitate to
do so.*

This alone convinced me that it was unlikely I was dealing with a
guilty man.

Elsewhere there had been some surprising developments. The death
of Rachel Ross had left its mark on both Waddell and McGuinness; both,
in different degrees, felt guilt that Meehan, a popular figure in the Glasgow underworld, should continue to be locked up indefinitely while
they were free. When Joe Beltrami found himself acting for Waddell on
a charge of being in possession of a loaded revolver and succeeded in getting him a lenient sentence, Waddell told him he felt sorry for Meehan
and that he would agree to take the truth drug believing that he could
not be prosecuted on that basis. Later, when he walked out of the prison
gates having served his sentence, he was met by David Scott and Ken Vass
of BBC Scotland, who were wearing tiny, concealed microphones
beneath their ties. To them Waddell admitted his part in the break-in,
and said that he would describe it in detail under the truth drug if that
was what they wanted: Meehan, he said, had been framed by the police.

In the end no media organisation would pay Waddell the £30,000 he
was demanding for his revelations, but BBC Scotland decided to mount a
programme anyway. It included Waddell's confessions to Scott and Vass,
Beltrami affirming his belief in Meehan's innocence, and one witness at
the ID parade saying that Abe Ross had been called to view the parade first

and two others stating that he had viewed it last. The programme went out in July 1972 and caused little interest; nor did I get a single letter in response to my article claiming innocence for Meehan when it was finally published in the *Scotsman* on 14 December the same year.

McGuinness was also scarred by the death of Mrs Ross, partly because his wife Agnes had been sickened by it and partly because fellow villains showed him how much they resented Meehan's continued and unjust incarceration. His hair began to go grey, then he developed alopecia and put himself under a psychiatrist in Oakley Terrace. And when Beltrami took him home from Barlinnie after he had been charged with another murder, held for sixty days, then released without further proceedings, he admitted that he had been Waddell's accomplice; information which Beltrami, because of the solicitor/client relationship, was at that time unable to divulge to anyone.

Two years went by. In February 1974 the Conservative government was defeated, Labour came back to power and William Ross returned as Scottish Secretary. When in August of that year Ross turned down the latest submissions of Meehan's advisers, Waddell, who had begun to revel in his notoriety, felt free to confess again, this time in some detail. To Gordon Airs and Charles Beaton, reporters on the *Scottish Daily Record*, he listed a number of observations he had made while in the Rosses' house, none of which had been revealed publicly before, but all of which Mr Ross confirmed: the gold bracelet he had ripped from the arm of Rachel Ross; the colour of the quilts on the twin beds (pink); the fact that much of the £3,500 haul from the safe had been in new £10 or £20 notes, in numbered sequence; the travellers' cheques they had stolen being contained in a black plastic folder; an alarm clock with a black face and green luminous hands standing in the hatchway to the kitchen … in all, some fourteen items unknown to either defence or prosecution. However, the editor of the *Record*, Bernard Vickers, like everyone else blinded by 'Pat and Jim', was not convinced of Waddell's confession and sent his reporters' findings to, guess who?, the Crown Office for the consideration of the Lord Advocate, who inevitably threw them out.

It was after this latest and, as I thought, final refusal of the Lord Advocate and the Scottish Secretary, Mr Ross, to review the case that I realised that unless someone wrote a comprehensive book on it, it would never be cleared up and Meehan would rot in Peterhead prison for ever. I was as familiar with the case as anyone and decided, despite earlier resolutions, to write the book myself. A little later I had the first of many meetings with Abe Ross, who showed me over his bungalow, including the bedroom where it had all happened and where, strangely, he still slept; after which we shared a congenial dinner in his favourite Ayr restaurant, the first of many such occasions. I was also in court in September 1974 when, in the same chamber in which he had been tried and sentenced, Meehan presented in person his Bill of Criminal Letters against Struthers and Inglis for perjury in the ID parade. Everyone in court, including the three judges, were as impressed by the vigour and lucidity of his pleading as by the diligence of his researches among the law books – indeed, at one moment the judges had to adjourn because their law books were different from his. But inevitably at the end of the day they turned him down, both then and when he presented a further bill in the spring of 1975.

By the summer of 1975 I had completed my book, which I called *A Presumption of Innocence*. Surprisingly, and in a welcome departure from his usual obduracy, William Ross wrote asking me if I would let him see a manuscript copy. Full of hope, and with the approval of the Meehan Committee and Meehan himself, I sent it to him. It took Ross and the Lord Advocate four months to read it, after which a minion wrote telling me that 'the Scottish Secretary has come to the conclusion that there are no grounds that would justify the exercise of the Royal Prerogative of Mercy or taking any other action in the case'.

This decision was even more disgraceful than the previous one, for if the Meehan jury had known, as I now knew, about the ID parade and the bits of paper, they would have been bound to acquit. I was beginning to think that the only explanation for the authorities' obduracy was no longer the seduction of 'Pat and Jim', but a fear of exposing the can of worms that any unbiased inquiry would reveal.

After five years in solitary confinement Meehan's health had begun to deteriorate and when he heard this negative news, he burst into tears. Abe Ross told ITN that he no longer believed that Meehan was one of the intruders. And Waddell, now certain that he would never be prosecuted, expanded on his previous confessions in an interview with the *Scottish Daily News*.

In October 1975, my book was serialised in the *News of the World*. Although Mr Beltrami had been scrupulous in observing his confidential relationship with McGuinness, the Meehan Committee now knew from other sources that McGuinness had been Waddell's accomplice. But to save Mr Beltrami any embarrassment, I used the pseudonym for him of McTurk. This led the Crown Agent to write to me asking for his real name. On the advice of the Meehan Committee I replied that I was unable to help them, adding that as the Lord Advocate had declined to prosecute Waddell despite his many detailed confessions, McTurk would also be willing to confess provided he too could be granted immunity from prosecution – a proposal that, needless to say, was not taken up.

The book was finally published in January 1976 with short prefaces from all Meehan's advisers – Nicky Fairbairn, Joe Beltrami, Ross Harper, Len Murray and David Burnside – affirming their belief in his wrongful conviction.

Any doubts in my mind that we had not made a convincing enough case for Meehan's innocence were dispelled by the reviews in the national press. First, and most encouraging of all, came an unsolicited letter from Patrick Devlin, to whom I had sent a copy as material for his committee then inquiring into the rules regarding identification evidence:

It is a very disturbing book. It needs to be answered one way or the other if confidence in the processes of justice is to be maintained.

Others were no less heartening. Louis Blom-Cooper, QC, in the *Listener*:

... this is a case of a double miscarriage of justice because Mr Kennedy has made out an overwhelming case for it. Is it so beyond the sense of fair-minded men that they cannot concede a public inquiry?

Lord Snow in the *Financial Times*:
It is impossible to pretend there is not a case to answer.

Julian Symons in the *Sunday Times*:
Patrick Meehan was convicted for a crime which he did not commit. The truth of the affair is now absolutely certain. If Meehan's conviction ought to astonish credulous boys, his continued imprisonment ought to jolt even cynics.

Bernard Levin in the *Observer*:
It is certain that certain irregular aspects of the investigation make some kind of inquiry now imperative.

Leo Abse in *The Spectator*:
necessitates a new independent inquiry ... there is too much in this case for matters to rest.

C. H. Rolph, the former police officer and writer on penal affairs, in *The Times Literary Supplement*:
If I was a Secretary of State for Scotland, I would recommend to the Queen that she grant what we still so oddly call 'the free pardon' by which the innocent are forgiven for what they have not done. For me that is the measure of the book's authority and power.

Finally, the Council of Justice, which included some of the most senior members of the English Bar, issued a statement demanding an official inquiry ...

Always an optimist, I sent William Ross and the Lord Advocate, Ronald King-Murray, extracts from the reviews, hoping that even their dim minds might be wakened and prejudices dented in the face of such unanimous opinion. I should have known better. From the Secretary of State's office came a brief acknowledgement, from the Lord Advocate nothing. So far as they were concerned, Meehan, guilty or innocent, could lie buried in Peterhead for ever.

This unholy pair compounded their obstinacy in January 1976 when Meehan was refused permission to bring a private prosecution against Carmichael, Waddell's alibi, for perjury. In dismissing the request, the Advocate Depute said that the Crown Agent had interviewed Carmichael and that the Lord Advocate had found nothing to convince him that Carmichael had committed perjury; while in the House of Commons William Ross refused a demand for an inquiry, claiming that it would be unlikely to bring out any facts not available to him, and that the 'alleged new evidence in Mr Kennedy's book' had not convinced the Lord Advocate that a prosecution against Waddell would be justified. Malcolm Rifkind, MP, also chucked his hat into the ring by telling the House that 'Mr Kennedy's alleged new evidence' was obtained almost entirely from those with criminal convictions. Mr Rifkind, a lawyer who should have known better, was talking nonsense. As readers of my original book and this one know, the verdict was almost entirely based on perjury given by police officers and others, and on Lord Grant's misleading charge to the jury.

And there, as they say, the matter rested. Both the Meehan Committee and Meehan himself were profoundly depressed by the prolonged, wilful stubbornness of William Ross and the Lord Advocate. We had done everything in our power, and we had failed.

February and part of March went by without any further developments. And then a most dramatic and unexpected thing happened. On 12 March 1976 'Tank' McGuinness was found lying unconscious with severe head injuries in a Glasgow street. He was taken to hospital, where thirteen days later, without regaining consciousness, he died. Afterwards, Agnes McGuinness telephoned Mr Beltrami to say that she had something important to say to him in relation to Paddy Meehan.

The next morning, she and her elder son came to Beltrami's office where she gave him a detailed account of her husband's and Waddell's participation in the Ayr robbery and murder. Having obtained a waiver of the confidentiality with his former client McGuinness, Joe Beltrami informed the Crown Agent of this latest development; the Crown Agent in turn interviewed Mrs McGuinness and her son and appointed two Strathclyde police officers of the highest integrity and calibre, Assistant Chief Constable Bell and Chief Superintendent McDougall, to carry out the investigation which we had been demanding for months, years, into the whole case.

From now on events moved at a gratifying pace, though the authorities, having clung to their false beliefs for so long, took their time to admit that an injustice had been done. Facing the inevitable, at the end of April they did something commensurate with their shabby conduct in the past – they offered Meehan parole, which he courageously refused, knowing that he was soon to be released unconditionally. A month later, William Ross retired as Secretary of State, to be replaced by Bruce Millan, MP. On 20 May Millan informed the House of Commons that he had decided to exercise on behalf of Meehan the Royal Prerogative of Mercy. It would have been a gracious gesture if William Ross, who was in the House at the time, could have expressed regret for his previous errors of judgement and congratulated his successor on his decision. But all that blinkered and mean-minded man could say was, 'Was this the only action open to you?' The contribution of George Younger, the MP for Ayr, was little better. He hoped, he said, that there would not be a witchhunt against the Ayr police, obviously unaware that Chief Superintendent Struthers, Detective Superintendent Cowie and Detective Sergeant Inglis of the Ayr police were, through their perjury at Meehan's trial, more responsible for his conviction than anybody.

The same day the gates of Peterhead prison were opened and, after six years and ten months' imprisonment, mostly in solitary confinement, Meehan walked out a free man. Later there were pictures in the papers of him in bed being served bacon and eggs by his son Garry while on a fishing holiday in a Highland hotel. Presently he was awarded an interim compensation payment of £2,500 and he and Betty took a further holiday in Majorca before returning to Old Rutherglen Road.

For the next six months Bell and McDougall continued their investigations, at the end of which Waddell was charged with acting along with the late William McGuinness in the murder of Rachel Ross. At the time he was back in Barlinnie prison serving a sentence for stabbing a man with a knife and a saw.

The court appointed to try Waddell first sat in Edinburgh in October 1976 to hear legal arguments. The judge was to be Lord (Ian) Robertson, one of the few judges of the Court of Session before whom Meehan, in his many court appearances, had not appeared. A year or two earlier Robertson had achieved a certain notoriety when his sentencing of a nurse to life imprisonment for murdering a patient was overturned by the Court of Appeal, on the grounds that, in his charge to the jury, he had accepted the police account of her telling them that she had given the patient a fatal dose of insulin, but made no reference whatever to the nurse's denial of that account or of her own version of the police interview. 'In the circumstances', read the judgment, 'it was a fault of commission and not just one of omission. It was so highly prejudicial to the appellant that it constituted a misdirection in law on a vital matter which called for the quashing of the conviction …' Not the best of auguries for the trial that now lay ahead.

Joe Beltrami, my wife Moira, Meehan and I turned up to hear the legal arguments but, although neither defence nor prosecution had any objections to our presence, Lord Robertson barred us from attending – 'the first court in my life,' quipped Meehan as we sauntered up the Royal Mile to a coffee shop, 'that I've ever been turned away from'. We wondered in what way Lord Robertson feared that our presence might contaminate the legal arguments.

And what did these legal arguments amount to? Incredibly, to decide whether the free pardon which had been granted to Meehan also quashed his conviction. Robertson invited two other judges to join him to try and reach a conclusion. All three, it turned out, were unaware of the fact that in 1963 the Lord Chancellor had ruled in the House of Lords that a free pardon wiped out a conviction and all its consequences and that the accused was therefore to be regarded as having been acquitted. Again in 1966 the Lords came to the same conclusion when considering Timothy Evans's free pardon. Yet this trio could not decide on the matter, a ruling or rather lack of one that, as they must have realised, would radically affect the course of Waddell's trial; for had they ruled, as they should have done, that a free pardon does annul a conviction, Waddell's defence of impeachment would have been weakened; now, as Robertson had intended, it was greatly strengthened.

During the next few days I watched Robertson closely and came to the conclusion he was one of the stupidest men I had ever come across, as arrogant as he was ignorant. In appearance he was a large man with a pronounced Morningside accent and a florid face that he was in the habit of rubbing continually with his hand. A member of the Honourable Company of Edinburgh golfers, as captain he had presented to them at their clubhouse at Muirfield a photograph of himself in a wig; it still hangs in the dining room there today, a source of some merriment among the junior members.

If Lord Grant's prejudices against Meehan at his trial were more implicit than expressed, Robertson made his plain for all to see. As Waddell's trial proceeded it became clear that Robertson had held for many years, in common with most of the Scottish legal and political establishment, a deep-rooted belief that Meehan and Griffiths had committed the Ayr murder, and that so paltry a matter as overwhelming new evidence to show that they had not but that Waddell and McGuinness had, was not going to sway him. It was a shocking exhibition of prejudice and in a fairer society should, after the trial, have resulted in his impeachment and dismissal from the Bench.

As Meehan's main defence at his trial had been an impeachment of Ian Waddell, so Waddell's main defence was allowed to be an impeachment of Meehan. This meant that, despite Meehan's pardon, the proceedings to some extent were to be a retrial of Meehan as well as a trial of Waddell. One of its more lunatic aspects was the Lord Advocate, Ronald King-Murray, who for two years had strenuously refused to entertain the notion of either Meehan's innocence or Waddell's guilt, now deploying arguments to show that very thing, although his heart did not seem to be in it; and consequently Waddell's counsel echoing the arguments of Ewan Stewart at Meehan's trial to demonstrate his guilt.[2]

The evidence against Waddell was devastating. First, Agnes McGuinness:

My husband went out on the Saturday and I didn't see him again until the Sunday morning. He told me he had done a job at Ayr … and Waddell was with him.

Then Waddell's alibi, Donald Carmichael, who had maintained that Waddell had stayed with him on the night of the break-in, now admitted that this was a lie. Several women friends of Waddell testified that within days of the murder Waddell had given them sums of money amounting to many hundreds of pounds, and a barman named John Mullen spoke of the time when Waddell came in with Carmichael and handed him £1,000 in brand new £10 notes which he said he had won on the horses and asked him to keep for him. Waddell would then come in each day to collect forty or fifty pounds; a week later all the money had gone.

---

2   Ewan Stewart gave me much assistance in the preparation of my book and was generous enough to admit that he too now believed in Meehan's innocence.

Next the two Ayr police officers in the panda car, whom Mr Beltrami had been trying unsuccessfully to trace for years, Hepburn and McNeil, at last surfaced and admitted to picking up McGuinness near Blackburn Place in the early morning after the break-in. Had this information reached the ears of the defence in 1969, as it should have done, it would have been enough for Meehan to have been spared his indictment and for McGuinness to have taken his place. Next, an employee from a Glasgow car hire firm testified that on the day before the break-in a William McGuinness had signed for the hire of a Ford Cortina.

In Waddell's confession to the *Daily Record* he stated that he had thrown ammonia in Rachel Ross's face to silence her. Now two doctors, Dr Bremner from Ayr County Hospital, the other an eminent pathologist, agreed that ammonia poisoning was the most likely cause of Mrs Ross's death.

Then came William McIntyre, to whom Waddell had confessed when both were prisoners in Barlinnie prison. Questioned as to whether he thought Meehan was innocent of the Ayr break-in and murder, he said he had been telling the police that for seven years and he had also said the same to Mr Beltrami. Waddell's counsel then asked, 'Wasn't that a last-minute attempt to help your exceptional friend Mr Meehan?' This got him on the raw.

'Just a minute, sir, none of this exceptional friend Mr Meehan. Waddell is a friend and Dick is a friend. I am not throwing one friend to the wolves to save another. I told the truth at Meehan's trial and don't you beat about the bush with me. If you can go to jail for telling the truth, I'm quite willing to go to jail.'

It was an impressive spontaneous outburst.

When King-Murray asked McIntyre who he believed had committed the Ayr murder, he raised his finger and pointed it at Waddell.

Then we heard evidence of all Waddell's confessions; to Ken Vass and John Scott of the BBC; to Gordon Airs and Charles Beaton of the *Daily Record*; to George Forbes and Jock Wallace of the *Scottish Daily News*; and his confession on television for a Birmingham-based programme called *Night and Day.* Cumulatively, and with so many detailed descriptions of the interior of Abe Ross's bungalow already confirmed by him, it was a damning indictment. It would have been even more damning if other telling evidence in Meehan's favour had been admitted to the court. One of the most glaring omissions on the Crown's part was not to lead evidence about the rigging of the ID parade. Why the Lord Advocate ignored this it is impossible to say; possibly to avoid embarrassment to the officers supervising the parade, Struthers and Inglis.

Robertson gave a further hand to the defence when he barred Mr Beltrami from giving evidence. Mr Beltrami would have told the jury that on many occasions during the past four years McGuinness had spoken to him in detail about his participation in the murder. As he has a commanding presence and deep authoritative voice, his evidence would have gone far to confirm to the jury what they had already heard from Agnes McGuinness. But Robertson barred him on two grounds. The first was because of the confidentiality of the solicitor/client relationship. When it was pointed out that the Scottish Law Society had granted him a waiver for this, it was still disallowed *on the frivolous grounds that the waiver had not been lodged in the court* (the Scottish Law Society's Edinburgh office was not far away and it could have been brought to the court within minutes). The second reason for barring Beltrami, said Robertson, was that evidence against McGuinness was not competent against Waddell. Yet at Meehan's trial this same argument – that evidence against Griffiths in relation to the bits of paper should not be competent as evidence against Meehan – was rejected by Lord Grant (he being as determined to see Meehan convicted as Robertson was to see Waddell acquitted). One ruling for one trial, a contradictory one for another!

There were other vital pieces of evidence either omitted or disallowed. The solicitor William Carlin was not permitted to recount how Waddell had lied at Meehan's trial in denying that he had given Carlin £200 to defend him if charged with the Ayr murder. Assistant Chief Constable Bell and Chief Superintendent McDougall (who, as the trial progressed, saw the case they had laboriously built up against Waddell dissolve in ashes) were not permitted to describe documents they had found in the files of the Ayrshire police. And had Abe Ross been called, he would have told the court what he had told me, that he now accepted the passage in my book that he knew before he viewed the ID parade what the police suspect looked like.

Since no evidence was led on the rigging of the ID parade (even though both Mr Falconer and the two girls, Isobel and Irene, were questioned on other matters), when Superintendent Struthers and Detective Sergeant Inglis were asked if they had heard of the parade being rigged, they could answer that such allegations were absurd. Struthers did let in a chink of light when asked if the two girls *followed* Mr Ross and he replied, '*I would have to say I can't be positive.*' But this was not taken up by counsel, which enabled Robertson to say that over a period of years very experienced and senior policemen had been maligned, defamed, and accused by Meehan of very grave dereliction of duty, including perjury and planting evidence without, as it turned out, any shred of justification whatsoever. It had turned out thus because the evidence which would have told the true story had been either suppressed or omitted.

But it was when Robertson came to his charge to the jury that he finally abandoned any attempt at judicial impartiality. He began by saying that seven years earlier Meehan had been found guilty by a jury 'on evidence which was amply justified' and went on, 'some public support was whipped up over the years for reasons which were not entirely clear and for motives which might be imagined'. What possible reasons could the Meehan Committee consisting of a QC, an MP (Frank McElhone, Meehan's constituency member, whom we had co-opted) four solicitors and myself have had other than a belief in Meehan's innocence and a wish to see his name cleared? Robertson lacked the courage to tell us.

He then referred to the free pardon. 'The reasons for it,' he said, 'had not become apparent at this trial.' (They had, but he had ignored them.) He then attacked Bruce Millan, the Scottish Secretary of State, for what he called 'usurping the functions of the judiciary', once again seemingly ignorant that recommendations for free pardons have always been vested in the executive.

Turning to the evidence, he stressed those aspects of it which told against Meehan and in favour of Waddell. He said that there were no fingerprints of Waddell found at Ayr, but he did not add that the same was true of Meehan. He explained away the list of things Waddell had seen in the Rosses' house as having been published at the trial or in the newspapers, which was quite untrue and also showed that he had not done his homework. He said that all of Waddell's confessions had been made for drink or money, which was also untrue, the clandestine confession given to Scott and Vass having self-evidently been made for neither. He said that Abe Ross might have been mistaken in thinking both burglars had Scottish accents (impossible). He gave the jury a list of Meehan's past convictions, none for violence, knowing that he was barred by the rules of evidence from both disclosing that Waddell had been brought to court from Barlinnie, where he was serving a sentence for wounding, and that he had been given three years by Lord Cameron for committing perjury at Meehan's trial. 'There can be no legal justification whatever,' he thundered in his ignorance, 'in saying that Meehan was wrongly convicted, and having heard the evidence in this case you might well have come to the conclusion that he was rightly convicted.'

At some point during this barrage of nonsense Meehan stormed out of the court, saying his pardon was not worth the paper it was printed on. I, too, had a strong urge to do the same, saying, 'This trial has been a farce, my lord, and you are the chief clown', but either wisely or cravenly (as I have come since to believe), I refrained; and was not surprised to see another miscarriage of justice take place before my eyes when the jury found Waddell not guilty.

The rest of this lamentable story can be told quite briefly. Instead of being handed the life sentence he so richly deserved, Waddell was released from Barlinnie the following year, when he gave yet another confession to the *Glasgow Evening News* ('It was me all right'). A few months later he was back in court charged with being in possession of a gun with intent to commit a robbery. Waddell's sticky career in crime finally came to an end a year or two later when he and a friend called Gentle – who was anything but – murdered a woman called Josephine Chipperfield on a housing estate in Easterhouse and wounded several of her family. The two went into hiding immediately after, but when they heard that a warrant had been issued for their arrest, Waddell told Gentle he was going to give himself up. To prevent this Gentle strangled him, put the body in his bath for a day or two and was then spotted at night trying to bury it. He was arrested, tried and sentenced to life imprisonment. Had Waddell's trial in Edinburgh not been the farce it was, had he been found guilty of the murder of Mrs Ross as he should have been, and had he been sentenced to life imprisonment as he should have been, Mrs Chipperfield might have lived to a ripe old age. Did Robertson, yet another opponent of the true course of justice, ever have the death of Mrs Chipperfield on his conscience? I rather doubt it.

Even that was not quite the end of the story. The Meehan–Waddell case had caused such a lengthy controversy that in 1977 Bruce Millan invited another Scottish judge, Lord Hunter[3] to conduct an inquiry into it. He laboured long – he took five years to complete and publish 1,200 pages – but at the end brought forth not so much a mouse as an abortion; and in the process proved himself almost as great a dumbo as Lord Robertson and the rest of the former Scottish legal and political establishment.

Stated baldly, and cheerfully ignoring Bruce Millan's instructions not to impute guilt to either Meehan or Waddell, Hunter's conclu-

---

3   All Scottish judges are given the courtesy title of 'Lord'. At one time wives were not allowed to share the title, which meant that when, say, John Macdonald became Lord Strathpeffer and his clerk booked a hotel room while on circuit with a Mrs Macdonald, eyebrows were understandably raised; to avoid any future embarrassment, the courtesy title of 'Lady' was extended to wives.

sions were that, while Waddell and McGuinness had probably carried out what he called the initial assault, 'it cannot be disproved that Meehan and Griffiths were not a follow-up team with the role of dealing with the safe or safes believed to be in the bungalow'. Apart from the worthlessness of double negatives, apart from the fact that McGuinness was a far more accomplished safe-breaker than Meehan, in all the verbiage spilled out by Meehan, McGuinness and the loquacious Waddell to lawyers, journalists and others over the years, not one of them had so much as hinted at the idea of a quartet. Meehan and McGuinness had never met, so there was not a worthwhile scrap of evidence to support Hunter's conclusion: it was speculation with a vengeance, shocking to find in a report by a judge of his standing.

And once again we had the by now familiar pattern of judicial complacency in the face of police corruption. 'Reliance is rightly placed,' he wrote, 'on the integrity and competence of police officers', a ukase which meant that, when he asked the officers who had planted the bits of paper in the safe and Griffiths's car coat whether they had done so and they continued to deny it, he deluded himself into thinking that no planting had taken place – showing that he lacked either the wisdom or the courage to face the truth.

So an alternative explanation had to be found; hence the fantasy of Meehan and Griffiths as a follow-up team. Claiming that in the end 'their services had not been required', Hunter concluded, 'they would have expected and received some share of the proceeds'; and it was presumably while Griffiths was being handed his share of the proceeds that bits of brown and white paper had found their way into the car coat he had not been wearing.

Hunter, like Robertson, being unable to accept that Pat and Jim was anything more than a coincidence, was as fixed on the idea that Meehan had participated in the Ross burglary as Sir Daniel Brabin had been that Timothy Evans had killed his wife. Because of prejudice, neither could bring himself to admit that the miscarriage of justice had been total, that neither Meehan nor Evans had played any part at all in the crimes for which they had been charged.

But there was one saving grace. Full compensation for Meehan for his nearly seven years' imprisonment, which had been held in abeyance during the five years that Hunter spent cogitating on his findings, was now given clearance for payment; and after negotiations between Mr Beltrami and an assessor, he was awarded, in addition to his interim payment of £2,500, a final settlement of £50,000.

6

WICKED BEYOND BELIEF –
THE LUTON POST OFFICE MURDER
1969–

If I had thought that the Meehan case was to be the last clear-cut mis-carriage of justice case to come my way, I was in for a surprise. Towards the end of the 1970s, my wife and I bought a house in Edin-burgh on the water of Leith, the stream that runs through Scotland's capital from the Pentland hills to the sea, and a few hundred yards downstream from the house in Belgrave Crescent where I had been born. It was here one morning in early 1979 that a large brown envelope came through the letter box.

It was from my then literary agent Michael Sissons. Enclosed was a handwritten manuscript of some 100,000 words written by a prisoner named David Cooper who ten years earlier had been sentenced to life imprisonment for his part in what became known as the Luton Post Office murder. Michael had been sent the manuscript by another of his clients, the writer and broadcaster Bryan Magee, who also happened to be Cooper's MP. Cooper claimed that he had been wrongfully con-victed. His book was not publishable as it stood, said Michael, but might it be of interest to me?

All I knew of the Luton Post Office murder case was what I remembered reading in the papers and having seen on television at the time. Its bare outlines were that in 1969 in a Luton car park a gang of four men had (probably accidentally) shot dead a sub-postmaster, Reginald Stevens, while trying to obtain from him the keys of his post office safe. The gang had then fled. One of them, an ageing grey-haired villain named Alfred Mathews, had subsequently been found and arrested. In exchange for not being prosecuted, he had agreed to turn Queen's evidence and name the three men he claimed were his accomplices: David Cooper, Michael McMahon and Patrick Murphy, all minor criminals from London's East End. At their trial, at which Mathews was the chief prosecution witness, all three were sentenced to life imprisonment with a recommendation they serve not less than twenty years. Patrick Murphy was freed not long afterwards when an alibi witness came forward, and his conviction was quashed on appeal. I also remember reading at the time that, as the evidence of Murphy's alibi witness was so contrary to Mathews' evidence that he was with him in Luton, Cooper and McMahon should have had their convictions quashed, too.

Having struggled through the first part of Cooper's handwritten manuscript I was sufficiently beguiled by what he said to write to McMahon's solicitors to ascertain his version of events; and was astonished when, in reply, they sent me another 100,000 word manuscript, this time by McMahon and this time, thankfully, typewritten. Its theme was the same as Cooper's; a passionate denial of having played any part in the Luton Post Office murder case at all. Having read both manuscripts carefully, I was left in little doubt that both men were speaking the truth. By now I thought I had plumbed the depths of police corruption and judicial incompetence, but this case exceeded them all and, once again believing I had it in me to put the record straight, I decided, despite other writing and broadcasting commitments, to bring the miscarriage to public notice as speedily as possible.

My initial reasons for believing in the men's innocence were ones of which the law takes no cognisance. First, there was the fact that these two East Enders, both of whom had left school at fifteen and were quite untutored in writing, had felt so passionately about their situations that in different prisons and unknown to one another, each had set himself the daunting task of writing the equivalent of a full-length book. Would they have done this if they were guilty? It seemed beyond the bounds of possibility. Secondly, the bitterness and resentment with which they expressed themselves could not, in my view, have been simulated. Thirdly, it was not just the bald declarations of innocence that impressed me, but their nature and quality: there were passages in both manuscripts which, as in many of McMahon's subsequent letters to me, had the sharp ring of truth.

Having been segregated into different prisons following their arrest, the three men came together in Brixton prison just before their trial at the Old Bailey. Cooper was pleased by the move, because he badly wanted to find out where the others stood.

I did not give much thought to the possibility of their innocence and in fact thought they were both involved with Mathews in the crime. This of course was a quite natural reaction, and perhaps subconsciously I was hoping they were guilty, in which case they would vindicate me.

Soon after speaking to McMahon and Murphy, it was clear they were as bewildered and anxious as I was. Unless they were very good actors, they sounded very convincing to me when they said they were innocent.

Then McMahon:

If the air needed clearing, then our first conversation did exactly that, for it saw each man strongly protesting his innocence and strenuously denying any involvement in the murder. Given my own predicament, I was left in no doubt that Cooper and Murphy had also been fitted up. Cooper was in a state of disbelief, tempered only by his reluctance to believe he could possibly be convicted.

Ten years later, both men were completing their manuscripts. Here is Cooper again, after long periods of nightmares, hallucinations, cold sweats, the depths of depression and (like Meehan) self-imposed solitary confinement:

I shall be vindicated. I am more certain of that than I am of anything in my life and although it is a slow and often agonising road I tread, the time will come when I shall be heard and cleared of the indictment held against me.

And McMahon:

For the past ten years I have been keeping vigil in a nocturnal maze and will continue to do so until daybreak. I am sometimes weary, sometimes depressed, sometimes afraid of being struck down by illness, but throughout even these moments, the driving force created by the injustice never deserts me ... in or out of prison I will relentlessly fight my case until my conviction for the murder of Reginald Stevens is finally quashed.

Were these two men both callous thugs who had helped in the shooting of an innocent postmaster and at the same time brilliant actors hoping to con the world into believing that they had not? I was unable to believe it. Having travelled south to visit Cooper, a little fellow with the build of a jockey, in Maidstone prison in Kent, and McMahon, wonderfully articulate, in Long Lartin prison in Worcestershire, and spoken to their two solicitors, Gareth Peirce of Birnberg and Co. for Cooper, Wendy Mantle of Bindmans for McMahon, as well as Tom Sargant, the secretary of Justice who had also taken up the case, I was convinced that both were as innocent of the Luton murder as I was.

During the next few months I uncovered a tale of wickedness, depravity and judicial boneheadedness that even I found hard to credit. Until then I had always held the view that police officers do not fabricate evidence against those they believe to be innocent, only those whom they genuinely, though mistakenly, have deluded themselves into thinking are guilty – 'the noble cause corruption',[1] as Sir Paul Condon, who disapproved of it, once confirmed to me. But in the Luton case there was no question of the officer in charge, Detective Chief Superintendent (later Commander) Kenneth Drury believing that Cooper and McMahon were guilty. A burly, domineering chain-smoking bully of a man, *he knew for a fact that they were innocent.* With twenty commendations for detective work to his name, he had come to believe he was omnipotent, and when Mathews declined to disclose the names of his accomplices, saying it was more than his life was worth, Drury, obsessed with clearing up another case, offered him a deal: make a statement that three men, whose names I will give you, were your accomplices, testify against them in the witness box and we will come to an arrangement about the reward money offered by the Post Office. Mathews, who otherwise faced the prospect of life imprisonment, had little option but to accept.

In addition, Drury persuaded one witness to amend his evidence so as to incriminate Cooper; arranged for another to be shown a photograph of McMahon before picking him out in an identification parade; omitted to tell the defence of two witnesses crucial to their case; cited an alibi witness vital to Cooper's defence as a prosecution witness, thus preventing the defence from calling him; and, to cap it all, bribed two prisoners on remand in Leicester prison to say that McMahon had admitted to them his part in the crime.

In his summing-up Mr Justice Cusack told the jury that the nub of the case was Mathews's evidence, and that for him to have implicated

---

1   The phrase was first coined by Sir John Woodcock as Chief Inspector of Constabulary in September 1992.

three quite innocent men, as the defence had claimed, would be 'wicked beyond belief'. The jury thought so, too. After an absence of two and a half hours, they returned guilty verdicts against all three.

Soon after, Drury was instructed to decide on how the Post Office reward money of £5,000 was to be allocated. There were to be nine recipients, all of whom had either deliberately or inadvertently given information that had led to the arrest of Mathews, and through him to the convictions of the three innocents. The biggest slice – £2,000 – went to Mathews himself, although Drury took half of this as his cut. Then there was £500 for Mathews's brother Albert, in whose house Mathews had been skulking since the murder and who had persuaded him to give himself up; £500 to a villain named Michael Good, whose shotgun had been used to kill the postmaster; £500 to each of the two inmates of Leicester prison, Weyers and Jackson, whom Dury had bribed to give false evidence that McMahon had admitted his guilt to them; £400 to a Mr Andrews, who had made a note of the number of Mathews's get away van; and £200 each to other witnesses for, on Drury's instructions, falsely identifying McMahon, Cooper and Murphy. There is evidence that Drury took a cut from these, too.

If the success of Drury's frame-up was breathtaking in its audacity, the failure of successive appeal courts to correct it during the next ten years was no less crass. The courts heard or reheard the case an unprecedented five times, three times on referral back from the Home Secretary. At the first appeal the judges rejected the evidence of two Luton witnesses previously suppressed by Drury whose description of the driver of the getaway van, whom Mathews declared had been the 26-year-old Murphy, more or less fitted the 53-year-old Mathews. They said it did not matter. To Cooper and McMahon it mattered very much. 'If Mathews was prepared to lie to that extent,' wrote McMahon, 'who was to say he wasn't lying when implicating the three of us in the murder instead of naming the real culprits?' At the second appeal Murphy's conviction was quashed, a man called Edwards having seen him in his car in London at the time when Mathews claimed he was in Luton.

Because Mr Edwards' evidence showed that Mathews was wrong in identifying Murphy, the Home Secretary, Roy Jenkins, asked the Appeal Court to consider whether this did not raise suspicions about Mathews's indentification of McMahon and Cooper, which indeed it did. Incredibly the Appeal Court (Lord Chief Justice Widgery, Lord Justice James and Mr Justice Ainsworth) ruled that *Mathews was not necessarily lying* when he said that Murphy was the driver of the getaway van *but he could have been mistaken* (a decision described by Gareth Peirce as an absurdity). Not even the evidence of two other villains named Stephen and Leonard that Mathews had invited them twenty months before to join him in a similar assault on the Luton sub-postmaster (which they had declined) could sway them. The appeals were dismissed in a ruling so contrary to both common sense and justice as to cause quite a flurry in the press and on television. Cooper and McMahon, who imagined they would be walking out of the court as free men, were shattered. When McMahon received a letter from the Archbishop of Canterbury telling him that God Almighty still loved him, he replied that a certain quotation (from Handel's *Acis and Galatea*) always stayed with him: 'I rage, I melt, I burn. The feeble God has stabbed me to the heart.'

After the pair had served more than six years in prison came a new twist to the case. A man called Slade made a statement that he had seen Cooper twice on the day of the murder, indeed had had a cup of tea with him in a café. This was enough for the Home Secretary to send the case back for a fourth hearing to the Court of Appeal, with a recommendation that they summoned Mathews as a witness to test his credibility. This they did. At times rambling incoherently (one observer in court thought him demented) Mathews repeated all the lies he had told at the original trial and added several more.

Here are two examples of his gibberish. First, his reply to Brian Capstick, QC,[2] who asked if he had not been worried that he might be arrested after the crime.

---

2   Son of Detective Superintendent Capstick (see chapter 4).

In a sense, no I reasoned myself. I knew I had not been near the scene of where the crime had been committed. I could not really believe it had been committed. No one could say they had seen me, so why shouldn't I walk back? But at the same time under the circumstances, one's mind can be in a turmoil and, well, anyone can reason how one feels under the circumstances. Under the panic and one thing and another, something must have happened drastically for me, and I saw this. I must have seen it had happened. One would not be a fool, and people don't joke over things like that.

Then Capstick suggested that he had brought the gun that killed the postmaster with him in a hold-all which one of the gang had thrown, while escaping, over the fence into a station yard.

Now you are being a comedian. I am sorry to say it like this because it is funny to me. You are saying such a ridiculous thing to me. In my life I have done a lot of things, and I thank God I have left it all behind me now, anything like that. I live quite a reasonable and good life as the next. But never in my life have I ever had to use a gun and would never use one. I see no reason for it, and it wasn't fair. We all had the greed for money. It is ridiculous to insinuate such a thing to me.

The three judges, however – Lord Justice Roskill, Lord Justice Lawton[3] and Mr Justice Wien – were inclined to believe him. 'Each of us watched him [Mathews] closely while he was giving his evidence. The conclusion that each of us has independently reached … on the vital part of his story is that he was clearly telling the truth … we see no justification for disturbing the verdicts which in our view were entirely correct.' Bryan Magee saw it differently. 'The judges did not watch Mathews

---

3   See chapter 4, page 84.

closely while he was giving evidence. I watched them and Mathews closely throughout both days and for most of the time all three judges had their heads and eyes down on the notes they were keeping.'

Cooper, fearing the worst, had stayed in the cells during the hearing, but the effect on McMahon was explosive.

One moment I was sitting bent over in the dock in utter despair, the next I was on my feet with arms outstretched, screaming at the judges, 'I am fucking innocent – innocent. Can't you understand that?' Lawton, who was sitting only a few yards away, rapidly shifted towards the edge of his seat in readiness for a quick getaway. He needn't have worried, as I was immediately dragged from the dock by the screws and led to the cell downstairs.

The Times, more restrained, came to the same conclusions: 'To most sensible, rational people, a verdict which depends on the evidence of a man like Mathews … cannot be safe.'

In 1979, yet another alibi witness surfaced, one Richard Hurn, who knew nothing of the case nor of McMahon's imprisonment but who had told a friend that he remembered seeing McMahon in London on the afternoon of the murder, a date which he had cause to remember for other reasons. The Home Secretary referred the matter for a fifth, unprecedented time to the Court of Appeal, who considered it in private and then rejected it. By now McMahon expected nothing else.

I am here in my cell writing this, having served almost nine years of a life sentence for a murder I did not commit. I also know that I sit here, not because of any evidence against me but because of the legal establishment's concern for its own pretensions to infallibility. Is this the statement of an embittered, biased man? I do not think so.

Throughout 1979 I was busy preparing my book on the case, which I decided to call *Wicked Beyond Belief, pace* Mr Justice Cusack. I was fortunate in being able to include in it, in addition to my own account, a contribution by Patrick Devlin, a friend of Bryan Magee, in which he took the fourth appeal court to task for usurping the functions of a jury in assessing Mathews's veracity, and a chapter by Bryan Magee telling of his efforts over many years to try to persuade the Home Office to reconsider Cooper's case. He, too, had some harsh things to say about Roskill, Lawton and Wien:

> *Their general demeanor was like that of elderly clubmen determined that it should be clearly understood that they were men of the world, fully alive to all the tricks of your Tom, Dick and Harry; yet their actual questions and comments revealed that they had not the remotest notion what sort of a world it was that these East End people they were listening to actually lived in, or how to evaluate their characters and the plausibility of what they said.*

I also included contributions from Tom Sargant of Justice and from solicitors Gareth Peirce and Wendy Mantle. All three unequivocally asserted the men's innocence.

From my own experience and that of others, I knew that books about miscarriages of justice tended to be published in a kind of vacuum where they remained for months, if not years, totally ignored by those whose business it was to evaluate and act on them. I had had to wait seven years for Evans's pardon and another seven years for Meehan's, and, knowing the reluctance of the Home Office even to consider whether a mistake might have occurred, far less admit it, I had little hopes of any remedial action.

But this time, quite fortuitously, I was in luck – or rather, as will be seen, partly in luck. Among those to whom I sent a copy of the book was Quentin Hogg, Lord Hailsham, then Lord Chancellor, with whom, despite our differences of opinion on political matters, I had been friendly over the years. His permanent secretary at that time was my cousin Wilfrid Bourne, who wrote back to me:

*Your book landed up with a pile of others on the desk of Hailsham's
private secretary. He did not know what to do with it, Hailsham
being far too busy to read it at the time. I happened to look in on
the Private Office before going home in order to see whether there
was anything I ought to take account of. Your book caught my eye.
I had, for once, no official papers to read and picked it up to read
in the train. I was so disquieted by it that I finished it that evening.*

Next day Wilfrid spoke of his disquiet to an old friend, Dick Thompson, the Registrar of Criminal Appeals, who read the book and felt a similar concern. Approaches were then made to Brian Cubbon, the Permanent Under Secretary at the Home Office responsible for criminal matters, with the result that within three weeks of publication the Home Secretary, Willie Whitelaw, announced to the House of Commons that, because of continued unease about the case and after discussions with the Lord Chief Justice (Geoffrey Lane), he had ordered the release of Cooper and McMahon from prison and that the remainder of the minimum sentence recommended by Mr Justice Cusack (i.e. a further nine years) should be remitted. He added that it was not a case for a free pardon because – wait for it – *there was no proof that Cooper and McMahon were innocent.*

As the reader knows, and as Willie's advisers should have told him, there was all the proof needed to say that Cooper and McMahon were innocent and should never have been indicted in the first place. So why was a free pardon not granted? I did not obtain the answer to this until several years later when, as a fellow guest with Willie in a friend's holiday house, I tackled him on it. 'I was all in favour of a pardon,' he replied, 'but Geoffrey Lane objected.'

I had known Willie since the days of boys' cricket matches and paper chases on summer holidays at Nairn, and Geoffrey I had also come to know later, but, while I was fond of both, I found this closing of Establishment ranks deeply shocking. Willie should have ignored Geoffrey's objections, and Geoffrey (presumably to protect the wretched judges of the appeal courts from further criticism) should never have made them. It was not justice these two were dispersing but the veneer of justice. And so, without a pardon or any monetary compensation for eleven years' wrongful imprisonment, Cooper and McMahon were shuffled discreetly out of prison to rejoin society, still branded for the rest of their brief lives as convicted murderers.

What was it Bryan Magee had written in his chapter in the book? 'We ought none of us to lose sight of the fact that human beings count far more than institutions or procedures or precedents, and we ought always to be willing … to sacrifice the latter to the former.' But that is not a view held by those who lack the imagination to enter into the hearts and minds of others and to do to them as they would be done by; among them the then Home Secretary and the then Lord Chief Justice.

What is the great lesson to be learned from this case, apart from its being yet another example of the absurdity of our adversary system of criminal justice? Surely the simple one is that the bigger and more outrageous the lie, the better the chance of its being believed.

There is a tailpiece to this case, which I am now writing in the late summer of 2001.

In May 2000 Gareth Peirce sent the Criminal Cases Review Commission (CCRC) a submission for the case to be reconsidered by the Court of Appeal. Peirce ended with the following words:

Tragically, first David Cooper and now Michael McMahon have died[4] without knowing the extent of the further evidence that could finally lead to the undoing of their convictions. The writer of these submissions has no doubt that the life and health of each was

---

4   Cooper in 1993, aged 51, McMahon in 2000, aged 55.

drastically affected by the eleven years each spent in torment in prison. Michael McMahon's widow was his fiancée when he was arrested; they have a son now of seventeen. It is clear both consider that they will have failed Michael McMahon if they do not continue until they have cleared his name: for many years McMahon's son did not know of his father's conviction. He, in particular, has expressed his deep regret that his father, concerned to protect him, turned down opportunities to discuss his wrongful conviction with interested journalists lest his notoriety be revived and his son suffer the stigma he bore himself.

David Cooper's family, she added, were equally haunted by their brother's case and their own inability to alter past history.

The CCRC had already made some inquiries of their own and in March 2001 they incorporated these and Gareth Peirce's findings into a composite submission which they sent to the Court of Appeal. This then joined the queue of cases waiting to be considered, though with a lesser priority than those made on behalf of applicants still living. I had hoped to have been able to say before this book goes to press that Cooper's and McMahon's convictions of 1969 have finally been quashed, but the Appeal Court now inform me that it is unlikely a hearing can take place before October 2002 – or twenty-two years after their unconditional release from prison.

That Michael Good, whose gun was known to have been used in the robbery, did participate in the crime Gareth Peirce now considers 'an overwhelming likelihood' – especially in view of new evidence that his brother-in-law, Terence Langstone, had recently taken possession of it for safe keeping and that on the morning of the murder a man called Alf, i.e. Mathews, had collected it. This claim is reinforced by four Luton witnesses who described one of the gang as either Italian or

Greek looking, and that while this fitted the appearance of Good, it in no way corresponded to that of Cooper, McMahon or Murphy.

It is hardly surprising that Chief Superintendent Drury, quite apart from the Luton case, should also have fallen prey to corruption. During the early 1970s he was found to have been accepting bribes from a Soho pornographer named Humphreys, and was committed for trial[5] for dishonesty just before Cooper and McMahon's 1976 appeal; and before Drury gave evidence at the appeal the presiding judge, Lord Justice Roskill, in order not to prejudice Drury's own forthcoming trial, said he did not want to hear any evidence alleging Drury's dishonesty in the Luton case. So McMahon was persuaded by his counsel to withdraw two planks of his appeal alleging that very thing (one being that Drury had shared Mathews's reward money). 'This,' commented Roskill smugly, exemplifying once again that English adversary justice is not concerned with truth, 'does McMahon nothing but credit.' 'Nothing but damage to his appeal' would have been nearer the mark.

Both submissions also referred to the role played by Thomas Weyers who, instructed by a Detective Sergeant Horn as to what to say, had given false evidence at the trial that while in Leicester prison McMahon had admitted his part in the crime to him. He had said that they had had adjoining cells and communicated through a water pipe that ran between them. This had not only earned him £500 of reward money but concessions by the Court of Appeal which at first reduced his sentence from thirty-three months to eighteen and later to nine months, suspended for two years, which led to his immediate release. 'The court,' said the CCRC submission, 'were very guarded in their reasons for reducing the sentence.' I bet they were. In the course of my own researches into the case I interviewed Weyers in the offices of my solicitors in London, Lee and Pemberton, where, in a written statement, he admitted that he had given false evidence:

---

5   Subsequently convicted and sentenced to eight years' imprisonment, reduced to
     five years on appeal.

I wish to state now that there is not a word of truth in any statement I made implicating McMahon in the Luton murder. At no time while we were in Leicester prison did McMahon confess to me his participation in it … The details of the Luton crime which I put into McMahon's mouth … were all fed to me by Detective Sergeant Horn. I said what I did because of the threats and promises made to me by Mr Horn and the local CID Inspector.

Earlier in the statement he had written, 'McMahon told me he was innocent of the crime of taking any part in the Luton murder.'

In all the Appeal Court hearings the heaviest criticisms in both the CCRC submissions were that, *pace* Lord Devlin, the judges were too ready to substitute their opinions for those of a jury; and the most telling part of them was that the European Human Rights Act, since incorporated into English law and deemed to be retrospective, had been doubly breached in Article 3, which guarantees a fair trial, and in Article 6 (3) (d), according to which a defendant has the right '*to examine or have examined witnesses against him and to obtain the attendance and examination of witnesses on his behalf under the same conditions of witnesses against him*'.

Certainly McMahon and Cooper were never granted that; so it is hard to see how the next appeal court hearing, which will be the sixth and hopefully last, can again deny them justice.

7

THE AIRMAN AND THE
CARPENTER – THE LINDBERGH
BABY KIDNAPPING AND THE
FRAMING OF RICHARD
HAUPTMANN
1932–85

One morning early in September 1981 I was in New York on an assignment for BBC Television. While awaiting in my hotel bedroom for the arrival of orange juice and coffee, I was flicking through the numerous TV channels before finally settling on an item in the NBC *Today* programme, in which an old woman with a strong German accent was saying that her husband was innocent of the murder for which he had been executed some forty-five years before. Initially I had no idea who she was, but I was impressed by the passion and conviction with which she spoke, which did not seem to me to be feigned. As the programme went on, I realised that I was listening to Anna Hauptmann, widow of Richard Hauptmann, who in 1936 had been electrocuted for the 1932 kidnapping and murder of the baby son of Colonel Charles Lindbergh, the first man to fly the

Atlantic solo (in 1927). The occasion of the interview was the opening up of the papers on the case, held in the New Jersey State police headquarters.

Anna Hauptmann was then in her late eighties. And the more I listened to her, the more I was persuaded that she was telling the truth. It was clear that she and her husband had been very close and, had she known him to have been the kidnapper and murderer a New Jersey jury had found him to be, it was unlikely that at her age she would have been willing to travel all the way to New York from her home in Pennsylvania to assert his innocence publicly and with such vehemence.

For the rest of that day the interview stayed in my mind; increasingly it both troubled and excited me. Was this yet another miscarriage of justice, admittedly in a different jurisdiction yet employing the same fallible adversary system that we maintain to our cost in England and Scotland? I knew I had to find out. Before leaving for home I went down to Yeadon, Pennsylvania, where Mrs Hauptmann lived and had a long talk with her. By the time I boarded the plane for England, my mind was made up. The Hauptmann–Lindbergh case would occupy me for the next four years.

First, though, a word about the American criminal justice system and how it works. Basically, it is the same as ours, with a single presiding judge, a jury of twelve men and women, prosecuting and defence counsel and state and federal appeal courts; the only difference being that, whereas we have one indictment for murder attracting a mandatory penalty of life imprisonment, the Americans have two degrees of which, in those states which retain the death penalty (not all do), only the first permits execution. I also applaud the rule whereby judges in criminal cases are only permitted to sum up in regard to the law, not the facts – which, it is reckoned, the jury have already heard and digested for themselves.

Like the British, however, or any other adversary system, they also experience a very large number of miscarriages of justice, the extent of which has been reported in a book entitled *In Spite of Innocence.*[1] In a survey of capital cases (i.e., those attracting the death penalty) from the years 1900 to 1990 the book's authors claim to have found *no less than 416 cases* of defendants wrongly convicted,[2] *of whom no less than twenty three* were electrocuted,[3] hanged, shot, strangled or despatched by lethal injection. The most common causes of miscarriages in the US, say the authors, are: 'perjury by prosecution witnesses and mistaken eye-witness testimony'; poor police work, 'whether from neglect and incompetent investigations or from more sinister motives'; coerced confessions and 'the prosecution withholding from the defence exculpatory evidence'. They add, presumably so as not to disturb their readers' belief in due process, 'Most Americans do not seriously distrust our criminal justice system or the efficiency and dedication of the law enforcement officers.' Hardly surprising in a nation fed on a diet of *Kojak, Ironside, Cagney and Lacey* and similar pap, which lulls viewers into believing that the cops always get their men. It is no different in Britain where, despite a spate of miscarriages in recent years, hardly anyone thinks there is anything fundamentally wrong with our justice system.

Where the two countries differ is in Britain's willingness and America's unwillingness to make amends after a mistake has been discovered. 'To the best of our knowledge,' say the authors of *In Spite of Innocence*, 'no state or federal officials have ever acknowledged that a wrongful execution has taken place.' And the reason? 'There is no legal forum in which the innocence of the dead can be officially confirmed or even sat-

---

1   Michael L. Radelet, Hugo Adams Bedau and Constance Putnam, *In Spite of Innocence* (Boston: Northeastern University Press, 1992).

2   The Autumn 2001 edition of the *Amicus Journal* records that in August of that year Charles Fain, after eighteen years on death row in Idaho state penitentiary was proved innocent of having raped and strangled a 9-year-old girl and released from prison. This, says the *Journal*, makes him the ninety-seventh innocent man to be released since the re-introduction of the death penalty in the USA in 1977.

3   They include Richard Hauptmann.

isfactorily investigated.'[4] We, on the other hand, do try to make amends through the Criminal Cases Review Commission, which, as the reader knows, has already proved its worth: some of the cases they have sent back to the Appeal Court, like that of Iain Gordon, go back forty or fifty years. And in my lifetime there has rarely been a time when press and/or public have not been agitating for some case to be reviewed. In America such *arrières pensées* are rare.

The reluctance of Americans ever to admit error, whether in correcting miscarriages of justice or in the fondness of their armed forces for opening fire on friendly troops or in the frequent cock-ups in everyday business or social life, would seem to stem from the macho image they have of themselves and their philosophy of 'never apologise, never explain'. When a mistake is pointed out – often after glowing promises of matchless efficiency – the invariable rejoinder is the dismissive 'Too bad!' There is a restlessness in the American psyche, a dissatisfaction with the present that militates against reassessments of the past and can only think and feel in terms of the future and attainment of the American dream.

The macho self-image, based on the delusion of many that theirs is still a frontier society, seems to me also responsible for America being the only country in the western world not only to permit its citizens to buy and use – and abuse – lethal weapons, but to have re-introduced the death penalty, in 1976, in the mistaken belief that it is a unique deterrent, thus putting America on a par with China, Singapore, Jamaica and Afghanistan: and this, despite the Supreme Court having suspended the death penalty in 1972 as a cruel and unusual punishment. At the time of writing (August 2001) it is a fact and not an opinion that in the USA states that exercise the death penalty have higher homicide rates than those

---

4   The only case I can recall is that of Sacco and Vanzetti, Italian immigrants who were executed in 1927 in Boston for the murders of two men in a payroll robbery. This troubled the American and European public for many years until in 1977 Governor Michael Dukakis of Massachusetts publicly announced that in his view the conduct of judge and prosecutor at Sacco and Vanzetti's trial had been riddled with errors, as well as being racist, prejudiced and misleading.

that have abolished it; and it is also a fact and not an opinion that after an execution the homicide rate in that state tends to increase.

Most executions in the US today take place, as they have always done, in the South. Here the macho self-image allows few objections to killing the mentally impaired, or abused teenagers or those unable (at least until recently) for lack of funds to appoint effective counsel to defend them, the majority of whom are poor blacks.

Bedau's and Radelet's conclusions: 'During this century in the United States more than seven thousand men and women have been legally executed for capital crimes.' And yet, they continue, 'The errors, blunders and tragedies recounted in the pages of this book barely scratch the surface of this vast output of the nation's criminal justice system. Hundreds of cases, many involving miscarriages of justice as serious as any we describe, almost certainly remain to be investigated.' But they never will be. Too bad!

Lindbergh's solo flight from New York to Paris had electrified the world. At the start it had been touch and go whether he would become airborne at all, the field in New York being sodden with rain, and he only cleared the telephone wires at the end of the runway by twenty feet. By the time he reached Newfoundland he had already been airborne *ten hours* but still had the Atlantic to fly. It was an epic voyage on many levels: the boldness of it, the sheer affrontery of this boy of twenty-five who looked eighteen, relying on his skills and the endurance of his frail single-engine craft, the *Spirit of St Louis*, to take him where no one had ventured before. When he saw Ireland beneath him, he knew he had made it: all he had to do now was to land in Normandy, for the rules of the Orteig Prize for which he was competing stipulated only that he land in France. But he knew it had to be Paris; it was where the crowds were and where he was expected. Dropping out of the night sky at Le Bourget would be, and in the event was, a dramatic end to the most dramatic of journeys.

No wonder Americans and Europeans, too, took Lindbergh to their hearts. In an age of hedonistic materialism, he had shown courage and self-denial of a high order; in an age of corporations and committees he had acted alone. From afar, people worshipped Lindbergh for doing what they would like to have done and never would, and so made of him a kind of god. From now on the gangling mechanic from the woods of Minnesota was a creature of the past: henceforth Lindbergh would walk in glory and sup with presidents and kings.

In Paris the President of the Republic decorated Lindbergh with the Cross of the Légion d'honneur, the Mayor with the city's Gold Medal. In London he was received by King George V, who asked how he had peed on the flight, to which he replied that he used a container which he had ditched before landing. President Coolidge sent an admiral in a cruiser to fetch him home and when he arrived decorated him with the Distinguished Flying Cross. Congress voted him the US Medal of Honor and the entire Cabinet entertained him to dinner. Then it was the turn of New York and a vast ticker-tape parade watched by between three and four million people. His response to the adulation was typical. 'I was so filled up with all this hero stuff,' he told a friend, 'I could have shouted murder.' Five years later at Hauptmann's trial he was to shout just that, and because of who he was everyone believed him.

At the end of that year, 1927, Lindbergh received an intriguing invitation from the newly appointed American ambassador to Mexico, the banker Dwight Morrow, to take the *Spirit of St Louis* there on a goodwill mission. He left Bolling Field in the afternoon, flew through the night and landed at Mexico City the following afternoon: it was another first, for no one had made that flight non-stop before. When he arrived, he was greeted by a vast crowd headed by President Calles, who handed him the keys of Mexico City. Then the ambassadorial car took him and Morrow through cheering crowds to the American embassy where he met Mrs Morrow and their youngest daughter, Constance. Her sisters, Elizabeth and Anne, would be arriving for Christmas the following week.

Anne Morrow was twenty-two then, a tiny brunette with an air of shy fragility which disguised a strong will. A lover of music and litera-ture, she longed to be a writer but felt she lacked the talent. When her father and Constance met her at Mexico City station and told her of Lindbergh's arrival, she was not impressed. 'All this public hero stuff breaking into our family party', she wrote in her diary, 'a nice man perhaps but not of my world at all, so I wouldn't be interested. I was certainly not going to worship "Lindy" (that *odious* name) anyway.'

But when they met it was a different story.

He is very, very young and was terribly shy – looks straight ahead and talked in short direct sentences which came out abruptly and clipped ... his sentences were statements of fact, presented with such honest directness, not trying to please, not trying to help a conversation along. It was amazing, breathtaking. I could not speak. What kind of boy was this?

Next day Lindbergh took the family for a spin in a big three-engined plane. The three sisters sat in wicker chairs behind the cockpit, 'so terri-bly and ecstatically happy', wrote Anne, 'alone and together and able to watch him. He moved so very little and yet you felt the harmony of it.'

And then, early next morning when it was still dark, he was gone. Already in love, Anne wrote in her diary that the very idea of him 'has swept out of sight all other men I have ever known, all the pseudo-intellectuals, the sophisticates, the posers, all the 'arty' people ... my little embroidery-beribboned world is smashed'. She thought that she would never see him again.

But he had not forgotten her. Having undertaken more goodwill trips across the Americas, Lindbergh presented the *Spirit of St Louis* to the Smithsonian Institute in Washington (it hangs there today, a source of wonder to all who see it, that something so small and flimsy could remain airborne for 3,500 miles and the thirty-three hours it took to fly from New York to Paris). Then he telephoned Anne and visited her at Next Day Hill, the mansion set in a fifty-acre estate that her father had recently had built just across the Hudson from New York. And from there, early in the New Year of 1928, as Anne Morrow wrote to a friend, 'apparently I am going to marry Colonel Lindbergh'.

To avoid publicity they were married secretly at Next Day Hill, left separately afterwards (Lindbergh on the floor of a taxi) and for their honeymoon embarked on a cabin cruiser in Long Island Sound; but a day or two later they were recognised refuelling at Block Island and soon the press were after them in planes and motorboats, one cameraman bawling at them through a loudspeaker to come and pose on deck. Lindbergh had experienced the razzmatazz before, but Anne was experiencing it for the first time. 'Fame', she wrote to a friend, 'is a kind of death.'

For most of the first two years of their marriage the Lindberghs were on the move, taking part in proving flights across America, the West Indies and Central America to survey possible commercial flight paths. This meant a succession of one night stopovers, and Anne found the non-stop socialising and need to adopt a tight-lipped public persona immensely wearing. 'There are so few people in the world who treat us *naturally*', she wrote to her mother, 'and if they aren't natural, I can't be.'

She increasingly longed for a home of their own and, finding herself pregnant in late 1929, stepped up the pace of looking for one. Eventually they found a plot of land on which to build, four miles from Hopewell in the Sourland mountains of New Jersey, within commuting distance of New York. Until it was completed they would stay in a suite the Morrows had put aside for them at Next Day Hill; and there, on 22 June 1930, Anne's birthday, she gave birth to a son, Charlie.

In July the Lindberghs embarked on another proving flight, this time to map a route along the great circle to China via Hudson's Bay, Alaska, Siberia and Japan, leaving Charlie with his Scottish nanny, 27-year-old Betty Gow, at the Morrow house on North Haven Island off the coast of Maine. The Lindberghs completed their mission successfully but when their plane was damaged in Shanghai and they heard that Anne's father had died, they curtailed the rest of the journey and embarked for home.

Upon their return, Anne found a new Charlie, 'a strong, independent boy, swaggering around on his little firm legs'. Every night, she said, he used to take his grandmother's toy lamb or pussycat to bed with him, hide it under the bedclothes, then like some artful conjurer pull it out with shouts of glee. 'And Charles says "Hi, Buster" to him whenever he sees him, so the other day when C came into the room, Charlie looked up and said, "Hi! Hi!" and when C left the room, Charlie said, "Hi all gone."'

By New Year 1932 the Hopewell house was more or less completed. Set in 500 acres of woodland and meadow, it was approached from a narrow country road by a half-mile winding drive. It was a modest establishment, the oblong central section of the house being flanked by two small wings. On the ground floor of the eastern wing was Lindbergh's study and above it Charlie's nursery and sleeping quarters.

At first the Lindberghs used Hopewell for weekends, allowing Betty Gow to have a break from her duties and stay at Next Day Hill, to be summoned only if necessary – an arrangement which suited Anne admirably, as it meant she could look after Charlie herself. 'It is such a joy', she wrote to her mother-in-law, 'to hear him calling for me instead of Betty.'

On the last weekend of February 1932, all three Lindberghs were at Hopewell, due to return to Next Day Hill on the Monday. But Charlie developed a cold, so Anne decided to stay over with him until Tuesday, 1 March. On Tuesday Charlie's cold was no better, so she decided to stay that night too, rang Betty at Next Day Hill and asked her to come over to help her look after him. This decision to stay on was taken on the spur of the moment; Charlie had never spent a Tuesday night at Hopewell before.

The first of March was bleak and cold and for most of the day the rain fell steadily. It cleared in the afternoon, so Anne went out for a walk. On the way back she threw a pebble against Charlie's nursery window. Betty came to the window, holding him. He waved to his mother and she waved back. It was the last time they would ever wave to each other.

In the evening the rain cleared but then the wind got up and blew for most of the night. Shortly before six, Betty gave Charlie his supper in the nursery, which he ate at a little maplewood table, surrounded by his toys. Then Betty and his mother prepared him for bed. Betty put drops in his nose, rubbed Vick's ointment on his chest and wrapped him in a little flannel shirt stitched with blue thread she had run up especially to keep out the cold. She also put on him a sleeveless woollen shirt, diapers and rubber pants, completing his attire with a Dr Denton's one-piece sleeping suit. The two women placed the draught screen with its pictures of farmyard animals at the head of the cot and opened the south window to let in some fresh air; then they closed the two east windows and one of the two green lattice shutters. The other had become warped and would not close; it had been like that for three weeks but no one had thought to fix it.

At 8.35 p.m. Lindbergh returned by car from New York and joined Anne for dinner. Afterwards, they went briefly into the living room. While they were there Lindbergh heard, above the moaning of the wind, the sound of what he described as a sharp crack, like the top slats of an orange box falling off a chair.

Betty, meanwhile, had her own supper with the resident married couple in the staff sitting-room. At ten she went upstairs to take Charlie on his final visit to the loo. On entering the nursery she did not switch on the light so as not to startle him but closed the open south window and turned on a heater to take the chill from the room. Warming her hands before it, she began to sense that something was amiss: she could no longer hear Charlie's regular breathing. 'I thought perhaps that the bedclothes had got over his head. In the half-light I saw he wasn't there and felt all over the bed for him.'

Puzzled and concerned, Betty went to Anne's bedroom next door to ask her if she had him. 'No,' said Anne, surprised, 'perhaps the Colonel does.' Lindbergh was reading in his study immediately below. Betty, by now alarmed, ran down to ask him. 'No,' he said in even greater surprise, and dashed upstairs to join Anne in the nursery.

In utter disbelief husband and wife stared at the empty crib, suddenly having to think the unthinkable, to register an event of such shocking enormity that the mind recoiled from it.

The Colonel was the first to accept it.

'Anne,' he said, 'they've stolen our baby.'

Outside in the darkness the wind howled like a dog as if to articulate their anguish.

'Oh my God!' cried Anne.

It was also what Anna Hauptmann said, sixty miles away in the Bronx, when she heard the news the next morning. She added incredulously, *'You mean someone stole a baby?'*

The local police were telephoned and arrived in force soon afterwards. When the fingerprint officer arrived, Lindbergh showed him an envelope left by the kidnappers on the radiator grille by the window and he opened it. Inside was a ransom note written in crude English, demanding $50,000 in various denominations. Instructions for delivering it would follow in two or three days, and there was a warning against informing the police. Future letters would bear the same symbol as at the bottom of this one – two interlocking circles coloured blue, and in the interlock an oval coloured red. The ransom note contained several misspellings such as 'mony', 'singnature' and 'gute' (for good). Meanwhile, more police with flashlights were searching the area outside and found a homemade ladder in three sections, the uprights of the bottom section having broken and split, an old Buck's chisel and a large footprint in the dirt beneath the nursery window, which they measured. During the next few days the police searched every building within five miles of the house and interviewed thousands of people, but without success. And no fingerprints were found on the ladder, chisel, ransom letter or envelope.

The head of the New Jersey State police was 37-year-old Colonel

Norman Schwarzkopf (father of the US commander in the Gulf War of 1991), described as a handsome young man with a crewcut and waxed blond moustache who had never patrolled a beat or arrested a criminal. The present case was beyond anything in his previous experience. However, he worshipped Lindbergh and said publicly that there was nothing he would not do for him.

Then the press arrived – four hundred of them – but found there was little newsworthy to write or photograph beyond the bare facts. But their leading articles did report on, and reflect, the sense of outrage and desire for retribution felt by millions of Americans. For Lindbergh's Atlantic odyssey had given him the status of a god. People saw an assault on his child as an assault on him, an act of sacrilege. In churches all over the world prayers were offered for Charlie's return. President Herbert Hoover himself and the presidents of France and Mexico sent messages of condolence, and the Governor of New York, Franklin D. Roosevelt, put his entire police force at Schwarzkopf's disposal. As the days went by without further developments, people felt increasingly angry, frustrated, burning with a desire for revenge but with no prospect of attaining it. A newsreel commentator expressed the mood of many. 'I know what I'd like to do with that kidnapper if only I could get my hands on him.'

Lindbergh had made it clear that his first priority was not to catch the kidnappers but to pay the ransom money in exchange for Charlie's safe return. He had inquiries made in New York's underworld about possible intermediaries but they all fell through. Then a most unlikely candidate did offer himself, a 72-year-old retired Bronx schoolteacher named Dr John F. Condon, who had a white mane of hair and a large white walrus moustache, and who wore a black bowler hat in winter and in summer a boater – a sanctimonious old bore whose aim was to see himself and to be seen by others in the best possible light. For many years he had been a contributor to the *Bronx Home News* with poems and pieces signed P. A. Triot, J. U. Stice, etc. Now he sent a letter proposing himself as intermediary between Lindbergh and the kidnappers; and the editor gave it front page coverage.

Surprisingly, the kidnappers responded; and the upshot was that after delivering a letter from them to Lindbergh at Hopewell and negotiating with one of them in the Bronx's Woodlawn Cemetery, Condon put an advertisement in the *Bronx Home News* as instructed saying 'Money is ready' and signed it JAFSIE (J. F. C. being his initials) to mislead the New York press. Fifty thousand dollars, mostly in gold certificate bills (easier to trace), were then counted out and stacked in bundles in the offices of J. P. Morgan, Dwight Morrow's bankers, with the help of the US Treasury's chief law enforcement officer who insisted, against the kidnappers' instructions, of a record being made of the serial numbers. With the box containing this on the back seat and Lindbergh at the wheel (and strict orders to the New York police not to follow them), Condon and Lindbergh drove to another cemetery, St Raymond's, where Condon was to hand over the money. At first, it being very dark, Condon was unable to find the man the gang had sent to meet him and so shouted to Lindbergh, still sitting in the car a hundred yards away, 'There's no-one here. We'd better go back.' Almost immediately another voice from the cemetery called out so that Lindbergh heard it, 'Hey, Doc!' It was the voice of the man Condon had met in the Woodlawn Cemetery, who had become known as Cemetery John.

Condon retraced his steps into the cemetery, made contact with the kidnapper and handed over the money. In exchange he received a note which said 'the boy is on Boad Nelly, a small boad 28 feet long', which could be found between Horseneck Beach, on the mainland, and Gay Head, near Martha's Vineyard.

Next day Lindbergh took a plane to search the waters around the Elizabeth Islands, between Martha's Vineyard and the mainland, but found nothing. A month later a truck driver in need of a pee found something else: the decomposed body of Charlie, lying in a shallow ditch in the woods some four miles from the Lindbergh house and half covered in leaves. His left leg was missing from the knee down, so were his left hand and right arm and all his major organs except his heart and liver. Beside him lay the remains of a burlap bag in which it was later thought he had been taken from the nursery and possibly dropped to the ground and killed when the ladder broke. Mrs Morrow gave the news gently to Anne. 'The baby is with Daddy,' she said.

The day after the discovery of Charlie's body, President Hoover announced, 'I have directed the law enforcement agencies and the several secret services of the Federal Government to make the kidnapping and murder of the Lindbergh baby a live and never-to-be-forgotten case, never to be relaxed until the criminals are brought to justice. Its agencies will be increasingly alert to assist the New Jersey State police in every possible way until the end has been accomplished.' Later, the New Jersey legislature authorised the Governor to offer a reward of $25,000 for information leading to the kidnap gang's arrest and conviction and in June Congress passed a bill making kidnapping a federal offence.

The police forces of New Jersey and New York were untiring in their efforts to make an arrest. They collected the names of all those renting safe-deposit boxes in New York in March and April and photographed their signatures. They checked on the origins and background of every unclaimed corpse in New York after the handing-over of the ransom money, on the grounds that Cemetery John might have been bumped off by the rest of the gang for fear that Condon would identify him. And they checked out individually *all* the former pupils of the school where Condon had been headmaster for twenty-five years in case any with criminal records had responded to his ad.

They also interrogated the only two witnesses who had had contact with the gang. One was a taxi driver named Joseph Perrone, who had been given a letter by one of the gang to deliver to Condon. But it happened in the dark, and, pressed as to whether he thought he could recognise the sender, he said emphatically he could not. Then they showed Condon hundreds of rogues' photographs in police files to see if he could identify any as Cemetery John. He either could not or pointed excitedly at one or two who were not in the country at the time. Lieutenant Finn of the New York City police thought him 'a screwball', while Lieutenant Keaton of the New Jersey police called him 'wacky- if not guilty, then mentally deranged'.

Nor were the only two artefacts left by the gang – the ransom notes and the makeshift ladder – of much help. A close examination of the style of writing on the notes and the formation of individual words led experts to conclude the writer was a German or Austrian living in the Bronx; and that some of the spelling mistakes like 'nihgt' and 'singnature' were to be expected from a German not well versed in English (although the fact that more difficult words like 'instructions' and 'arrangements' were correctly spelt led to one view that the mistakes may have been deliberate and that the notes had been composed by one person and written by another).

An examination of the ladder by the Forest Service of the Department of Agriculture revealed that it was made up of a miscellaneous collection of odd pieces of lumber from a variety of woods which, because of a lack of moisture in them, had probably been under cover for some time. Months later an independent wood expert named Arthur Koehler was called in and said that the ladder was very crude and that its maker showed little skill in the use of carpentry tools. He labelled the side rails of the three sections 12 and 13 (bottom), 14 and 15 (middle) and 16 and 17 (top). Rail 16, he said, was the odd one out. Whereas the other rails contained nail holes made by round nails, the holes in rail 16 had been made by old-fashioned square nails. It had been a board, or part of one, and had probably been part of the interior of a building, possibly an attic, shop, warehouse or barn.

Later Detective Lewis Bornmann of the New Jersey police, who had been seconded to Koehler to help with his work, was to remember what he had said.

But their best bet, the police knew, was to wait for the marked gold certificate ransom bills to show up in banks, department stores or restaurants: *all* the East Coast banks had been supplied with their serial numbers. Unfortunately, between the day that the money was handed over (2 April) and the end of 1932, only twenty-seven marked bills were found and most, being of small denomination, proved impossible to trace. None turned up during the first three months of 1933, though more were expected later that year when it was announced that America was going off the gold standard and no individual could hold more than $100-worth of gold certificates. New York banks did receive deposits of several thousand dollars worth, but once again it proved impossible to trace the depositors. Through most of 1934 more ransom money, mostly in $5 bills, was deposited, some in places as far away as Minneapolis and Chicago. Then in September without warning, a quite different pattern emerged, the passing of bills previously rarely seen, $10 and $20, in New York shops between 84th and 103rd Streets on the East Side.

One of these, a $20 bill, was proferred and accepted for payment for gas at a filling station at Lexington and 127th Street; and the attendant there, uncertain whether gold certificate bills were still legal tender, jotted down on the bill the vehicle licence number: 4U13.41. The bill was deposited at the Corn Exchange Bank at 125th Street and Park Avenue, where the police telephoned the Bureau of Motor Vehicles to ask for the name and address of the owner. Bruno Richard Hauptmann, they said, 1279 222nd Street, New York City.

Hauptmann had been born in 1899 in Kamenz, Germany, a small town seventy miles south of Berlin, not far from Dresden and the Czechoslovak border. The youngest of five children, he was the son of a stone mason. From an early age Richard adored his mother but had a poor relationship with his father. As he grew up he developed a lasting love of the local countryside and this led to him enrolling in the Pathfinders, an organisation for boys which twenty years later was to form the core of the Hitler Youth. On summer weekends they camped in the woods, swam and ran races, practised field crafts and marched home singing. At Christmas Richard's mother used to make up a basket of food for him to take to the needy, 'for while we were poor, she never forgot there were those even poorer'. At Easter 1913, when he was fourteen, Hauptmann was confirmed in the Lutheran church. He and four others became apprenticed to an old joiner to learn carpentry, at which he became quite proficient. Then came the Great War. Two of his three elder brothers were killed early on and when he was eighteen he too was called up, to serve as a machine gunner on the western front.

Slightly wounded twice in enemy artillery barrages, Hauptmann was demobbed in 1919 and returned to Kamenz where, as in so many German towns, food and clothing were scarce and work unobtainable. 'I thought I was no different when I returned', he wrote in his memoirs, 'but I deceived myself. My moral view was no longer the same.'

He started pilfering: stealing a lump of coal from a local mine where he had found temporary work as a night repair machinist, then a goose from a farm which had rejected his plea for work. Worse was to follow. He met a pre-war friend, Fritz Petzold:

How we came to think of stealing, I can no longer remember.
Before I entered the army I never had such a thought, even though
I often had to forgo pleasure which required just a little money …

Richard admitted to taking part in three burglaries, two from houses in nearby villages and the last in Kamenz itself; between 14 March and 20 March 1919 he and Petzold took money and watches they found in desks, which they forced open.

Five days later they committed a crime which was to haunt Richard and play some part in determining his ultimate fate; a crime negligible in cash terms but deplorable in human ones and which Richard was to call 'the greatest shame of my life'. On the morning of 20 March he and Petzold, to whom he had given his army pistol, accosted two women wheeling a pushcart laden with foodstuffs. At first the women refused to stop but did so when Petzold pointed his pistol and threatened to shoot. From the pushcart Petzold and Hauptmann took nine bread rolls, eight food ration cards and a pocketbook containing three marks. That night they broke into a house near Richard's home and stole 200 marks and another watch.

Six days later they were arrested, taken to the country court and sentenced to two and a half years' imprisonment for the burglaries and another two and a half for robbing the pushcart. It was a harsh punishment for first offenders, but unemployment and food shortages were rife in Germany then and deterrent sentences were thought essential.

For four years the conduct of both was exemplary. Hauptmann sang in the prison choir, learned to accompany himself on the mandolin and in the library read scores of travel books. He and Petzold walked together in the prison garden, 'but we never talked about our past, we were too ashamed of it'.

After finishing his sentence, Richard again looked for work back in Kamenz, but there was still none on offer. So he decided to walk to southern Germany and try there, sleeping in 'nature cabins' when he could find them, or else in the open, always looking for work and never finding it. Eventually he returned to Kamenz footsore, penniless and frustrated.

Before long he was back in prison on a charge of having stolen three leather drive belts, which he denied. But whatever the verdict, he had come to believe that he had no future in Germany and resolved, like many young Germans then, to seek his future in America, to which his sister had successfully emigrated a few years before. Discipline at the prison must have been lax, for he found himself able to walk out through the gates without being stopped. Before leaving he promised his mother he would never do anything seriously wrong again and, many will claim, he kept his word.

Unsuccessful in his first two attempts to stow away in German ships (on both occasions he reached the other side of the Atlantic but was apprehended upon landing and returned to Germany), the third time he chose an American liner and, after spending ten days hidden in the coal bunkers, walked ashore unmolested into Hoboken, on the

Hudson. "'God, I thank you!" were my first words as I trod the pavements of the New World.' The state of New Jersey, in which Hoboken lies, welcomed Hauptmann to his new life. Twelve years later it was to help usher him out of it.

Hauptmann had only one German contact in New York, a friend called Diebig, but after he had crossed to Manhattan on the ferry and walked some sixty blocks to the address he had been given, he was told that Diebig had moved. Yet nothing could dampen his spirits: to be alive and free, with the prospect of working and of earning and saving money, was exhilarating. 'I was so happy I wanted to sing. I was in the best of health and had recovered my inner peace. And I thought no more about my past. I had locked it behind me.' Luck was with him. Richard met a young German in the same rooming house who invited Richard to stay at his parents' apartment until he could find a place of his own: the young German's name was Fred Aldinger, and his mother, Lena, was a washerwoman. At first Richard found work as a dish washer, and then, having saved enough money to buy himself a cheap set of tools, he found employment at the trade for which he had been trained – carpentry – at treble the wages.

One of the families for whom Aldinger's mother Lena (with whom Richard was still staying as a paying guest) worked was a Jewish couple called Rosenbaum. They had a maid, Anna Schoeffler, to whom Lena often spoke about Richard, describing him as a 'quiet young man who is like a second son to me'. Anna came from the same part of Germany as Lena and one evening Lena invited her to her house, where she met Richard for the first time. 'We talked and listened to the radio,' she said, 'Richard and another friend sang. It was like our home in Germany.'

One Sunday Anna and Lena visited the famous Coney Island where they saw Richard sitting on the sand. 'He joined us,' she said, 'and we did the rounds of all the amusements and had a fine time.' Anna and

Richard began seeing each other regularly and later Richard would write, 'During that summer I knew I had found my dear wife.'

Anna was then twenty-six, a year older than Richard, handsome rather than pretty, with the same moral principles as her future mother-in-law. 'An upright Christian woman', Hauptmann once called her, 'to whom truth is sacred' – and all of us who came to know her would agree.

Richard and Anna took walks together in the evening after work. 'He loved nature,' she said, 'and all kinds of animals and birds.' And, painful though it was, he felt he must tell her about his past. 'I passed over everything as superficially as I could', he wrote, ' for fear I might lose her love.' But Anna accepted it. 'It was not hard to understand,' she said, 'if you were in Germany after the war. Food was scarce and there was no money: it was difficult to live'. She told him: 'That is all behind you now and will not affect our happiness and love.'

Their engagement lasted more than a year, for they wanted to save as much as possible before their wedding. On 10 October 1925 they were married in the home of a cousin of Anna in Brooklyn, intending to spend their honeymoon, and possibly settling, in California. But the second-hand car they had bought for the trip broke down soon after they left New York and they had to abandon it. Had they reached California and stayed on it is unlikely the world would ever have heard of them.

For the next four years Richard and Anna prospered, he contracting with various firms for carpentry work, she as an assistant at Fredericksen's bakery and café. Soon between them they were making around $100 a week, and saving most of it. By 1931 Richard was telling friends they were worth between $10,000 and $12,000, in today's money, $90,000–100,000. 'We worked hard but we were happy', wrote Richard, 'our future looked rosy.' As if in confirmation, Anna said, 'When he came home, I heard him whistling and singing as he came up the stairs.'

Most evenings they stayed at home, listening to the wireless and going to bed early. On the first Saturday of each month they held musical evenings: Richard played and sang to the mandolin, his great friend Hans Kloppenburg played the guitar and another German friend the zither.

And on most weekends, in winter as well as summer, the Hauptmanns visited a conservation area known as Hunter's Island, on Long Island Sound, along with other members of a little close-knit group of German immigrants. In the winter the men played football; in the summer, when wives and girlfriends came too, they swam, boated, fished, sunbathed, cooked meals and, in the evenings, gathered round the fire to play music and sing songs that reminded them of home. 'Everyone seemed to know Hauptmann,' commented a woman friend and, said his great friend Kloppenburg, 'everyone seemed to like him'.

In 1931 there was an economic slump; the stock market was in the doldrums and the demand for carpenters diminished. With money from savings at their disposal, now was the time for Richard and Anna to make the trip they had intended to make on their honeymoon – drive to California to see Richard's sister Emma and explore the rest of America on the way. Hans Kloppenburg joined them. They took camping equipment, cooking utensils, field glasses, a small pistol for protection, a mandolin and a guitar. In Los Angeles they stayed with Emma and her husband, a Hollywood chauffeur; for Emma and Richard it was an emotional reunion after twenty-two years apart. An air circus was in town and Richard took a ten-minute flip, the nearest he would ever come to the world of Charles Lindbergh.

Richard, Anna and Hans returned to New York by the traditional tourist route, through New Mexico, then along the Mexican border to New Orleans and across to Florida. By the time they had reached New York again they had covered 14,000 miles; the Dodge car Richard had bought for the trip had never once let them down. All three were bowled over by what they had seen. 'After the beauties of America', wrote Richard, 'I cannot understand why so many people go to Europe to see nature.'

In October 1931 the Hauptmanns moved into a new apartment, the upper floor of 1279 East 222nd Street; the landlord, name of Rauch, lived with his mother on the ground floor. There was no garage for the Dodge but Mr Rauch owned an adjoining plot and gave Richard the timber to build a garage on it, rent free.

Anna, meanwhile, took up her old job at Fredericksen's bakery and café. Every morning Richard took her there in the Dodge and on Tuesdays and Fridays, when she worked late, he fetched her home. One morning in February 1932 Richard met a man in the café who worked at the Reliant Employment Agency on 6th Avenue. He sounded him out about prospects of work and was advised to go along to the agency and inquire. There a Mr E. V. Pescia told him there would probably be an opening for a skilled carpenter quite soon; so as not to miss the opportunity when it arose, Richard started to call in at the agency every morning and afternoon. In America, as in Germany, no one could accuse Richard of not exerting himself in order to find work where there was the least chance of it.

Pescia's records show that towards the end of February a job came up for Hauptmann at the Majestic Apartments, a big block on 72nd Street and Central Park West. Having handed over a $10 booking fee, Hauptmann and another carpenter, Gus Kassens, were instructed to report to the construction supervisor, one Joseph M. Furcht. Hauptmann duly reported to the supervisor on Saturday, 27 February and was told to start work on Tuesday, 1 March (the day of the Lindbergh baby kidnapping) at $100 a month.

Later that Saturday Richard Hauptmann and Hans Kloppenburg drove to Hunter's Island to play football with friends, and again the following afternoon. On Monday Richard took his tools to the Majestic Apartments and left them in the carpenters' room in the basement.

'On 1 March 1932 at 8 a.m.', declared Mr Furcht, 'Bruno Richard Hauptmann and Gus Kassens reported for work at the Majestic Apartments and worked throughout that entire day until 5 p.m. … Hauptmann was a skilled carpenter who, much against my wishes, I was forced to put on maintenance work which is ordinary work instead of skilled carpenter work.' Gus Kassens also recalled working with Hauptmann that day.

That night, at about the time that the kidnap gang were removing little Charlie from the nursery, Anna worked late at Fredericksen's and, as was his usual practice, Richard drove there to fetch her so she would not have to walk home alone.

Anna, as has already been stated, heard the news of the kidnapping when she arrived for work at Fredericksen's the next morning. Richard read about it in the paper he bought at the 225th Street subway on his way to work. That evening the two of them, as shocked and saddened as the rest of America, talked about it; there were few across the country who did not.

Mr Furcht said that for the rest of that week Richard Hauptmann worked at the Majestic Apartments from 8 a.m. to 5 p.m. every day.

The $100 a month that Richard was earning at the Majestic Apartments for unskilled carpentry was about half of what he had been earning on contract work before the trip to California; indeed, Anna's wages at Fredericksen's, plus tips, were more than that. So, after work on the evening of Saturday, 2 April (the night that Condon was handing over the $50,000 in St Raymond's Cemetery) Richard gave in his notice, collected his tools and went home for another musical evening with Hans Kloppenburg. The next week he resumed what he had already been practising with some success before the Californian trip – buying and selling shares at the brokerage firm of Steiner, Rouse.

In June that year Anna left on the liner *Europa* to visit her mother in Germany; she would be away until September. During her absence Richard paid daily visits to Steiner, Rouse, did occasional carpentry work and joined the Hunter's Island crowd at weekends. Among the many pretty, lightly dressed girls he met there, he found himself attracted to Gerta Henkel, wife of Carl Henkel, who were fellow tenants with Hans Kloppenburg in Mrs Kohl's rooming house at 149 East 127th Street; and soon hardly a day passed without Richard dropping in there for coffee on his way to Steiner, Rouse.

One morning, when he was with Carl and Gerta, Richard met for the first time the man who was to prove his nemesis. The door opened

and in came a small, skinny-looking German Jew whom Carl introduced as Isidor Fisch, another of Mrs Kohl's lodgers. Before his marriage, Carl said, he had shared rooms with Isidor and another friend,
Henry Uhlig, who were both in the fur trade. Isidor was then twenty-
seven, five feet five inches tall, under 150 pounds in weight, had brown
hair and eyes, two outsize ears and a persistent, hacking cough (the
first signs of the tuberculosis that would eventually kill him). Uhlig
was the opposite, a big handsome man with blond hair and grey eyes,
'a chubby, happy sort of fellow', as Hans Kloppenburg remembered
him, 'always making jokes and being the life and soul of a party'.
Richard and Isidor seem to have hit it off that day and when Richard
invited him to see the souvenirs he had brought back from the California trip, Isidor accepted.

From Isidor and other mutual friends, Richard learned that the
Fisch family were originally Polish but had settled in Leipzig where
Isidor's parents still lived. After school in Leipzig, Isidor was appren-
ticed to a firm of furriers, where he met Henry Uhlig, who became his
lifelong friend; the foreman who supervised their work was Hermann
Kirsten.

During the later 1920s the Kirstens and their daughters Gerta and
Erica, Isidor Fisch and Henry Uhlig all separately emigrated to America, where at first Isidor and Henry shared an apartment.

Reports of Isidor vary. To his friends he never seemed to have any
money, although reportedly he earned between $50 and $100 dollars a
week in the fur trade. At Mrs Kohl's he had the cheapest room in the
house, in the attic, for which he paid only $3.50 a week – and even then,
said Mrs Kohl, he was often behind with the rent. Carl Henkel said he
thought Isidor was as poor as a church mouse and fellow members of
the Chrzanower Young Men's Association thought he was destitute.

But there was another side to Fisch of which his friends were ignorant. Because working for long hours in chilled fur storage rooms was
bad for his damaged lungs, he looked around for some more congenial
activity; and in doing so found he had an uncanny gift for persuading

people to invest money in dubious enterprises. In short, he became a con man. In 1930 Fisch advised a Mrs Kuntz that an investment of $3,000 in something called the Long Sign Company would yield good dividends; she gave him $500 which she never saw again. The next year he was involved in an implausible scheme for showing movies in parks, for which he persuaded one Alois Motzer to part with $1,000. Wisely, Mr Motzer had insisted on collateral (some real estate that Fisch had bought on Long Island) so that, when the scheme folded, he got his money back.

But Fisch's biggest con was an outfit called the Knickerbocker Pie Company. Already on its last legs when he joined, it was being run by two crooks, one of them a gangster who had robbed a woman of $5,000 and then fled to his native Italy; the other a professional gambler who had served a prison sentence for grand larceny (which shows that Fisch was already associating with other crooks). Early in 1931, the two per-suaded Fisch to put $1,000 into the company to try and rescue it, in return for becoming its president.

In a desperate attempt to keep the company afloat Fisch persuaded Carl Henkel's mother, Mrs Hile, to invest $1,250 in it and the parents of another young friend to part with $2,500. But the Knickerbocker Pie Company was beyond salvation. In July 1931, with the gas cut off because of non-payment of bills and money owing to various creditors, including the landlord, it finally went bust.

Having developed an addiction to winkling money out of the unsus-pecting, Fisch was reluctant to discontinue. Long after the Knicker-bocker Pie Company had closed its doors, Fisch sang its praises to anyone who would listen; he also persuaded people to invest in non-existent furs. The results were gratifying. Gerta's mother, Mrs Kirsten, gave him $4,000; Mrs Hile a further $2,850; Max Falek $800; Uhlig $400; and others various undisclosed sums. Uhlig reckoned Fisch must have raked in a total of some $13,000, and, apart from Carl Henkel, none of his investors saw their money again.

What Fisch did with this money is a mystery; for his mode of existence continued as frugally as before. When Hauptmann told him how well he was doing on the stock market, he impressed Hauptmann with how well he was doing selling furs, so they agreed to form a partnership. But with this difference: Hauptmann's dealings with Fisch were on the level, whereas Fisch was preparing to con Hauptmann just as he had conned all the others. So that when the Hauptmanns gave an evening party and Otto Wollenberg, rather the worse for drink, pointed at Fisch and said, 'Who is that little shrimp over there?' Hauptmann replied, with some heat, 'That guy is worth thirty thousand dollars. He is my partner in furs and the stock market. We have an agreement to go half and half on everything.'

Fisch was also dabbling in other fraudulent activities. When his elder brother Pinkus sent him a shipment of cat skins from Germany worth $84, he sold them at a profit and pocketed the proceeds for himself. He then got a secretary to type out a list of non-existent furs which he valued at two or three times their actual worth; and it was because he had invested in these so heavily, he told Hauptmann, that he was unable to pay into their joint account the $5,000 he owed it. About this time, Fisch also involved himself in buying 'hot' money at 40 or 50 cents for a dollar's worth. Evidence that Fisch was involved in the sale of hot money, including the Lindbergh ransom money, comes from several sources: Oscar J. Bruchman told *The New York Times* that Fisch had asked for his help in disposing of hot money; and Henry Uhlig told me that he was informed by a private detective that Fisch had been seen exchanging hot money in a pool room at 3rd Avenue and 86th Street. And in this same pool room, says Anthony Scaduto in his book *Scapegoat* another friend of Fisch by the name of Trost heard that Fisch was offering hot money for sale.

During the spring of 1933 Anna found she was pregnant, and told friends how good to her Richard had been, bringing her presents of flower and candy. The baby, a boy they called Manfred, was born on 3 November and Richard was overjoyed. 'My wife and child', he wrote, 'my heaven on earth'.

Earlier that year Fisch had told Richard that he would be returning to Leipzig for Christmas to set up the German end of an export–import business in furs and that he had booked a third-class cabin for himself and Uhlig on the S.S. *Manhattan,* leaving on 6 December. On 14 November Fisch paid the steamship company agent, a Mr Steinweg, the balance of what he owed for the two tickets and bought some travellers' cheques for both of them, over $1,000-worth. He paid for these in gold certificate $10 and $20 dollar bills, which later Mr Steinweg told a private detective was Lindbergh ransom money (this has been confirmed by Sidney Whipple in his book *The Lindbergh Crime*).

Never wishing to pay for anything himself he could get others to pay for, Fisch approached Richard later that day and asked if he would advance him $2,000 for the steamship tickets and living expenses in Germany from their joint partnership account and Richard, unaware that Fisch's furs existed only on paper, gave him a cheque.

On 4 December, Richard and Anna gave a farewell party for Fisch, who, flush with the $2,000 he had conned from his host, sportingly provided the drinks. Hans Kloppenburg was among the guests and saw Fisch hand Richard a package, asking him to look after it until his return: it was wrapped in brown paper, he said, tied with string, about the size and shape of a shoe box. 'Fisch said to keep it in a dry place,' said Richard. 'I stuck it on the top shelf of the kitchen closet and forgot about it.' And for the next eight months Richard continued to forget about it.

Time marched on: 1933 gave way to 1934, winter to spring, then in April 1934 Richard heard from Pinkus that Isidor had died of consumption. When Uhlig returned to New York alone, they began a search for Fisch's assets, the furs he was always boasting about, the contents of his safe-deposit box, which they needed a court order to examine. But there was nothing, no furs or skins, and the safe-deposit box contained only dust. Richard was dumbfounded, for, as he wrote to Pinkus, 'our relationship was founded on trust', and to Kloppenburg he said, 'I think Fisch is the biggest crook I ever met.' By this time he had quite forgotten about the package Fisch had given him. He spent an uneventful summer doing the odd carpentry job, playing the stock market at Steiner, Rouse and visiting Hunter's Island with his friends at weekends. Often he took Anna and Manfred with him. Of Richard's relationship with Manfred Henry Uhlig said, 'I always felt he never wanted to let him out of his sight. He liked to play with him and march him around and carry him on his shoulders.' At home Richard built his son a high chair and rocking chair and, before the baby went to sleep at night, he would play the mandolin and sing to him, especially Brahms' Lullaby.

Then, in mid-August 1934, Richard made the discovery that was to be his undoing.

Late one afternoon I had transplanted some flowers and some soil had fallen on the floor. I went to the kitchen closet to get the broom. In taking out the broom I touched the things on the top shelf with it and … saw the little package which Mr Fisch had given me to keep for him. I had broken through the wrapping which was soaked with water and saw the yellow shine of money.

He put the package in a bucket which he took to the garage and found it crammed full of $10 and $20 gold certificate bills. They were so wet through and glued together that when he tried to separate them, they tore. So he put them in a basket to dry. When they had dried he counted them and found they came to $14,600.

What was he to do? What would any of us have done? What a truly honest man would have done, and what Anna with her high standards of morality would have insisted he do, would have been to inform Pinkus of his find and ask for instructions. But truly honest men of this world are rare and Richard was not one of them. For months past he had been searching for Fisch's assets in order to repay himself the $5,500 plus $2,000 travel expenses that Fisch owed him, without success. Now it was here for the asking. If he disclosed his find, Pinkus would almost certainly claim it, for he had no written proof of what Fisch owed him.

And what about the balance of around $7,000 after he had subtracted Fisch's debt? No doubt he told himself he would cross that bridge when he came to it.

But where to put it? Had the money been in regular greenbacks, Richard could have put it on deposit in his bank or at Steiner, Rouse. It being in gold certificates, which it was now illegal to hold in bulk, he could do neither. So he had to hide it, but where? If in the apartment Anna might find it and tell him to send it to Pinkus. The garage was safer; no one went there except himself. So he secreted it, in shellac tins stuffed with rags, in holes drilled for bits and on a boarded-in shelf wrapped in copies of old newspapers.

He then drew out a dozen bills for himself and began to spend them at local stores; and on 15 September used one bill to pay for petrol at the Warner-Quinlan gas station on Lexington and 127th Street, which led the attendant to jot down the Dodge's registration number and for the police to call the Bureau of Motor Vehicles for Hauptmann's name and address.

Three days later, three police cars containing officers of the New York and New Jersey police forces and the FBI assembled outside Hauptmann's house at 1279 222nd Street. A little before 9 a.m. they saw Hauptmann leave his house; he fitted the Motor Bureau's description of him: aged thirty-four, 180 pounds, 5 feet 10 inches, blue eyes, blond hair. Lieutenant Finn of the New York City police, who was scheduled to make the arrest, had already made up his mind about Hauptmann, as millions of Americans were to do in the coming weeks, without a scrap of evidence to link him with either the kidnapping or the murder. 'A creature,' wrote Finn, 'who had not hesitated to go into the house of another man, and had so destroyed the happiness of that home that the owner and his wife had been forced to abandon the house of their dreams and flee to scenes that had not been blighted by the filthy creature's foot.' The police saw Hauptmann back out of the garage, tailed him for five miles, and then, afraid they might lose him at a red light, closed in.

With guns at the ready they surrounded the car, opened the driving door and looked into Hauptmann's bewildered face. 'What is happening?' they heard him say. 'What is this?' He imagined he had been stopped for speeding, but why so many officers, why the hostility and why the guns?

'Get out,' said Finn.

They put the handcuffs on him, searched him and found another ransom money gold certificate bill in his wallet. 'Where did you get this counterfeit money?' Finn asked and Hauptmann replied that he was collecting gold certificate bills against inflation and at one time had $300-worth. Then Finn asked how much more of it he had at home; and Hauptmann, thinking of the $14,600 hidden in the garage, knew that if he did not want to face charges of hoarding and maybe stealing, he had to lie. Remembering some gold coins he kept in a tin, he said, 'About $120-worth.' 'We'll check on that,' said Finn. Allowing his fantasies to run away with him, he wrote later, 'He was the bird we were looking for all right. I could defy any man to like him. I felt that he would kill a baby in a crib and never turn a hair.' Then Finn went off to telephone headquarters, telling two other detectives to sit with Hauptmann in the back of his car.

'So you're the Lindbergh kidnapper!' one said.

The what? *The what?* First it was speeding, then passing counterfeit money, now this. It must all be some horrible mistake. When would it end?

The other detective looked at him with venom.

'You're going to burn, baby,' he said. And he was right.

From now on events followed a kind of dreadful inevitability. Hauptmann was taken back to his apartment and had to sit and watch as police officers turned the rooms upside down in their search for more ransom money. He realised now the deadly peril he was in. Was Fisch aware when he passed the shoe box to him that it contained Lindbergh ransom money? With Fisch dead, he would never know. Who would believe his story as to how the money had come to him? Now and again he rose a little to look out of the window at the garage where the bulk of the money lay hidden. 'What are you looking at?' one officer asked, and Hauptmann said, 'Nothing'. He would be all right, he reckoned, so long as the search did not extend there.

Then they took him to the Second Precinct police station, on the Lower West Side, to face a sea of grim police faces. They looked at him with wonder and a certain awe. This was the man – they were certain of it – who for the past two and a half years had filled their waking thoughts, the human fiend who had kidnapped and then murdered the Lindbergh baby. Strange, some thought, that he didn't look more the part. Asked about his early life and arrival in America, he answered with what they called apparent frankness. 'There was nothing in his face to tell us he wasn't innocent,' wrote one of the FBI men. 'It was distressed and tired but free of guilt.'

Asked what he was doing on 1 March 1932, Hauptmann said he had been working at the Majestic Apartments until five or six – and they said they would check on that. Asked how he had acquired the ransom money, he foolishly said from the banks. How much, they asked, and where did he keep it? Only $300-worth, he replied, even more foolishly, and in the same box where he kept his gold coins; the $20 they had found on him that morning had been the last of it. With all these untruths he was digging his own grave.

Expecting Hauptmann to confess, and despite giving him a severe beating to persuade him to do so without success, the police were baffled by his continued protestations of innocence, a claim at first supported by the opinions of two of the best-known handwriting experts in the country, the Osborns father and son, that there was no resemblance between Hauptmann's writing and that of the writer of the ransom notes. Nor was there a scrap of evidence to connect him with either the kidnapping or the murder.

Despite this, and like everybody else in America, the police had no doubts about Hauptmann's guilt and dismissed his claim that Fisch had left the ransom money in the shoe box as 'a fishy story'; an opinion much bolstered the next day when Hauptmann's garage was taken apart and the $14,600 hidden within it was discovered. Who would then believe his explanation of having hidden it, not because it was ransom money and he knew it, but firstly because the money was strictly speaking not his and secondly because he knew it was now illegal to hold gold certificate money in bulk.

The discovery of the money had two immediate consequences. It enabled the two Osborns, who had so emphatically denied that there was any resemblance between Hauptmann's writing and that of the author of the ransom note, to have second thoughts and tell the police that there were *some* similarities between the two after all; and secondly it led the *New York Daily News* to print a front page banner headline LINDBERGH KIDNAPPER JAILED. Under UK law this would have been regarded as a contempt of court prejudicial to the outcome of a trial.

But Hauptmann's ordeals had only just begun. That first night at the Second Precinct police station the police hauled in Hans Kloppenburg (who as a friend of Hauptmann they thought might be involved, too) and made both write out some of the words which had been mispelt in the ransom notes: 'singnature' for 'signature'; 'were' for 'where'; 'ouer' for 'our'; 'haus' for 'house'; 'gute' for 'good', and others. The two were also asked to copy out facsmile photographs of some of the ransom notes. Naively, Hauptmann agreed to do this, thinking it would help to clear him. Later he said that if he had known the use to which the authorities would put it, he would never have complied.

Then he was taken to be interviewed by the Bronx district attorney, one Samuel Foley, whose failure to winkle a confession out of Hauptmann so enraged him that he attacked his prisoner with an outburst of quite shocking prejudice and brutality, concluding by saying that Hauptmann had killed one baby and wrecked the life of another, his own child.

Your wife is being held in the Women's Jail [not true] with a lot of prostitutes. She is separated from the baby. It has no one who loves it. It may die of under-nourishment. Your wife is hysterical. She will probably become an imbecile over the shock of this. If you have any speck of manhood left in you, you will come clean on this and do one manly thing in your life.

The wretched Hauptmann's response was to break into uncontrollable sobbing and shout out, 'Stop it, stop it! I told you everything, I don't know any more.'

Yet the New Jersey police had a problem, too. They wanted to apply to the Bronx for Hauptmann to be extradited to New Jersey but lacked any evidence on which to base the extradition. So for the second time they approached an impoverished woodcutter, a known liar named Millard Whited, who lived in a shack quite close to the Lindbergh estate. The day after the kidnapping the police had asked him whether he had seen any suspicious-looking persons in the area the day before and he had twice said that he had not. Now they approached him again and asked if, in exchange for a fee of $150, $35 expenses and a share of the reward money, he would travel to the Bronx District Court and testify[5] that he had twice seen Hauptmann in the neighbourhood either on or just before the day of the kidnapping. For Whited the promise of such riches was irresistible – enough for Hauptmann to be extradited to the little New Jersey town of Flemington, the nearest court house and prison to where the crime had been committed. Colonel Schwarzkopf kept Whited away from the press as part of his deal with him, but told them that he was 'a poor man who is absolutely upright and honest.'

Hauptmann's trial for murder opened at Flemington on 2 January 1935. Five hundred press and spectators crammed into the tiny court

---

5   There is a film of this still extant showing Whited tapping Hauptmann's
     shoulder to identify him.

room which before then had seldom seen more than a handful of people; among the journalists were the writers Damon Runyon, Ford Madox Ford and Edna Ferber and the broadcaster Walter Winchell; and among the spectators Ginger Rogers, Jack Benny, Lynn Fontanne and Moss Hart and the *haut monde* of New York with accompanying Pekinese, ferried there by liveried chauffeurs. Forty-five telegraph lines were set up for direct filing to Paris, London, Berlin, Buenos Aires and Sydney. H. L. Mencken called it 'The Greatest Story since the Resurrection', others 'The Trial of the Century'.

His savings by now exhausted, Hauptmann accepted an offer from the Hearst Press to pay for his defence lawyers in exchange for exclusive access at the trial. Leading the team was a fat, flamboyant, alcoholic and syphilitic clown called Edward Reilly, nicknamed Death House Reilly because of all the capital cases he had lost. Yet his team included a much-respected Flemington advocate, C. Lloyd Fisher, who, unlike Reilly, believed in Hauptmann's innocence from the outset. Chief counsel for the prosecution was New Jersey's newly appointed Attorney-General, the dapper David Wilentz. It was his first, and last, murder trial.

In those countries that employ the adversary system of justice, it is generally considered bad form and unethical to present the case against the accused other than dispassionately and without prejudice, letting the facts against him speak for themselves. But David Wilentz was not of that breed, at one point in the trial asking the jury what sort of man it would be that killed the child of Colonel and Mrs Lindbergh.

He wouldn't be an American. No American gangster ever sunk to the level of killing babies. Ah, no! It had to be a fellow that had ice water in his veins, not blood, it had to be a fellow that was an egomaniac, who thought he was omnipotent ...

And let me tell you, men and women, the State of New Jersey and of New York and the federal authorities have found that animal, an animal lower than the lowest form in the animal kingdom … Bruno Richard Hauptmann, and he is here for your judgment.

His tirade continued:

I never even walked into his cell to ask him a word, I wouldn't get close enough to him, I wouldn't become contaminated, I wouldn't breathe the same air. I just couldn't stand being anywhere near him. I feel itchy, I feel oozy.

By now almost hysterical with prejudice, Wilentz offered the jury a scenario which was without a shred of evidence:

This fellow took no chance on the child awakening. He crushed that child right in that room into insensibility … the child never cried, never gave an outcry. The little voice was stilled right in that room. He wasn't interested in the child. Life meant nothing to him. Take a look at him as he sits here. Look at him as he walks into this room, panther-like, gloating, feeling good.

'Either this man is the filthiest and vilest snake who ever crept through the grass,' concluded the chief prosecutor, 'or he is entitled to an acquittal. And if you believe as we do, you have got to convict him … of murder in the first degree.'

The distinguished defence lawyer Sam Leibowitz, who was in court, was appalled by all this. 'No prosecutor had the right to use inflammatory arguments calculated to arouse the passions of the jury instead of cold arguments based on reason and logic.'

So utterly convinced was the prosecution that Hauptmann was guilty that, lacking the evidence to prove it, they had no compunction in inventing it. In addition to Whited's false evidence they bribed a half-blind 87-year-old Prussian war veteran called Amandus Hochmuth, who lived at the foot of the road leading to the Lindbergh estate, to say that he too had caught a glimpse of Hauptmann on the day of the kidnapping, driving a car with a ladder in the back! The taxi driver Perrone, who had said that he would never be able to recognise the member of the kidnap gang who had given him a letter to deliver to Dr Condon in the dark, now identified Hauptmann as that man. And Dr Condon, who had failed to pick out Hauptmann as the member of the gang he had met in the two cemeteries, was told by the police that if he did not change his mind he would be indicted as an accessory himself – and so obligingly changed his mind.

But the worst perjuries came from those who should have known better. The misspellings in the ransom notes which the police had ordered Richard Hauptmann and Hans Kloppenburg to write out were proffered as evidence that Hauptmann must have written the notes, as the likelihood of anyone else making such a combination of mistakes was inconceivable.

The final nail in poor Hauptmann's coffin was the evidence of Charles Lindbergh himself. Before his extradition from New York, Hauptmann had been made to stand in the Bronx District Attorney's office and shout, 'Hey, doc' or 'Hey, doktor' in a variety of voices – the words that Lindbergh had heard a member of the gang shout to Condon in the St Raymond's Cemetery – while a disguised Lindbergh listened. Although he had told the DA that he could not possibly say the two voices were the same, he was then assured by Colonel Schwarzkopf that there was no doubt at all that Hauptmann was guilty, and was persuaded to testify at the trial that the two words he had heard in the dark a hundred yards away two years earlier were from the same voice he had heard in the office of the Bronx DA – that of Hauptmann. Although *The New York Times* considered this piece of evidence 'too slender a thread' to be believed, coming as it did from the mouth of the national hero, for the jury trying Hauptmann (as Ethel Stockton, who was one of them, told me) it was conclusive.

What could and should have saved Hauptmann were the time sheets showing that he was working at the Majestic Apartments from 8 a.m. to

5 p.m. on the day of the kidnapping and so would not have had time to go home after work, pick up a ladder and any accomplices and reach the Lindbergh house before the baby went missing. Both Wilentz and Foley saw these time sheets but declared, without evidence, that on that day Hauptmann had quit work early. The time sheets were then handed over to the New York City police and, despite many inquiries, have never been seen since. Other time sheets still in existence were then doctored to show that Hauptmann did not start work at the Majestic Apartments until after the kidnapping (thus contradicting Wilentz's assertion that on the day of the kidnapping Hauptmann was at work but left early).

Finally, and in order to clinch Hauptmann's presence at Hopewell, the prosecution sought to show that one rail of the kidnap ladder had come from a floorboard in Hauptmann's attic. This evidence had been fabricated by two detectives. Aside from the ludicrousness of Hauptmann, a skilled carpenter who always kept lengths of timber in his garage, climbing up the cleats of the airing cupboard with hammer and chisel to reach the attic (the only way up and down) and then chopping up bits of his landlord's flooring, two wood experts for the defence categorically denied that the wood of the rail from the ladder matched the board from which it was claimed to have come. By this time, however, the mountain of false evidence that had been built up against Hauptmann was too strong to dislodge. As one of the FBI agents wrote, 'Hauptmann was foredoomed. He *had* to be found guilty.'

And on the morning of 13 February 1934, when the jury returned to court, he was. Because the charge was one of first degree murder, Hauptmann was sentenced to death by electrocution. 'What a terrible wedding anniversary present,' he told Lloyd Fisher, who visited him soon after in his cell, 'for my poor Annie!' She took the news bravely, adding, 'I hope and pray the true facts will come out before they can do anything to my poor man.'

All that afternoon Hauptmann sat motionless on his bed, staring at the floor. Now he knew that everything that had gone before was no empty formality. They really did mean to kill him.

Was there nothing or nobody who could help him? He remembered hearing that Colonel Kimberling, the warden of the prison at Trenton to which he had been transferred to await execution, owed his appointment to New Jersey's recently elected governor, Harold Hoffman; and Hoffman was the *ex-officio* chairman of the Court of Pardons, the only body that had the power to commute his sentence to life imprisonment. Hauptmann sent word to Kimberling that he would like the Governor to come and see him.

At thirty-nine, Hoffman was the youngest governor in the country, a stocky, chubby-faced man whose secretary said he had an enormous capacity for work, an astonishing memory and an independent mind. He had already taken an interest in the case, perturbed by what he saw as the railroading of the defendant. 'I have never in my life,' he told his secretary, 'seen more hatred shown to a man than at that trial.' He also knew that an old friend, a brilliant investigator named Ellis Parker, had been asked by his predecessor as governor to look into the case and had assured him that Hauptmann was not guilty.

But what did Hauptmann want to see him *about*? Was he now ready to confess, to 'thaw', as Wilentz had so crudely put it, when faced with the certainty of the electric chair? If so, then as the state's chief executive it was his duty to comply. In any case, the temptation to meet and talk with the man who for months had gripped the attention of the world must have been well nigh irresistible. Nevertheless, to avoid unnecessary publicity, he decided to visit Hauptmann after dark and under the personal supervision of the warden.

Hoffman's account of his visit later appeared in *Liberty* magazine. He describes how he entered the prison by way of the darkened execution chamber where the flashlight of the deputy warden picked out the electric chair 'covered in white muslin like a seated ghost', and from there to Hauptmann's cell. Hoffman noticed that Hauptmann was wearing an open shirt and dark blue trousers, that on a table were the bound transcripts of the trial and a Bible, and on the wall photographs of Anna and Manfred.

Expecting to have to listen to a plea for mercy to be conveyed to the Court of Pardons, Hoffman found himself instead confronted by an angry and frustrated man. 'Vy does your state do to me all this, Governor?' was Hauptmann's opening remark. 'Vy do they want my life for something somebody else have done?' Hoffman interrupted to point out that Hauptmann had been found guilty. 'Lies, lies, lies!' Hauptmann shouted back. 'All lies! Vould I kill a baby? I am a man. Vould I build that ladder? I am a carpenter.'

In four months his own counsel, Edward Reilly, had given Hauptmann no more than thirty-eight minutes to discuss his defence. Now Governor Hoffman was giving him an uninterrupted hour. Why, Hauptmann asked, hadn't it been said at the trial that not a single fingerprint of his had been found on the ladder or in the nursery, and that the footprint found under the nursery window didn't match his own? Why was it said that the chisel found on the lawn was his, when his chisel, which they had taken away, was a quite different type? Why had all the letters Fisch had written to him from Germany been suppressed? Would he as a carpenter build a ladder that would not bear his own weight? Why would he tear up one of his landlord's boards in the attic when he had plenty of boards of his own in the garage? And would he have told the gas station attendant that took his car licence number that he had a hundred more gold certificate bills at home if he knew they were Lindbergh ransom money?

All this and much more. He finished bitterly, 'The poor child haf been kidnapped and murdered, so somebody must die for it. For is the parent not the great flyer? And if somebody does not die for it, then always the police will be monkeys. So I am the one picked out to die.'

Much shaken by what he had heard, Hoffman returned to his suite at the Hildebrecht Hotel and wrote down all he could remember of what Hauptmann had said far into the night; and the next day motored over to Flemington to collect all twelve volumes of the trial transcript.

In mid-January 1936 the Court of Pardons, with Hoffman in the chair, met to decide if there were any grounds for clemency. The most impressive submission (because its author had no axe to grind) came from one of Hauptmann's two spiritual advisers, the Revd James Matthiesen:

I have had fifteen very intimate and soul searching interviews with Bruno Richard Hauptmann and am convinced he tells the truth. If Hauptmann had had a reliable defence lawyer at the outstart and if he had asked for an interpreter during the trial, the very evidence used against him would have spoken in his favour …

First, know Hauptmann as he really is and his wife Anna and then study the evidence and you will arrive at the same conclusion. Hauptmann does not fit into the frame of circumstantial evidence. I bring these findings to your honourable members of the Court of Pardons not because of sympathy for Hauptmann … but I want to see justice prevail.

I would ask for the supreme penalty if Hauptmann were guilty. My creed has no objections to that. There is nothing else in my mind than this: that I may serve the state of New Jersey in my findings. I feel it is a sacred duty I have to discharge.

For having the courage to discharge this sacred duty, the Revd Matthiesen was rebuked by his parish council, so angry were they at his having questioned the received wisdom. And Richard's other spiritual adviser, the Revd D. C. Werner, was punished even more severely for expressing publicly the same view. Although a pastor for thirty years and not in the best of health, his church, the Seventh Day Adventists, declared him unfrocked and took away his pension.

Nor did their joint pleas have any effect on the Court of Pardons who, like their parishioners, did not want to have their conclusions disturbed. When the vote was taken, Hoffman alone declared in favour of a commutation to life imprisonment, all seven members of the court against.

All his appeals having failed, Richard was scheduled to be electrocuted on Friday, 17 January 1936. A few days before this he turned down an offer from Sid Boehm of the *New York Evening Journal* to pay Anna $90,000 if he would give the paper a full and exclusive confession of his part in the crime, to be published after his death. Hoffman knew how devoted Richard was to his wife and son and how concerned he was about their future. How could he possibly reject such an offer unless his protestations of innocence were true?

Meeting David Wilentz by chance in New York on 15 January, Hoffman persuaded him to agree to a proposal he made: that if Hauptmann could be persuaded to make a statement admitting whatever part he had played in the affair, whether large or small, Wilentz and Hoffmann would jointly recommend to the Court of Pardons that the death sentence be reduced to life imprisonment. So, on his return to Trenton, Hoffman saw Anna in the manager's rooms of the Stacy-Trent Hotel where she was staying to be near Richard up to the end, and asked her to convey to him what he and Wilentz had agreed. If her husband would tell the truth now, his life would be saved.

Anna, red-eyed and exhausted by worry and lack of sleep, was galvanised into life.

'*No, no, no!*' Hoffman reported her as saying. 'My husband has only a few hours to live. Could I do that to him – make him think that I too believe that he would kill a baby. No, no! Never would I do that. Not even to save my Richard's life!'

Hoffman telephoned Wilentz with the news and Wilentz said, 'The hell with it, Harold. If that's still his attitude, I'm damned if I'm going to do anything to help him.'

Hoffman did not have the power, as some governors did, to commute the death sentence himself, but New Jersey's constitution did permit him to grant a reprieve of up to ninety days, and so, because of his own strong feelings that on very flimsy evidence Hauptmann was being railroaded to his death, he did grant a sixty-day reprieve. Anna and Richard's old mother back in Kamenz were naturally elated but

A GALLERY OF 'NOBLE CAUSE'
PRACTITIONERS

14

Sgt Fairfax and PC Harrison

15

PCs Harrison and McDonald

INCRIMINATING MATERIAL	TRIAL OF	CONSEQUENCES
Evidence	Derek Bentley	Executed

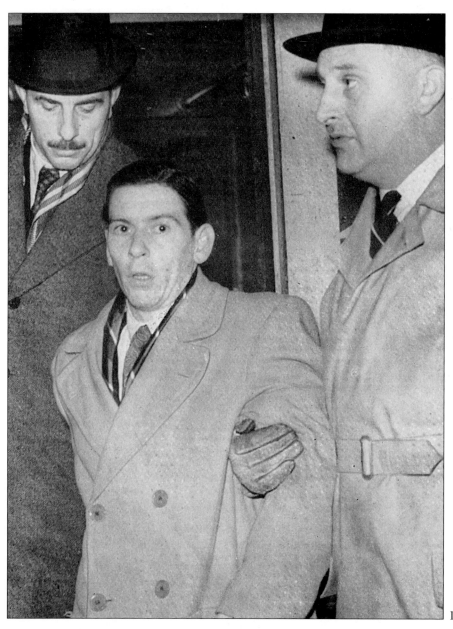
16

Det. Inspector Jennings and Inspector Black with Timothy Evans

INCRIMINATING MATERIAL	TRIAL OF	CONSEQUENCES
Confession	Timothy Evans	Executed

17

Det. Chief Inspector Herbert and Det. Sgt Burrows

INCRIMINATING MATERIAL   TRIAL OF   CONSEQUENCES

Evidence   Stephen Ward   Suicide

18

Det. Chief Superintendent Drury

INCRIMINATING MATERIAL	TRIAL OF	CONSEQUENCES
Evidence	McMahon, Cooper	11 years

19

Det. Chief Superintendent Capstick and Det. Sgt Hawkins

INCRIMINATING MATERIAL	TRIAL OF	CONSEQUENCES
Confession	Iain Hay Gordon	7 years mental institution

20

Det. Superintendent Reade and others

INCRIMINATING MATERIAL	TRIAL OF	CONSEQUENCES
Confessions	Birmingham Six	16 years

Asst Chief Constable Rowe

Det. Chief Superintendent Simmons

INCRIMINATING MATERIAL	TRIAL OF	CONSEQUENCES
Confessions	Guildford Four	16 years

23

24

Chief Superintendent Struthers   *Det. Superintendent Cowie*

INCRIMINATING MATERIAL	TRIAL OF	CONSEQUENCES
Evidence	Patrick Meehan	7 years

25

Col. Norman Schwarzkopf (left) and others. With Charles Lindbergh

INCRIMINATING MATERIAL	TRIAL OF	CONSEQUENCES
Evidence	Richard Hauptmann	Executed

public opinion in America was outraged, fearing that the catharsis and expiation that Hauptmann's death would provide was about to be denied them. An hysterical editorial in the *Trenton Times* declared that by granting this reprieve Hoffman had 'dishonoured himself, disgraced the state and converted New Jersey into an international laughing stock … sacrificed every legal and moral right to serve as Chief Executive of New Jersey', and called for the state's House of Assembly to institute immediate proceedings for impeachment. Even the staid *New York Times* called his action 'a desperate gamble' and 'indefensible'. Death threats began arriving in the mail at Hoffman's house. Schwarzkopf, as severe a critic of the reprieve as anyone, ordered guards to be posted outside it.

Unfazed by all this, Hoffman issued a statement that the letters he was receiving applauding his action far outnumbered those critical of it; and if impeachment was the price he had to pay for following his conscience, he was ready to pay it. He had never expressed a view as to Hauptmann's guilt or innocence and he did not do so now:

I do however share with hundreds and thousands of our people doubt as to the value of the evidence that placed him in the Lindbergh nursery on the night of the crime. I do wonder what part passion and prejudice played in the conviction of a man who was previously tried and convicted in the columns of many of our newspapers … I do doubt that this crime could have been committed by any one man, and I am worried about the eagerness of some of our law-enforcement agencies to bring about the death of this one man so that the books may be closed on the thought that another great crime mystery has been successfully solved.

For Hoffman the purpose of the reprieve was to allow time for further investigations to be made into the case, and he appointed a small team of selected detectives to undertake them. In the files of the New Jersey State police (requisitioned against Schwarzkopf's strong opposition) they found Whited's statement made soon after the kidnapping that he had seen no suspicious strangers in the neighbourhood, and a statement by a state trooper admitting to having offered Whited a share of the $25,000 reward money; a statement by the half-blind Hochmuth (who had recently mistaken a vase of flowers for a woman's hat) that he too had seen no one suspicious in the area at the time of the kidnapping (the *quid pro quo* was that he would not be indicted for drawing on social security funds to which he was not entitled); a record of the police informing Condon that if he did not identify Hauptmann as Cemetery John, he himself would be indicted. And the transcription of an interview with Mr Pescia, manager of the agency which had engaged Hauptmann to start work at the Majestic Apartments on the day of the kidnapping, in which he confirmed that he had done so; proof, he said, would be found in the firm's time sheets. However, when Hoffman applied for them, he was told that those for the relevant period (1–15 March) were missing. Finally, Hoffman paid a visit to Hauptmann's attic and found, as he thought he would, that the evidence that rail 16 of the kidnap ladder was part of an attic floorboard was a police fabrication.

In the light of all this and more, Hoffman had formed the view that Hauptmann's execution would be a gross miscarriage of justice. In a long statement issued only three days before the new date set for it to take place he declared that the whole case reeked of passion, prejudice and unfairness. He added that he had been to see the trial judge to ask if the evidence that had been unearthed would allow the judge to set aside the conviction and order a new trial, but the judge had said that the time limit for that had expired. There was no loophole left.

A day and a half before the execution date a nutter named Paul Wendel claimed that it was he who had kidnapped and murdered the Lindbergh baby, and in a last-minute attempt to save Hauptmann from the chair Lloyd Fisher asked for a recall of the Court of Pardons. The night before the recall, a handwriting expert named Samuel Small showed up at Hoffman's suite at the Hildebrecht to ask if he could testify to it that all eight handwriting experts at the trial who said that Hauptmann had written the ransom notes were wrong and that Hauptmann could not possibly have written them. When Hoffman said that the rules would not permit this, Small broke down and cried, saying it wasn't a question of *if* Hauptmann wrote the letters but of whether he *could*. 'I tell you, Governor, that if you were to say to Hauptmann that if he could write a single letter the way it was written in the ransom notes, he would have to stay in prison the rest of his life. A person cannot change his handwriting from one known system to another.' At 5 p.m. the court rejected Hauptmann's final appeal – a decision which Fisher called incomprehensible. And Wendel was unmasked as the nutter he was.

That same day Anna went to the prison to see Richard for the last time. They were allowed to hold hands through the bars and they cried together, aghast and incredulous that nine years of married happiness had to end like this. After she had gone and Fisher had brought him the news that his appeal had been rejected, Richard called for pencil and paper so that he could write a sort of last testament. Once more he emphasised his innocence ('I passed the money without knowing it was Lindbergh money … up to the present day I have no idea where the Lindbergh house in Hopewell is located') and there were notes to Wilentz ('Once you will stand before the same judge to who I go in a few hours. You know you have done wrong on me, you will not only take my life but also the happiness of my family. God will be judge between me and you') and to Hoffman ('I see it as my duty to thank you for what you have done for me. I write this with tears in my eyes. If ever prayers will reach you, they will come from me, from my dear wife and my little boy').

The execution was to take place at eight in the evening of the following day. That night Richard did not eat his supper, nor his breakfast or lunch the next day. In the afternoon he was moved from his own cell to cell 8, adjacent to the death chamber. He was only permitted to take with him his Bible, not even the photographs of Anna and Manfred. The prison barber arrived to shave the crown of his head where the executioner would fix the first of two electrodes. Then they brought in the clothes he was to die in – a blue shirt and some dark striped khaki trousers. Hauptmann queried a long slit in one of the trouser legs and was told this was the opening for the second electrode.

Then his attorneys, led by Lloyd Fisher in place of the absent Reilly, came to say goodbye. They tried not to show their distress at seeing this man whom they had grown to admire and like appear before them like some grotesque clown, ashen faced, hair shaved like a monk's tonsure, one trouser leg obscenely different from the other. They shook hands and he thanked them. Then Matthiesen and Werner came in, but when they suggested he might like to pray, Richard said his mind was too full to concentrate. They told him of the solace that St Francis of Assisi had derived from the single word 'God'. Then they read the Bible together.

A little before seven o'clock, the first of the forty-five witnesses to the execution, two-thirds of them journalists, arrived at the prison. Having been thoroughly searched by the guards, they were taken to Kimberling's office, where they were asked to sign affidavits that they were not carrying cameras, weapons, drugs or other contraband. Then Kimberling told them that they were to watch the execution in silence; anyone who cried out or spoke would be removed by the guards; if Hauptmann himself spoke or indicated he wanted to confess, then he, Kimberling, would give whatever response he deemed necessary. Lloyd Fisher now came to the death cell to bid Hauptmann a final goodbye. Matthiesen and Werner were still with the condemned man. Matthiesen handed Fisher a note written in German which Hauptmann told him was his final statement; Matthiesen, himself a German, translated it for him.

I am glad that my life in a world which has not believed me has ended. Soon I will be at home with my Lord. And as I love my Lord, I am dying an innocent man.

Should my death however serve the purpose of abolishing capital punishment ... I feel that my death has not been in vain.

I am at peace with God. I repeat, I affirm my innocence of the crime for which I was convicted. However I die with no malice or hatred in my heart. The love of Christ has filled my heart and I am happy in him.

Now it was time for the witnesses to proceed to the execution chamber. They set off two abreast in a file a hundred feet long, through the centre of the prison and out into the yard the other side. The clouds had cleared, the stars were out and there was a pale moon. Ahead lay the square shape of the death house, two guards with rifles and fixed bayonets patrolling its floodlit roof, presumably to thwart any last-minute attempt to rescue the condemned man. A sound like the murmur of the sea came to them; the voices of the crowd beyond the prison walls, believed to be 2,000 strong.

They went through the folding doors to the death house courtyard, then, having been searched a second time, were ushered into the chamber one by one. It was a bare, square, brightly lit room with poorly whitewashed walls and a skylight in the roof. Resting against the centre of the far wall, like some tawdry throne awaiting the crowning of a new occupant, was the chair. Between it and the ten rows of plain wooden chairs was a three foot high white canvas strip separating the spectators from participants.

Behind the chair was a cabinet enclosing an instrument panel and a large wheel, and standing beside it Robert Elliott, the executioner, and his assistant, John Bloom. Elliott, grey haired and wearing a grey suit, had a deeply lined face, not unconnected with his job. Later he was to write, 'I dreaded this assignment more than any other.' He had read the trial transcript, spoken to friends who had attended it and was much concerned about the rightness of the conviction. 'I wondered whether justice would be best served by snuffing out the life of this man.' His not to reason why: killing people was his job.

The witnesses took their seats. Kimberling, still wearing his hat and topcoat, asked everyone else to button up their own coats and keep their hands out of their pockets. Journalists who wanted to make notes could do so as long as pads and pencils could be clearly seen. Then he said to a guard, 'Before we call in Hauptmann it would be wise to telephone the central office and see if there is any message.' Like thousands of others, he was hoping for a last-minute confession.

The guard nodded and left. Elliott placed a wooden bar with light bulbs on the electric chair, then turned a switch on the instrument panel: the bulbs lit up. He removed the bar and now everyone waited the return of the guard. They were waiting outside the prison walls, too; while in New York's Times Square a huge silent crowd was waiting to see the announcement appear on the big, illuminated ticker-tape screen. All over the world families and individuals waited by their radios to hear the words that would at last end this terrible story.

The guard returned. There was no message. Kimberling looked at Elliott, who signified that all was ready. Kimberling still hesitated, as though reluctant to assume responsibility for this final, irrevocable act. Then he ordered Hauptmann to be brought in. A senior official, Lieutenant Robert Hicks, looked at Kimberling's face. 'I could read there', he wrote later, 'an immense distaste for the task.'

The guards went through the steel doors and closed them behind them. Now there was dead silence, for those in the room were about to see a live pornographic show, and live shows, whether of copulation or killing, instil a certain awe.

A minute later the doors re-opened. First came the guards and behind them the two priests, Werner and Matthiesen, chanting Psalm 23 in German: 'The Lord is my shepherd … he maketh me to lie down in green pastures … Yea, though I walk through the valley of the shadow of death, I will fear no evil: for thou art with me; thy rod and staff they comfort me …' They were followed by a semi-bald Hauptmann, one trouser leg flapping, shuffling to his doom in brown carpet slippers. He walked past the chair and would have collided with one of the three attendant doctors had not a guard guided him back. He sat down heavily, laying his elbows on the arm-rests as in the famous Abraham Lincoln statue. Some of the press men had their pencils poised for a confession. 'Here was Hauptmann's chance to talk,' said

Edward Folliard of the *Washington Post*, who seemed surprised he did not take it.

The guards strapped Richard's arms, chest and legs firmly to the chair. Elliott took one of the two cup-shaped electrodes dipped in brine, placed it on his head like a coronet and secured it with a strap under his lower lip, like the busby of a British Guardsman. It took but a moment to fix the second electrode through the slit in the right trouser leg. Then a mask was put over Richard's face, to spare the audience seeing the horrific contortions that 2,000 volts do to a man's features, almost forcing the eyes out of their sockets.

Elliott walked to the control panel, looked at Kimberling. A guard held up a big clock: it said 8.44. Kimberling nodded. Elliott turned the wheel, there was a drawn-out mournful whine from the dynamos, the bulbs on the control panel lit up as if on a Christmas tree and the full charge drove into Richard's body. He went rigid, strained against the straps, dropped back as the whine of the dynamos fell away. One rookie spectator, unable to contain himself, cried out, 'Christ, it's terrible!' The process was repeated a second and then a third time. Against it could be heard the chanting of the defrocked Revd Werner, continuing to give comfort to one already far beyond it, at 8.44 a sentient being, at 8.45 a corpse. 'Jesus said … I am the resurrection and the Life … whosoever liveth and believeth in me shall never die' – a debatable point at the best of times. The spectators observed a wisp of smoke rising above Hauptmann's head.

Elliott switched off the current, the three doctors put their stethoscopes to Hauptmann's chest. Dr Wiesler, the prison doctor, spoke for all. 'This man is dead,' he said; then again, 'This man is dead.'

The guards unstrapped the body and carried it into the autopsy room next door. The spectators, stunned and silent, rose from their seats and went out into the night. Kimberling made his way outside to give the news to the press. Under the arc lights movie cameras and microphones had been positioned, typewriters had been set up on little makeshift tables, press men stood poised with pads and pencils at the ready; most wore hats and many were puffing cigarettes.

There was only one question they wanted to ask. Did he make a statement before he went? Did he confess?

'No,' replied Kimberling, 'he made no statement after he left the cell.'

Why not? Brainwashed by months of having instilled into them a false belief in Hauptmann's guilt, they felt puzzled, cheated, let down. But then the whole case had been a conundrum from the beginning, and only a very few unprejudiced and clear-sighted thinkers – who, in addition to Governor Hoffman and Lloyd Fisher, included Eleanor Roosevelt, the writer H. L. Mencken and the famous advocate Clarence Darrow – understood why.

Presently in New York a sub-editor on *The New York Times* roughed out a front page headline for the next day's paper: HAUPTMANN SILENT TO THE END.

Silent? It was as great a lie as the headline that had told the world of Richard Hauptmann's arrest back in September 1934 – LINDBERGH KIDNAPPER JAILED. Far from remaining silent he had from the outset unceasingly asserted his innocence to anyone who would listen. But the American press and public remained deaf to what he had to say; it was not, never had been and never would be what they wanted to hear.

In the spring of 1982 I returned to America with a camera crew to make a documentary film on the case for the BBC. Having made contact with Mrs Hauptmann's lawyer, Robert Bryan, who had just obtained access to the FBI files on the case under the Freedom of Information Act, I visited the principal locations of the case and met those participants who were still alive. I had several long talks with Anna Hauptmann at her home in Yeadon, Pennsylvania, although I was disappointed that her son Manfred, now nearing retirement as a Pennsylvania state employee, was not interested in helping to clear his father's name. I also talked to two of Richard's close friends, Hans Kloppenburg and Henry Uhlig, and found that an hour with either was enough to convince anyone prepared to listen of the impossibility of Hauptmann's guilt. I also spoke to Lewis Bornmann, the detective who had taken over Hauptmann's apartment and thus prevented the defence from discovering how he had falsified the evidence about a plank used in the kidnap ladder having once been part of his landlord's attic floor.

Others I spoke to were Ethel Stockton, the last living juror at the trial, and Anthony Scaduto, author of *Scapegoat*, the first book to contest unequivocally Hauptmann's guilt; also, later in Glasgow, Betty Gow, the baby's Scottish nanny, who was the first person to find him missing from his cot. I inspected the former nursery at the Lindbergh's house at Hopewell (now a delinquent boys' home) from which the baby had been snatched, and the woods where his body had been found. I visited the Lindbergh Archive Room in the New Jersey State police headquarters in Trenton to inspect the kidnap ladder; the courtroom in the sleepy town of Flemington in which Hauptmann had been tried and the cell he had occupied there, as well as his cell on death row and the execution chamber in Trenton's state prison.

I went through back editions of *The New York Times* from 1932 to 1936 and also made notes from the 4,000 pages of trial transcript of the proceedings that had lasted more than six weeks; at every stage was prepared, as I had been in previous cases, to find some piece of evidence that would confirm beyond doubt Hauptmann's guilt. At no stage did I find it, although there were occasions when I did find people who should have known better clinging to entrenched beliefs. For instance, while I was discussing the case on the telephone with the columnist Joe Allsop, telling him of my certainty of Hauptmann's innocence, he almost exploded with disbelief. 'He was guilty as hell,' he shouted down the line. 'Everyone knows that. And if you'd been around at the time, as I was, you'd have known it too.'

I also found, in addition to a proliferation of still photographs of locations and participants, a surprising amount of archive film, including sound sequences of Lindbergh and Hauptmann giving evidence at the trial, which we were able to include in our film. The answer to our programme's questioning title, *Who Killed the Lindbergh Baby?*, we had to leave hanging in the air, because, like those few Americans who shared our beliefs, we did not know: all we could say for certain was that whoever it was, it was not Hauptmann.

The film, aired in Britain on BBC2 and in the States on the Public Service Network Channel 13, was well received, with most critics agreeing that I had proved my case. But from all the material I had already accumulated for the documentary I realised that I had more to say than the 7,000 words allowed for in an hour's film commentary, and that therefore another book was imperative. So once again, in 1983, I retraced my steps to New York and New Jersey, this time with my wife Moira, staying in New York at the Harvard Club and in New Jersey at the delightful Lambertville House Hotel on the banks of the Delaware, almost equidistant from Hopewell, Flemington and Trenton.

The Airman and the Carpenter was published in London and New York in 1985 and, as with the television film, critics on both sides of the Atlantic were almost unanimous in finding the case for Hauptmann's innocence proven. 'Gripping and horrifying', declared the *The New York Times*, while the *Detroit Free Press* called it 'a gripping story with chilling argument that justice went awry'. So when my American publishers launched me on a book-signing and speaking promotional tour of the United States, I was full of hopes that it would make the same sort of impact on the American public that long ago *10 Rillington Place* had made in Britain.

I should have known better. The first time I realised which way the wind was blowing was in New York on the first day of the tour. When I arrived for an important prime time radio interview I was told it had been cancelled: the reason, it seemed, was to make way for something more topical. Later in the tour a discussion programme on a Philadelphia TV station in which Anna Hauptmann had also agreed to take part was dropped for the same reason. A suit by Anna to persuade the then Governor of New Jersey to re-open the case, or at least call for an inquiry, also fell by the way. And to cap it all, an ass called Jim Fisher who styled himself Associate Professor of Criminal Justice (about which he was quite ignorant) at the University of Edinbro in Pennsylvania, aided by the New Jersey police officer in charge of the Lindbergh Archive Room at state police headquarters in Trenton, published a book called *The Lindbergh Case* which sought to maintain the once received and now discredited wisdom that Hauptmann had been rightly convicted and executed. It was a shoddy and disgraceful piece of work which omitted all the new information that had come to light in recent years which had been used by Mrs Hauptmann's lawyer Robert Bryan, Tony Scaduto and others, as well as myself to prove the exact opposite. Later Fisher published a second book, *The Ghosts of Hopewell*, which again ignored all the facts and arguments that pointed to Hauptmann's innocence. I sent a draft review of this book to the *New York Review of Books* and was disappointed when editor Robert Silvers, despite the magazine having reviewed Fisher's first book, proved to be as indifferent to the issue of Hauptmann's innocence as most of the popular press.

Apologising for holding on to my review for several months, he wrote telling me that he and his colleagues had talked with people who knew something about the case (though not, I guess, as much as I did), continuing:

> *What you say sounded convincing; but we still felt far from the evidence because of the passage of time. It is hard to assess just how the police 'made' Hauptmann spell certain words; it is hard to know whether the spelling … was decisive.*

The truth was that the police had *ordered* Hauptmann to misspell the words that had been misspelled in the ransom notes. Hauptmann, who had not been shown the ransom notes, had agreed to this in the mistaken belief it would clear his name. Later at his trial the police had offered these misspellings as evidence that he must have written the ransom notes.

As to its decisiveness, this misspelling was only one of very many pieces of false evidence (Lindbergh's, unwittingly, was almost the worst) which, when taken together, had led to Hauptmann's conviction and execution.

The final straw was the publication in 1998 of the Pulitzer Prize-winning *Lindbergh* by A. Scott Berg. You would have thought that the author of a book so comprehensive (628 pages) and minutely documented would have taken time out to study the case in depth and at least put forward arguments for a belief in Hauptmann's innocence. But no, as I wrote in my review of the book in the *Daily Telegraph*, Berg was too lazy, too cowardly or too ignorant even to attempt it, and his tired conclusions were that, although his trial may have been unfair, there was no doubt that Hauptmann was guilty.

There was better news, though, from other quarters. First, Mark Falzini, a civilian, was appointed curator of the Lindbergh Archives at Trenton police headquarters, and as part of his duties read most of the books published on the case. He wrote to me to say that he regarded *The Airman and the Carpenter* as the definitive one, and that whenever students asked for the best book on the case, it was his practice to recommend it. Also, out of the blue, word had come from my film agent, Norman North, that Barbara Broccoli, daughter of the producer Cubby Broccoli from whom she had inherited the rights to produce the James Bond films, was interested in buying an option to acquire film rights. A deal was struck and I met the delectable Barbara for the first time, the beginnings of a long, happy and fruitful relationship.

Barbara did more than just buy an option. She commissioned the brilliant writer Bill Nicolson, whose credits already included *Shadowlands* on the life of C. S. Lewis, and *Life Story*, on how two Cambridge scientists, Watson and Crick, unravelled the secrets of DNA, to write a screenplay based on my book. This turned out to be almost everything I could have wished for: true to the book and at times very moving. For several months, if not years, Barbara's company hawked this round the major Hollywood studios, but disappointingly there were no takers –

the puritanical element in the American psyche thinking it not right (and not box office) to question a verdict handed down in an American court by an American jury exposing yet another American cock-up.

As the years went by there were times when I doubted whether the film would ever be made, but I was buoyed up by Barbara's unflagging optimism. In 1995 her faith and persistence were at last rewarded. The American independent television network Home Box Office (HBO) announced that it had made a deal with Barbara's company to acquire the film rights and would soon put it into production.

And so it came to pass. Stephen Rea, a fine actor but in my opinion a little too old and bulky to represent the slim and youthful Hauptmann, was engaged for the leading part and Isabella Rossellini, daughter of Ingrid Bergman, was cast as the rather less exquisite though morally strong Anna Hauptmann. The film, directed by Mark Rydell, was shot in California in early 1996. I was not required there, though when I did see one of the earliest final copies, I was very pleased, my only regret being that there had been no room for a scene showing the clinching argument for Hauptmann's innocence – the evidence of Joseph Furcht, construction supervisor of the apartment block on 72nd Street at Central Park West that on the day of the kidnapping and for the rest of that week, Hauptmann had worked there every day from 8 a.m. to 5 p.m.; which would not have given him sufficient time to collect a ladder, motor to Hopewell and kidnap the baby before it was reported missing.

Moira and I were finally bidden to the film's premiere and supper party at the Guggenheim Museum on Fifth Avenue. The premiere itself, though not quite what some call a glittering occasion, went off well enough, although I was sorry that one guest I would dearly liked to have come, Harry Evans, my much valued co-combatant on the *10 Rillington Place* case, and now head of the great publishing company Random House, was unable to do so.

HBO broadcast the film several times, then moved on to other things. And that really was that. Any hopes that it might rouse the conscience of the American people, particularly the governor and leg-islature of New Jersey, were as firmly dashed as they had been after publication of my book. I had been given two chances to air my views and had failed to convince both times. It was the only one of all the cases I had looked into in a lifetime of investigating miscarriages of justice where, in seeking restitution for the wronged, I had to admit total defeat.

8

THE BIRMINGHAM SIX
1974–91

Within the last five years two people who should have known better have expressed to me the view that, despite having been finally cleared by the Court of Appeal in 1991, the Birmingham Six were guilty. The first was the wife of a Home Counties lord lieutenant, my neighbour at a lunch party, the second, and less agreeable, the former Labour MP and later confidant of Mrs Thatcher, Lord Wyatt of Weeford, a fellow member of a London dining club. To both I inquired whether they would object to my passing on what they had said to the Six's solicitors; when asked why, I replied, 'So they may serve you with a writ.' End of conversation.

From what I hear from others, these two are not the only ones, so one has to ask, what is the reason? A simple one – that most people's faith in British criminal justice is so innate that they cannot bring themselves to believe that such a monumental cock-up, in which six innocent men were imprisoned for more than sixteen years, could possibly have happened. Best therefore to deny it. It is basically the same attitude of judges of first instance and appeal who cannot accept evidence of police corruption even when it is staring them in the face.

I had always nursed some unease about the Six's conviction if for no other reason than that (as Lord Scarman pointed out) if they were members of an IRA active service unit (as they liked to be called), it was improbable that immediately after planting the bombs five of them (the sixth, Hugh Callaghan, only went to see the others off at the station) would, as they did, take the boat train to Heysham where they could expect to be interrogated by police. Also, did it really require *six* men to plant a bomb in two pubs? But it was not until the Labour MP Chris Mullin published his devastating book on the case, *Error of Judgement*, in 1986 that the full extent of the miscarriage was brought home to me.

Sure enough, when the five men's train reached Heysham to connect with the ferry to Belfast, the local Lancashire police, alerted by the Birmingham police, were waiting to interrogate them: they were all pretty tense, for the explosions in the two pubs, the Mulberry Bush and the Tavern in the Town, had killed twenty-one people with more than two hundred maimed. When the police discovered that the main reason the men were journeying to Belfast was not, as they claimed, to visit relatives but to attend the funeral of a genuine IRA bomber named McDade, who had just blown himself up while planting an explosive in the Coventry telephone exchange, they at once became suspicious, and had the five transferred to the nearest large police station, a few miles along the coast at Morecambe.

There they waited for the arrival of the forensic scientist Dr Frank Skuse, who had been summoned from his bed in Wigan to come to Morecambe and take swabs of the suspects' hands to see if they contained any traces of explosive. The five received this news with equanimity, knowing that they had nothing to fear from the examination. They had enjoyed the train ride, which they had spent playing cards, and were observed by the guard to be quite relaxed, having all lived and worked in the Birmingham area for many years and, while sympathetic to the Republican cause and willing to raise funds for IRA charities, having distanced themselves from IRA terrorism; the reason they were going to McDade's funeral was that most of them knew his family from their childhood days spent in the Ardoyne district of Belfast.

Dr Skuse, a portly character, arrived at Morecambe in the early hours of the next morning and spent some three hours setting up his equipment for carrying out the tests. Unfortunately, despite meticulous preparations, he was not a very competent operator who was later to be given early retirement; unaware that tests that showed positive for nitroglycerine could also show positive from contact with other substances such as playing cards coated with nitrocellulose and lacquer, he announced that Billy Power's right hand and Paddy Hill's right hand showed they had recently been handling explosives; tests on the other three, Richard McIlkenny, Gerry Hunter and Johnnie Walker, proved negative.

By now officers of the West Midlands police force, under the command of burly Chief Superintendent George Reade from Walsall, had arrived at Morecambe and, on hearing Dr Skuse's findings, were convinced that in not only Power and Hill but also (and without a scrap of evidence) in Hunter, McIlkenny and Walker, they had found the Birmingham bombers; and, appalled by the carnage in the two pubs, involving the wounding of many innocent young men and women, they were very angry. What they wanted now (the old story) were confessions which, they knew from experience, would ensure convictions.

And this, said Power, when interviewed by Chris Mullin, is how they set about it, when taken by two officers named French and Watson to an upstairs room:

As I walked through the door French punched me on the back of my head. I stumbled forward and they both set about me. I was pushed into a chair. They were shouting, 'You dirty, murdering IRA bastard. You got gelly on your hands.'

They and another officer, said Power, beat him up again and then French said that they would throw him out of the car on the way to

Birmingham and explain it away by saying that he had been trying to escape.

Then they started telling me there was a mob outside my house ready to lynch my wife and children. All that was saving them was the police who were searching it. The only way to save my wife and children was to tell them what they wanted to know.

He was taken to another room where, he said, several more officers set on him:

From all sides I was punched, hit and kicked. When I slid down the wall I was dragged up by the hair. This was repeated three or four times.

It was at this stage, said Power, that he fouled his trousers. Then one officer said, 'Stretch his balls', and another bellowed into his ear, 'You'll never have sex with your wife again.' 'I screamed "OK, OK." I had to say something to stop them. I just couldn't take any more.'

Yet even then they hadn't done with him. When he stalled over answering a question, someone shouted, 'Throw him out of the fucking window.' Power was not to know that the window was sealed. Some of the policemen dragged him over to it while another shouted, 'If the fall doesn't kill him, the crowd will.' Then Power screamed in his bottom-less fear, 'I'll tell you anything you want me to say', and they prepared to write his 'confession'.

The other men told broadly similar stories: of being slapped, punched and kicked, of hearing the screams of their friends as they were punched, slapped and kicked in other rooms. Hill said he was dragged round the room by his hair, told he would be shot and his body dumped on the motorway, but that if he signed a statement saying he had planted the bombs the beating would stop. Walker said he was punched repeatedly on an operation scar on his stomach, was also told he would be shot, had a gun pressed against his head and the trigger pulled, and endured a cigarette stubbed out on a blistered toe. 'In the end,' he said, 'I became completely deranged.'

In the late afternoon the five men, without shoes or socks, were bundled into police cars. Hunter said that as soon as he got in, Superintendent Reade, who smelt of drink, began slapping and punching him. In another car Walker claimed that an officer called Kelly, also smelling of drink, headbutted him. In a third car Hill complained that a Sergeant Bennett whipped his testicles with the leather thong of his truncheon. Later, Walker said, an Inspector Moore put a revolver into his mouth, pulled the trigger so that it clicked, then laughed.

Although the prisoners were kept segregated from each other, the police officers maintained that all their stories, so similar in what they alleged, were total inventions and that they did not assault any of them.

Yet worse was to come. Late that night the five were taken to Birmingham's Queens Road police station, where they were joined by their friend Hugh Callaghan, who had been mentioned in Power's and Hunter's statements. All were kept in custody until the Sunday afternoon. There, they claimed, they were further savagely assaulted, kept awake at night by the banging of cell door hatches and by an Alsatian dog that was made to bark repeatedly at them, continually forced to stand up or sit down and be abused. It was this sustained intimidation and violence that led all but Hill and Hunter to sign written 'confessions'.

These 'confessions' were a mass of contradictions and untruths. Three of them said the bombs had been carried in plastic bags (which, only the police knew, had been used for carrying earlier IRA bombs): in fact, forensic tests proved that briefcases and holdalls had been used to carry the bombs to the pubs. Callaghan's 'confession' stated that he and Hunter had planted their bombs *outside* the Mulberry Bush; again, forensic evidence proved that the bombs had exploded *inside* the pub; and despite Callaghan's claim that he and Hunter had bombed the Mulberry Bush, Walker claimed that Hunter was with him bombing the Tavern. Callaghan said there were six bombs, McIlkenny, three.

Subsequently, all four denied the voluntariness of their 'confessions'. Callaghan, who was of a very nervous disposition, said, 'I was in a state of shock. I do not know what I said. They said things to me. I agreed. At the end one of the officers put a pen in my right hand, placed it over the paper and guided my hand as I signed.'[1] After this traumatic weekend, the Six were taken to Winson Green prison, where they were again assaulted by staff and inmates.

In the course of their trial (held at Lancaster in June 1975 to avoid any local prejudice in Birmingham) neither judge nor jury either believed the allegations of beatings or disbelieved the 'confessions'; and when Mr Justice Bridge came to his summing-up, he laid bare his own prejudices for all to see. 'I am of the opinion', he told the jury pompously, 'not shared by all my brothers on the bench that if a judge has formed a clear view, it is much better to let the jury see that and not pretend to be a kind of Olympian detached observer' (which is surely more like what a good judge ought to be).

With amazing naivety he then proceeded to do so, describing the allegations of the Six against the police as being 'of the most bizarre and grotesque character'. 'If the defendants were telling the truth,' he said, 'I would have to suppose that a team of fifteen officers conspired among themselves to use violence on the prisoners and to fabricate evidence.' Poor innocent, he did not seem aware that when the police interrogate those whom they have already convinced themselves are guilty, especially in a case where the officers have been inflamed by deaths and injuries inflicted on so many, this sort of conduct is not exceptional; there was no conspiracy, because the officers involved, sharing the same beliefs, reacted spontaneously. 'All the officers,' he concluded, 'who gave their evidence of the circumstances in which the statements were taken, impressed me as being straightforward and honest witnesses.' Of course

---

1   Callaghan's description of how the Birmingham police abused him, as related in his book *Cruel Fate* (Dublin: Poolbeg Press, 1993) is so vivid and rings so true that I have included the greater part of it as an appendix on pp. 317–25.

they did: that is how they are trained to appear; that is why they lie and lie knowing they will be believed.

However bizarre and grotesque Bridge may have found the Six's allegations, he had a duty (which so far as I can tell he ignored) to put them to the jury; for every police handbook of the previous fifty years had stressed the dangers of confessions extorted by oppression, which is what the Six were alleging. 'Members of the jury,' he might have said, 'you have heard my views of these allegations but you may have a different one. Remember the specific allegations the defendants made about the brutality of police behaviour, little details like Power claiming that three or four times when he slid down the wall, the police dragged him up by the hair, and him hearing other officers threatening to stretch his balls and throw him out of the window; Walker having a gun pressed against his head and an officer clicking the trigger, being punched repeatedly on an operation scar and a cigarette being stubbed out on a blistered toe; Hill's charge that Sergeant Bennett had whipped his testicles with the leather thong of his truncheon. All these assaults, the defendants claim, so destroyed their morale as ultimately to lead them into making statements of self-incrimination. Do you think it possible that such statements made by not very well educated men could have been invented out of nothing? Do not some of them have the ring of truth? Or do you prefer the evidence of the police officers who you have heard deny these allegations as ridiculous? Well, it is a matter entirely for you.'

But his view of bizarreness and grotesqueness prevailed, indeed Bridge was considered to be so bright and unprejudiced that later he was promoted to Law Lord, as Lord Bridge of Harwich. And guilty verdicts were handed down, followed by sentences of life imprisonment, for all six defendants.

Frustrated and angered by the injustice of their trial, the Six tried another tack, bringing a civil action against the police and the Home Office for injuries they had received in police custody. For fresh evidence they relied on the findings of Dr David Paul, a former police surgeon and

City of London coroner who was a specialist in the interpretation of injuries from photographs. Shown enlarged photographs of the Six taken when in custody at Queens Road, he found signs of injury on all.

The action was allowed and application made for legal aid. But the police appealed and, in an astonishingly depraved judgement, the Master of the Rolls, Lord Denning, upheld that appeal:

> *Just consider the course of events if this action is allowed to proceed to trial. If the six men fail, it will mean that much time and money will have been expended by many people for no good purpose. If the six men win, it will mean that the police were guilty of perjury, that they were guilty of violence and threats, that the confessions were involuntary and were improperly admitted in evidence and that the convictions were erroneous. This would mean the Home Secretary would either have to recommend they be pardoned or he would have to remit the case to the Court of Appeal. This is such an appalling vista that every sensible person in the land would say, it cannot be right that these actions go any further.*

That is, better for six possibly innocent men to continue to rot in prison than to find there had been police wrongdoing. For such an 'appalling' (to use his word) perversion of the course of justice, Lord Denning should have been removed from office; yet such is the timidity of the British people in daring to question judicial pronouncements that there was no public demand for it; and even if there had been, no machinery for allowing it.

But the supporters of the Six, including some of the media, continued to press their case; and when a number of former police officers volunteered to come forward and confirm that they had witnessed intimidation and assaults on the prisoners at Queens Road, the Home Secretary, Douglas Hurd, announced in January 1987 that he was sending the case back to the Court of Appeal and ordering an inquiry into it by the Devon and Cornwall police.

At the appeal, presided over by the Lord Chief Justice, Lord Lane, sitting with Lord Justices O'Connor and Stephen Brown, the former police officers made impressive witnesses. They confirmed what the Six had claimed about measures employed to deprive them of sleep: cell door hatches being banged to and fro, a guard dog being continually made to bark at them, the Six being ordered continually to stand up or sit down; the evidence, too, of injuries they saw on the prisoners' bodies. One former officer, though in his own words 'thrilled to know we had got the right people', was disturbed at seeing on one prisoner's stomach 'a red weal turning bluish and measuring six inches by four. He had been hit so badly that, although I had wanted to see him dead, I was worried about him. He had had the hell of a hefty thump.'

Almost the most convincing witness was a woman called Joyce Lynas, who was on duty at Queens Road as a police cadet when the Six arrived, and who gave evidence on two occasions. On the first she confirmed what the others had said about the prisoners being kept awake and been called 'fucking, murdering bastards', but denied having seen any prisoner being assaulted. However, she was back in court a few days later to say that she *had* seen a prisoner being assaulted but had declined to say so before because of two telephone calls threatening harm to her family if she recounted what she had seen. Now, even though it meant admitting to perjury, she was ready to tell the court of the attack she had seen. This must have required the same sort of courage as I had witnessed at the trial of Stephen Ward when Ronna Ricardo had retracted the lies she had told at the magistrate's court.

Joyce Lynas had been asked to take tea, she said, to officers who were interviewing prisoners in an upstairs room. When she entered, she saw two officers holding down one man while a third kneed him in the groin; and heard this officer say, '"This is what we do to fucking, murdering Irish bastards", and other vile words.' In court she would not say what these words were but when I interviewed her after the appeal she told me, 'You won't be having sex with your wife again because I'm going to put your balls where your brains are.' I asked her if she was sure about this, and she replied that they were not the kind of words you forget.

And how did the three Appeal Court judges respond to the overwhelming evidence that over a period of three days the Six had been assaulted and intimidated by the police and so their 'confessions' were no longer tenable?

Those who attended the court, particularly the Six's counsel, said it was clear from the start that the judges had made up their minds that the appeals were not going to succeed, and in different ways they rubbished the evidence of the former police witnesses. The most shocking of their expressions of disbelief concerned Joyce Lynas. The writer Robert Kee was in court on the day of her second appearance, and he wrote in *The Times* that the way she gave her evidence was 'so totally convincing that, had I been a member of a jury asked to judge her credibility, there would have been no question in my mind that she was speaking anything but the truth'. Richard Ferguson, QC, agreed: 'Anyone who heard her give evidence must have known she was speaking the truth.' Yet the judges described her as 'a witness not worthy of belief' and her reasons for changing her evidence 'not acceptable'. Mrs Lynas, a committed Christian whose character as a police officer was assessed as exemplary, was upset and angered by these attacks on her integrity. 'I did not have to go back,' she told me. 'I went back because I felt I ought to, and I told the absolute truth.'

There was confirmatory evidence from another source of the prisoners having been beaten up at Queens Road. A prison officer at Winson Green, Brian Sharp, was on duty when they arrived on the Monday morning and had observed that when Walker undressed, 'his torso from the neck to the middle had numerous amounts of bruising, purple, blackish, some with tinges of yellow'. Sharp thought the injuries were so bad that he telephoned for a hospital officer to come down and look at them.

Next to the stand was Superintendent Reade, the officer who had arrested five of the Six at Morecambe. He claimed never to have touched them, yet he had to admit that earlier in his career he had been involved in an assault on a suspect. He had led a party of officers on a raid in a house in Walsall where, while Reade looked on, they had assaulted a Mr Buckley by punching, kicking and pushing him down the stairs, for which Mr Buckley had taken legal action and been awarded £800. Mr Reade was also found to have altered a document relating to interviews with the Six; and Dr Skuse, too, admitted to altering certain timings at the police's request.

When it came to the judgment, at the conclusion of what was then the longest criminal appeal court hearing in British legal history – fourteen days of evidence, seventeen days of counsels' speeches – Lord Lane took a side swipe at the Home Secretary: 'As has happened before in references by the Home Secretary to this court, the longer this hearing has gone on the more convinced this court has become that the verdict of the jury was correct' – words which, before another three years were out, should have come to haunt him, though one doubts they ever did.

My own feelings on hearing the judgment were ones of incredulity and anger, its being so at variance with the comprehensive and convincing account of the whole case in Chris Mullin's book, *Error of Judgement*, which showed that the Six had had nothing to do with the pub bombings and that their 'confessions', convictions and imprisonment were entirely due to errors made by the incompetent Dr Skuse and the violence and blackmail inflicted on them by George Reade and his merry men. Not only had Chris Mullin proved to my satisfaction that the Six were innocent, but also, on his own initiative, he had sought out the IRA men who had made and planted the bombs. The first he found was the bomb maker, who, he said, gave him a complete rundown of events on the night of the pub bombing. Locating the planters took rather longer:

One by one I traced and questioned the likely candidates,
eliminating each as I established their whereabouts on the night in
question. Gradually one name began to emerge. I did not make an
approach until I had the same name from three separate sources,
one who stated the name categorically and two others who hinted
at the same name.

In the spring of 1986, Chris said, he made his sixth visit to Ireland, to a bleak housing estate where he met the man he was looking for. He looked about thirty, which meant he must have been a teenager when he joined the Birmingham IRA in 1973 and took part in a series of bombings in the West Midlands before the plantings in the Mulberry Bush and Tavern in the Town. At first he denied any participation in the bombings, although when the conversation turned in that direction, Chris noticed that his voice began to tremble and almost fade away.

'Eventually I said to him, "I think you were in the pubs." There was a long silence. We were sitting on the floor. He stared straight ahead, smoking. Then it all came out:'

On the evening of the bombing a person came to see me and said,
'You're needed for an operation.' I went with him to a house. The
bombs were in the parlour. Behind the sofa. One was in a duffle
bag, the other in a small brown luggage case.

We walked into town. It was a good mile. The other guy told me
the targets about ten minutes before we arrived. He said, 'There'll
be plenty of warning.' Believe it or not I accepted it. He kept saying,
'Don't worry. Those people will be well out of there.' He kept on
about it and repeated there'd be a substantial warning.

We approached down Digbeth. Just before we arrived, we stopped
in the entrance to a row of shops. The other guy opened the case and
fiddled with something. Then he reached inside my duffel bag.
That's when the bombs were primed. We crossed the road without
using the underpass because the police were sometimes down there.

We did the Tavern first. Up New Street, past the Mulberry Bush. The other fellow went to the bar and ordered two drinks. I took both bags and found a seat. I was shitting myself. The other person came back with the drinks. We took a sip and then got up, leaving the duffle bag under a seat.

Chris then drew a diagram of the Tavern and asked the man to mark the exact spot where the bomb had been left and, without hesitation, he did so. The same procedure was repeated at the Mulberry Bush. 'Again without hesitation he marked a spot at the rear: for good measure he also drew in the rear exit which I had omitted.' Chris had inadvertently drawn in a staircase but the man said, as it turned out correctly, that he did not recall there being any stairs.

Chris's conclusion about the bomber's account of what he did in both pubs was as follows: 'It is hard to see how someone who cannot possibly have had access to the forensic evidence at the trial could accurately mark the spots where the bombs were placed. Unless of course he was present when the bombs were planted.'

The bomber finished his story:

We went outside. The other fellow ... told me to go home and keep my head down. Nobody would be hurt. No need to worry. I last saw the other guy walking off down Digbeth. I've never heard of him again. I don't know whether it was his intention to kill people. If they'd have said, 'We're going to kill people', there was no way I'd have gone. I'm not blaming anyone or making excuses. What's done is done.

I walked home. Took about an hour. Didn't hear the bang. Then all those people got killed. Jesus, I can't make excuses.

Who was this man's accomplice? Further inquiries from a variety of sources led Chris to believe he was a man he calls 'Z'. He met Z in Dublin, but apart from admitting that after the bombings he had, along with the three other Birmingham IRA men who had participated in them, been arrested, interrogated and released by the Birmingham police, he would say no more. Yet for all his reluctance to confide in Chris Mullin the part he had played in the bombings, confirmation of it was to emerge from another source. In 1987 there came into the hands of Granada Television a Special Branch archive consisting of a précis of an interview with a member of the Birmingham IRA who had agreed to co-operate with the police. The informant told the police that Z had admitted to him that he had actually planted the bomb in one of the pubs. This interview probably took place in late 1975, several months after the Six had started their twenty-one life sentences, yet the police took no action. No prizes, commented Chris, for guessing why!

Because of the strict rules of English criminal law, none of this new evidence would have been permitted to be heard by Lane, Brown and O'Connor because it was hearsay – though one hazards they would have been as dismissive of this as they had been of everything else. In France, however, and other inquisitorial systems, any evidence, including hearsay, is admissible if it can in any way help the court to reach the truth. For me, though, combined with Chris's persuasive arguments claiming the Six's innocence, it was more than enough to ask my agents to contact the *Sunday Times* and propose a lengthy article on the case and the miscarriage of justice perpetuated by Lord Lane and co.

But first, as by now was my usual practice, I talked to the two solicitors acting for the Six, Ivan Geffen for two of them and Gareth Peirce for the other four. Neither had the slightest doubts about their innocence. Gareth called Lord Lane's findings 'disgraceful' while Geffen said it was only what he had come to expect from the Court of Appeal. Next I talked to the three counsel for the Six at the hearing. Lord Gifford, QC, told me, 'The judges had no business dismissing the evidence of police malpractice and violence. To come to the conclusions they did on evidence which was 95 per cent written and only 5 per cent oral is to assume powers of divination which no one should arrogate to themselves.' Richard Ferguson, QC, said the findings had sickened him. 'The whole demeanour of the judges was not to find the truth but how to counter the good arguments on our side. They were also gratuitously offensive. Coming as I do from Northern Ireland, I find it particularly distressing when justice fails to live up to the high standards we were brought up to believe in.' And Michael Mansfield, QC, who thought there should have been a complete retrial since most of the participants were still alive, said the judgment had left him angry and upset: 'I think it did incomparable damage to people's concept of justice.'

Among others I spoke to were three scientific officers whose evidence contradicted that of Dr Skuse. One of them, David Baldock, a former scientific officer at the Home Office, told me, 'The judges quite failed to grasp the nettle of the scientific evidence', while Dr Hugh Black, a former Chief Inspector of Explosives, whose evidence at the original trial had been rubbished by Bridge, went further. 'Their findings,' he said of the judges, 'were an outrage.' In addition I travelled to Birmingham to visit the Queens Road police station and talk to some of the former police officers who had given evidence at the appeal and found them as angered and disappointed by the contemptuous dismissal of their evidence as I was.

So how come that, with the same evidence at my disposal as the judges of the Appeal Court, I could have come to such a diametrically opposed conclusion? I think there are two reasons. The first is that one advantage I had over Lane and co. was that I had met and talked with not only the wives of three of the Six when I was in Birmingham,[2] but also with two of the Six themselves,[3] whom I visited in Long Lartin prison in Worcestershire. Had Lane, O'Connor and Brown also had that experience, I am convinced that, unless they were even more myopic than I think, it would have been impossible for them to have brought in the findings they did. Why? Because, as I said about Paddy Meehan in chapter 5 and I have found about others since, those who are truly innocent

---

2   Eileen Callaghan, Sandra Hunter, Kathleen McIlkenny.
3   Hugh Callaghan, John Walker.

do not so much *assert* their innocence as *assume* it; only the guilty assert it. In a strange way the truly innocent convey an impression to interrogators of being quite arrogant; certain in the knowledge that they were wrongly convicted, they regard those who doubt them as misguided, and so are paradoxically disinclined to spend time converting them.

But the second and probably the most cogent reason for the Appeal Court judges arriving at such a radically different conclusion from my own is the age-old one that they refused to entertain the idea of any police corruption. This has been a feature of almost every judicial inquiry into miscarriages of justice since the Second World War: Scott Henderson and Brabin in the two Evans inquiries; Fisher in the Confait inquiry; Lawton and Roskill in the fourth Luton appeal; Roskill again at the appeal of the Guildford Four and of the Maguire Seven – all have preferred to accept dubious police evidence and so uphold police morale, recognising them as partners in the administration of justice. Lord Hunter spoke for them all when in the Meehan case he wrote of reliance being placed on the integrity and competence of the police – he could not bring himself to believe that the police in question had planted incriminating evidence in a dead man's pocket.

But, above all, why on earth hadn't the three judges read Chris Mullin's book, full of the most detailed and meticulous research, before coming to their perverse judgement? Too grand I suppose, or too incurious. Yet Chris's findings absolving the Six had seemed to me and others to be irrefutable.

The reaction of the press to their findings was mixed. The *Express* and the *Sun* claimed they brought the matter to an end, that justice had been done, but an editorial in *The Times* labelled them 'three unwise judges'. And the Six's disappointment and despair was only worsened by the pathetic Denning claiming on television that in the old days *The Times* editorial would have led to a charge of contempt of court, that Chris Mullin's book had done a disservice to justice and that *public confidence in the law was more important than 'one or two people being wrongfully convicted'* – which appalling views he later, to the further anger and distress of the Six, compounded in an interview in the *Spectator* by saying that if hanging had still been in force, by now the Six would have all been executed and forgotten about, with the community's full approval. Hugh Callaghan said that in his cell he brooded over this for weeks, as well he might.

But for the long-suffering and much maligned Birmingham Six, their hour was about to come. When the very thorough report of the Chief Constable of Devon and Cornwall's inquiry into their case alleging further police malpractice was received by the new Home Secretary, David Waddington, he lost little time in re-referring the case back to the Court of Appeal. This time it was heard by Lord Justice Lloyd presiding, sitting with Lord Justices Mustill and Farquharson, between 1 and 14 March 1991. Gifford and Mansfield again led for the appellants and a Mr Graham Boal, QC, for the Crown. I attended the court each day.

The nature of the police malpractices were indicated by something called ESDA, or Electronic Document Analysis Test. This showed that some of the Birmingham police officers' statements of interviews with the accused were not contemporaneous, as they had claimed at the trial, but had been written up at different times on different pads with different pens, and that some parts had been added to or altered afterwards; and an interview which the police claimed to have had with McIlkenny had been denied by McIlkenny as ever having happened at all.

For me one of the most refreshing aspects of the appeal was that instead of the hostility and impatience displayed by Lane and his colleagues at the previous hearing, the judges here clearly did want to understand what was being put to them. Michael Mansfield guided them most skilfully through the maze of highly technical evidence. The only sour note came at the end of the submissions when Mr Boal, powerless to challenge the new forensic evidence, solemnly told the judges that circumstantial evidence *alone* would have been enough to convict all six men. This was not only dotty and untrue, but, said in the presence of six men whom he knew had just spent their sixteenth consecutive Christmas in prison, extremely distasteful. But that's the adversary system for you: even if the man in the blue shorts has been knocked down by the man in the red to within a second of being counted out, the contest must be continued to the end.

I was sorry that Mr Mansfield did not raise the claim of four of the Six that their 'confessions' had been beaten out of them, as this partly enabled the judges to say that there was no evidence that they had suffered any injuries before their first appearance in court (there was, but Denning disallowed it) and then to support Lord Lane's rubbishing of the former police witnesses at the 1987–8 hearing (which I took to be a sort of damage limitation exercise). Yet if the Six were not guilty as charged, what other explanation could there be for the 'confessions' – which were detailed, varied and contradictory – than that they *had* been beaten out of them?

Having been in court throughout the hearing I had hoped to be there to congratulate the Six when Lord Justice Lloyd announced that their convictions had been quashed and they were free to go. Not knowing that 14 March was to be the last day of the hearing, I left the court for a speaking engagement in Cardiff. However Chris Mullin, the architect of their belated victory, was there to greet the Six and join in a celebratory photograph taken outside the courts.

An expression of apology from Lord Lane and Lord Justices O'Connor and Brown for their previous cock-up would not have come amiss, but that is not the English way. Yet Lane himself was not to escape censure for his crass mishandling of the previous appeal. Many thought he had undermined public confidence in the administration of justice and there were calls for his resignation. *The Times* urged him to take early retirement, and some 160 MPs of all parties signed a motion calling on the Queen to remove him from office. But he gave no indication that he intended to do anything but stay where he was, and would presumably have thought any sort of apology or expression of regret for his and his colleagues' ineptitude *infra dig*. Yet one cannot think of any other profession or business where, had the managing director been found guilty of similar incompetence (in this instance leading to a further three years' imprisonment of six innocent men), he would not have been faced with a call for his immediate resignation or dismissal. On a personal level I am sorry to have to say this because, after we had first met at Aviemore at a Scottish Law Society conference, we had become friends, played the odd round of golf together, and for my part, and I hope his, enjoyed each other's company. When he finally did retire at the age of seventy-three colleagues of Bench and Bar gave him a generous send-off. Tributes were paid to his capacity for work and interest in and encouragement of fledgling barristers. One judge was rash enough to say that his name would live on when those of his critics had been forgotten. He was wrong. By the public at large both Lane and his critics have already been forgotten.

To return to the after effects of the release of the Birmingham Six: predictably the legal establishment closed ranks. The Lord Chancellor, the Lord Mackay of Clashfern, described my *Sunday Times* article as 'clamour' and made soothing noises about judicial integrity, which on the previous appeal had been honoured more in the breach than the observance. The Attorney-General said that all judges do is see that the rules are kept, while former buck-passing judges like Sir Frederick Lawton were quick to point out that it is not they but juries who reach verdicts and judges can only be as good as the evidence put before them – conveniently forgetting that judges do not hesitate to discount good evidence they do not agree with, as Bridge had done at the trial of the Six, as Lane and co. had done at their appeal, as Lawton himself had done at one of the Luton appeals. The *Independent* summed it up:

> *Instead of taking a hard look at its own failings, the Court of Appeal has sought to exculpate itself. There could be no clearer evidence that judges are temperamentally inclined to protect the legal system rather than the lives of those with whom it deals. To them the dignity of the law seems to be more important than justice itself.*

And this from the *Economist*:

*The Birmingham trial underlines the need to scrap the peculiar
unwillingness of the English court to accept uncorroborated
confessions which openly invite police abuse.*

Thankfully the Home Secretary, Kenneth Baker, realised that after
the shambles of the cases of the Guildford Four, the Maguire Seven and
the Birmingham Six the criminal justice system in this country was in
need of review. On 14 March 1991, he announced the appointment of a
Royal Commission under Lord Runciman to look into it and endeav-
our to report within two years. When I heard this, I could not recall any
public pronouncement in recent years that had given me so much satisfaction; indeed, I saw it as a justification of part of my life's work. But
would the Commission have the courage and imagination to recommend the abolition of our outdated adversary system of criminal justice, with its invitation to corruption by police and judiciary, and
substitute some form of inquisitorial process where there are neither
winners or losers and whose only object is to ascertain the truth?
In time we would see.

9

THE GUILDFORD FOUR AND
THE MAGUIRE SEVEN
1974–1991

On 7 November 1974 or two weeks before the Birmingham pub bombings, two men were killed by an IRA bomb thrown through the window of the King's Arms public house at Woolwich. On 5 October of the same year IRA bombs exploded in two Guildford pubs, the Horse and Groom and the Seven Stars, killing five people in the former but fortunately none in the latter.

Four young people – three men from Northern Ireland, Paul Hill, Gerry Conlon and Paddy Armstrong, and the English girlfriend of one of them, Carole Richardson – were arrested, tried, found guilty and sentenced to life imprisonment for both bombings. Following a long campaign to clear their names their convictions were quashed seventeen years later.

Because of the many similarities between them, the Birmingham and Guildford cases are often spoken of in the same breath. Both resulted in the conviction and long imprisonments of the accused as a result of false confessions being beaten out of them by officers of the West Midlands and Surrey police respectively. These allegations the officers of both forces denied, but to any detached observer not that convincingly; and no one doubts that, had capital punishment still been in force, nine of the ten (at seventeen Carole would have been too young to hang) would have been executed. Indeed, in his summing-up at the Guildford Four trial Mr Justice Donaldson emphasised that that was the fate that would have awaited them. As it was, he handed down recommended minimum lengths of imprisonment (between twenty and thirty-five years (and told Armstrong and Hill not to harbour hopes that they would *ever* be released).

Both the Birmingham and Guildford pub bombings were planted and carried out by self-styled IRA Active Service Units (ASUs) whose identities were later disclosed – in the Birmingham case by Chris Mullin, MP, and at Guildford by members of the IRA's London ASU after their capture following the siege of Balcombe Street in December 1975. And in both the Birmingham and the Guildford cases injustice was further prolonged by the faulty, indeed fatuous, reasoning of two lots of Appeal Court judges, Lord Lane the Lord Chief Justice sitting with Lord Justices O'Connor and Stephen Brown in the 1988 Birmingham Six appeal, and in the 1977 appeal of the Guildford Four Lord Justice Roskill sitting with Lord Justice Frederick Lawton and Mr Justice Boreham.

I myself did not write a book or article about the Guildford case as I had done on the Birmingham bombings, but I had read the first book on the case, *Trial and Error* (1986), by my old friend from distant Panorama days, Robert Kee, and later accepted an invitation from Grant McKee and Ros Franey to write a foreword to their own comprehensive book on the case, *Time Bomb* (1988). And there are one or two things I would like to say about the case of the Guildford Four and that of the Maguire Seven.

The first is that, apart from their confessions, there was not a scrap of evidence against the Four. The first to be interrogated was Paul Hill, lately arrived in England from Belfast where he was suspected of having participated in an IRA murder. His was the old story, so in evidence in the Birmingham case, of being assaulted and intimidated by the police to bring about a confession: eventually, totally exhausted by the relentless questioning, he gave them one, not only admitting his own guilt but that of the others, as well as inculpating Conlon's aunt, Anne Maguire, who he claimed had accompanied them to Guildford. By now certain that they had smoked out one of the Horse and Groom bombers, the police felt free to intimidate and assault the others in order to obtain further 'confessions', in which they succeeded only too well. Here is what Gerry Conlon told his mother he had experienced, having suffered several sessions of prolonged interrogation in which the police called him (shades of Birmingham) a 'fucking, murdering Irish bastard', squeezed his testicles, hit him in the kidneys and slapped his face:

> *I was crying and frightened. Simmons said if I didn't make a statement, he would ring Belfast first thing in the morning and I would never see my mother or sister again. The last of my resistance shattered when he said this. I was crying and shaking uncontrollably. I said my family hadn't done anything. I fell apart. Simmons said what happened to my family was up to me. I said I would make a statement like they wanted, but it wouldn't be true as I really didn't do it …*
>
> *I started to write the statement, but as I hadn't done the bombing I didn't know what to write … I wrote a statement from what I read on Hill's. I just wanted to get it over. I didn't care any more. I was tired, frightened and to tell the truth I was beginning to believe I had maybe done the fucking bombing. I just couldn't take any more. It seemed easier to do what they wanted.*

Later he wrote home again, saying, 'Mum, we were fitted up something rotten.'

And this is what Carole Richardson wrote about the 'confession' she was said to have made:

The statements which I wrote were virtually dictated to me, and I wrote down what they said and suggested to me. When I wrote out my statement, I did not know what to write, Longhurst asked me questions and made suggestions and would indicate that I write down what he said. I was forced to go along with what was happening because I was terrified of them, and what further treatment I would get if I continued to deny my involvement.

Armstrong's 'confession' was on similar lines:

I said I knew nothing. I was struck in the face by Rowe with his fist under my right eye. He called me a fucking, lying bastard. I said that I knew nothing. Then Mr Simmons said, 'Let's try the other side.' He hit me on the other side of my face with his hand just above the lip … Atwell came in in the course of the taking of the statement … Atwell said, 'If these officers hear anything about you, they will come in here and throw you out of the window and put it down as suicide.' I was crying and shaking. I started to make the statement. Being hit and thrown against the wall had affected my mind. I was compelled by fear and force to make the statements, and the statements were taken by question and answer. The questions were put in such a form as to suggest an answer, to which I assented …

In addition to those three statements which to my mind have the ring of truth, there is a further consideration. In their way of life and general outlook all four defendants were about as far removed from the disciplined lifestyle of the IRA's Active Service Units as one could imagine: they were drifters and layabouts, living from hand to mouth, some in a variety of squats or empty houses, existing on the fringes of society in a twilight world of drugs, cigarettes and booze; and it speaks volumes for the boneheadedness of the Surrey police that they allowed themselves to believe for a moment that these four were IRA bombmakers and planters. As Brian Rose-Smith, one of the defence solicitors, put it, 'It would be like asking a wally to plant a bomb. No one in their right mind would want to have anybody involved who took LSD. It's nonsensical.' But when, as at Birmingham and in other cases, the police recognise an urgent need to assuage public outrage by the speedy nailing of the perpetrators, common sense and rational thinking go out of the window.

On 16 September 1975 the Guildford Four went on trial at the Old Bailey for the five murders committed at the Horse and Groom and for a further two at the King's Arms, Woolwich, committed by Hill and Armstrong only. Their defence was twofold: an explanation of how the 'confessions' had come to be made (threats and violence) and the assertion of alibis. These, however, failed. In Conlon's case, a statement by a man called Charles Burke, who had seen him in a north London hostel that night, had disappeared. In that of Carole Richardson, who established that she had been at a pop concert in London, the prosecution argued successfully that there would have been *just* time for her to have reached the concert hall after planting the bomb in the Horse and Groom; while the evidence of one of her companions that night, one Frank Johnson, who had come forward voluntarily to support her and then found himself being treated as a suspect, was effectively rubbished by the police.

Before sentencing all four to life imprisonment, Mr Justice Donaldson had a word to say about the 'confessions' evidence, particularly that of Paddy Armstrong. '*I* would not have made a confession', he is reported to have told the jury, 'but maybe Armstrong is different from me.' When I read this I thought, Oh for heaven's sake, Donaldson, do take a pull on yourself. *Of course* he was bloody different from you: different in background and social class, education, intelligence, moral fibre and lifestyle. But if you had suffered the sort of abusive treatment from three hostile and frightening police officers as he claimed he had done, two of them taking turns to hit you in the face, the third making threats that you would be thrown out of the window and your death reported as suicide, as well as throwing you against the wall, who's to say how long you would have held out before making a self-incriminating confession?

On 12 December 1975, only three months after the Guildford Four had been sentenced, four IRA men of the London ASU who had been holed up in a flat in Balcombe Street, Marylebone, after a car chase agreed to surrender. They were Eddie Butler, 24, from Castleconnell, County Limerick; Hugh Doherty, 22, from County Donegal; Harry Duggan, 21, from Feakle, County Clare; and Joe O'Connell, 21, from Kilkee, County Clare. A fifth man, Brendan Dowd, 24, from Tralee, County Kerry, had previously been in charge of this unit but had recently been captured on another bombing mission in Manchester and was now serving time in Strangeways prison.

The arrest of the Balcombe Street gang, or what remained of it, had been a great coup for the Metropolitan Police, for during the previous eighteen months it had carried out a series of bombings which had caused many injuries, widespread destruction, and thousands of pounds' worth of damage. Then Alastair Logan, the Guildford Four's principal solicitor, received a telephone call indicating that Eddie Butler had made a statement to the Metropolitan Police that neither Hill nor Armstrong had taken part in the Woolwich bombing, but that he himself and another man had done it. Through an intermediary Logan sent a message to Butler and the other members of the gang that he would like to make contact; and in an interview in Wandsworth prison, where the gang were on remand, O'Connell confirmed that Hill and Armstrong took no part in the Woolwich pub bombing, but that he was not prepared to say more without the agreement of Brendan Dowd. The same intermediary saw Dowd, who agreed to give Logan an interview.

This took place in the Albany prison on the Isle of Wight, to which Dowd had been transferred. Logan had taken the precaution of engaging a retired Metropolitan Police Superintendent, James Still, to do the questioning and to have a professional court stenographer present to record the proceedings. At the outset Still warned Dowd that anything he said might be handed over to the police and prosecuting service. Nevertheless Dowd admitted that his unit had been responsible for both the Woolwich and Guildford bombings, the accounts of which, says one writer, 'in terms of precise detail, far surpassed the accounts given by the Guildford Four.' Still produced a map of Guildford and Dowd correctly marked on it the location of the Horse and Groom, the Seven Stars and the multistorey car park where he said the gang had parked their car. He also made an accurate drawing of just where in the pub the bomb had been planted and gave details of its composition.

Logan and Still realised that what Dowd had said so far could have been fed to him by others; what they were after was some unique piece of evidence that had surfaced neither at the trial or in the press, to prove that Dowd had been there. And out of the blue, when questioned about anything unusual he had observed in the Horse and Groom bar, Dowd produced it. Having just marked on his drawing the positions of the jukebox and the dartboard, something jogged his memory. 'There were two old guys with shopping bags,' he said. 'Just sitting beside me. Carrier bags. They must have been waiting for a bus.' He drew a circle on the diagram to indicate where they were sitting. 'Had some large bags of groceries with them.'

He was spot on, although Logan did not realise it. These were Leslie Hutton, a 51-year-old labourer, and Arthur Jones, a 59-year-old bookseller, neighbours in the nearby village of Compton, who had come into Guildford to do some Saturday afternoon shopping. They *were* waiting for a bus and, after an hour or so in the pub, they left to catch it. When the Surrey police were tracking down everyone who had been in the pub that night, they took statements from Hutton and Jones in which the two had mentioned sitting next to a courting couple, the only two people in the Horse and Groom that evening the police had been unable to trace, and whom Dowd now revealed to be himself and a woman he had engaged to play the female role. The statements of Hutton and Jones had not been introduced at the trial of the Four, and nor had either of them been asked to take the witness stand. If Dowd's account of where he placed the bomb in the Horse and Groom was true, then Armstrong's 'confession' to having done the same thing was a lie.

After a break for lunch the interrogation moved on to the Woolwich pub bombing to which Hill and Armstrong had 'confessed' and at their trial been found guilty of carrying out. Dowd admitted that he had masterminded the operation and indeed had stolen and then driven the car which had taken the bombers there. He gave an accurate and convincing account of the whole operation, the exact window of the pub through which the bomb had been thrown ('after Guildford it wasn't possible to plant it by hand') and technical details of the bomb itself: 'About eight pounds of gelignite, I think. Safety fuse, what they call blue sump. The fuse was about two and a half inches. That would give you about five and a half, six seconds.' As was pointed out later, this description confirmed the forensic officers' report on the bomb; it was also very similar to another IRA throw bomb which had failed to explode, as well as five other bombs which had been thrown during the IRA London unit's terror campaign.

Dowd also added that the car he had stolen for the Woolwich bombing had been a Ford Cortina he had found in Earls Court the day before. It belonged to a woman called Anne Simpson who had reported its loss to the police. This fact had never been disclosed at the Guildford Four's trial and was further proof that it was the IRA and not Hill and Armstrong who had done the Woolwich pub bombing. Dowd also later admitted that he had worn a bush hat for the operation, and when the car was found abandoned, a bush hat was found on the back seat – another undisclosed fact! Nor had Dowd's admission that he had driven away from the scene so fast that he had forgotten to switch his lights on and that an oncoming car had flashed his lights at him (an incident recorded by a police witness by the name of Fairs) ever been made public before. Further confirmation that the King's Arms bombing was the work of the IRA came when Eddie Butler admitted to Commander Jim Nevill, head of the Bomb Squad, after his surrender at

Balcombe Street, that he was one of the two involved, although he would not say who his accomplice was. In fact it was O'Connell, who also admitted it.

Dowd concluded his statement to Logan and Still by saying, 'There are other people inside for something I did. I don't like that. Could you put a bit on the end to say as far as I am concerned those four people convicted on the Guildford and Woolwich pub bombs had no connection whatsoever with me or my colleagues and they are completely innocent?'

When the Balcombe Street gang came up for trial at the Old Bailey more than a year later, in January 1977, they each faced twenty-five indictments connected with the planting or throwing of bombs. Yet, in spite of the statements they had made admitting culpability for the explosions at Guildford and Woolwich, these did not feature in any of the indictments, and because this had angered them, they refused to plead. 'I took part in both,' Joe O'Connell said, 'for which innocent people were convicted.'

One result of this was that when the chief scientific officer at the government's Research and Development Establishment (RARDE) at Woolwich, Douglas Higgs, was called, and admitted that all the IRA throw bombs whose characteristics he had studied had certain common features, he was asked by O'Connell's counsel why he had eliminated from his report references to the Woolwich bombing which followed the same pattern. After some humming and hawing, he said that the police had instructed him to remove all such references. Questioning of other witnesses revealed that, although Commander Nevill of the Bomb Squad had thought there was sufficient evidence by way of the four's admissions combined with Hill's and Armstrong's denials to mount a prosecution, and had recommended it to the Director of Public Prosecutions, the Director himself, fearful of having to live with the admission of a monstrous miscarriage of justice, declined. This was the first of a number of instances of the authorities embarking on a damage limitation exercise. More would follow.

O'Connell's counsel then turned to Guildford. Here again evidence was produced to reveal that for the trial of the Guildford Four Mr Higgs had prepared a document that showed that the debris at the two pubs shared a number of characteristics with debris recovered from explosions known to have been the work of the IRA. 'It is my opinion,' Higgs had written,

> *the extensive use of Smith's pocket-watches, particularly the Combat variety, the use of Ever Ready type 126 batteries, similar types of adhesive tapes and detonators and above all the great similarity of explosive types are too much of a coincidence to be other than a reflection of an underlying common source of supply, information and expertise.*

This devastating document had naturally not been led at the Guildford Four trial nor, again unforgivably, had it been disclosed to the defence. And the Guildford Four were not to know that the bombings they were charged with had similar characteristics with others *which had taken place after their arrests.* Higgs was followed into the witness box by another, even more experienced scientific officer, Donald Lidstone, who confirmed everything Higgs had said. Asked by O'Connell's counsel, 'You thought that there was a likelihood that because of those forensic links, you found that they were done by the same person or persons?' Lidstone replied, 'Yes, I certainly do'.

Reading these accounts in the papers in Wakefield prison in Yorkshire Gerry Conlon felt exhilarated and wrote to his mother:

> *It's the first time I shed a tear in prison. Mum, you'll never know how happy I was to read it and see for the first time since I was arrested that the truth is coming out, now it has been publicly admitted in a court of law that we were not responsible for the charges on which we were convicted. I'm feeling confident about the outcome, everyone must now know that I should be out as the police fitted up the wrong people and it's out in the open now, Mum.*

So convincing was all this evidence to anyone of common sense that I doubt if any surprise would have been expressed had the Home Secretary decided then and there (as with McMahon and Cooper) to order the release of the Guildford Four on parole pending a public inquiry. But the wheels of British justice and injustice alike grind exceedingly slow, so Conlon and the others would have to endure further unnecessary vicissitudes and setbacks before gaining their liberty.

Commander Nevill of the Bomb Squad was then called and asked why he had not pursued Dowd's and O'Connell's claims to have bombed the Horse and Groom. He replied that he was not the investigating officer on the case. However, he did admit that it was the Director of Public Prosecutions who had given orders that anything about Woolwich was to be removed from Higgs's statement.

There were no closing speeches for the defence. Instead, O'Connell made an unsworn statement on behalf of all the defendants from the dock. The judge tried to interrupt him on several occasions to tell him not to bring politics into it but, according to what one of the jurors told Franey and McKee, he just ignored him and spoke through the interruptions directly to the jury. 'He stood up in the dock and wouldn't be stopped. He was very impassioned and emotional about how, in their terms, they were fighting a war, but he was also very controlled', and, in the process, touched on some embarrassing home truths:

We have recognised this court to the extent that we have instructed our lawyers to draw the attention of the court to the fact that four totally innocent people – Carole Richardson, Gerard Conlon, Paul Hill and Patrick Armstrong – are serving massive sentences for three bombings, two in Guildford and one in Woolwich. We and another man [Dowd] now sentenced have admitted our part in the Woolwich bombings. The Director of Public Prosecutions was made aware of these submissions and has chosen to do nothing. I wonder if he would still do nothing when he is made aware of the new and important evidence which has come to light … during this trial.

He then singled out three prosecution witnesses for blistering criticism: Mr Higgs at the trial of the Guildford Four for deliberately concealing that the Woolwich bomb was part of an IRA series and that the Four were in custody at the time of similar bombings; Mr Lidstone at this trial for making little of the suggestion that the Guildford bombings had been part of a series until forced to backtrack and admit there was a likely connection; both Higgs and Lidstone for giving untrue evidence at the trial of the Guildford Four which, together with police lies, made the evidence against the Four stick; and finally Commander Nevill for saying at this trial that he wanted to reach the truth about the Guildford and Woolwich bombings but clearly had not done so. And thinking of all the IRA bombings for which innocent people had been convicted – the Guildford Four, the Birmingham Six, Judith Ward, (found guilty of the M62 army coach bombing which was to rob her of nineteen years of life) – and one or two similar cases where justice had miscarried, he made a scathing attack on 'what we as Irish Republicans have come to understand as British justice'.

> *Time and again in Irish political trials in this country, innocent people have been convicted on the flimsiest of evidence, often no more than statements and even 'verbals' from the police*

Then the judge passed sentence. O'Connell, Butler and Duggan were given twelve life sentences to run concurrently, and it was recommended that they served a minimum of thirty years; Doherty was given eleven life sentences. Certain other offences were ordered not to be proceeded with and left on the file. The Guildford and Woolwich bombings, which had not been part of any indictment, were not even mentioned. Yet if the trial had done one positive thing, it had led the Guildford Four to think that the quashing of their convictions and early release was now a foregone conclusion.

Asked later why he had named his aunt Anne Maguire (his mother's sister) as having accompanied him to Guildford in his 'confession' to the bombing of the Horse and Groom, Conlon said that, under intense police pressure to identify his companions, and knowing she was innocent, he had thought she would be able to convince the police of it and at the same time clear him.

Anne Maguire, then forty, lived with her husband Paddy, 43, in a house in Third Avenue, Queen's Park, north-west London. They had been there since the day they had been married in Belfast eighteen years earlier, and two more unlikely candidates for involvement in IRA activities it would have been harder to find. Paddy had served in the British army, in the Royal Iniskilling Fusiliers, which had taken him to Egypt and Cyprus. He was now a pillar of his local Conservative Party and the Royal British Legion, while Anne had two morning jobs as a cleaning lady. They had three sons, Vincent, aged 16, John, 15, Patrick, 13 and a daughter Anne-Marie, 9. For the first eleven years of living in London Paddy had been employed as a fitter by the North Thames Gas Board. Then, aghast at the violence taking place in Ulster and fearful for the safety of his mother who was still living there, he became increasingly depressed and started drinking heavily – ten to twelve pints of Guinness at lunch time as well as whisky, wine and cider during the rest of the day. Paddy's being unable or unwilling to find work and in and out of the house most of the time put his marriage under considerable strain, and Anne, to whom he now rarely spoke, threatened to leave.

On the evening of Monday 2 December 1974 a telegram was delivered to the house. It was from a Belfast firm of solicitors saying that the Maguires' nephew Gerard Conlon had been arrested and was being held in custody at Guildford and asked Paddy to ring either them or a London solicitor whose number they gave. Next day, sitting in a chair in the front room, Paddy saw, to his astonishment, his brother-in-law, Joseph (known in the family as Giuseppe because of an Italian godfather), Gerry Conlon's father, approaching the house. He knew that

Giuseppe was suffering from advanced tuberculosis and would only have made the long journey to London from Belfast for a matter of great urgency. It was: he, too, had been told of his son's arrest and had come over to see what he could do to help him. Paddy told him that if he had been involved in the Guildford bombing he deserved everything coming to him. Giuseppe agreed but added, 'He's my son. What can I do?'

At around 8 p.m. that evening the situation at 43 Third Avenue was as follows: Anne Maguire was putting to bed the children of a friend, Helen O'Neill, who was in hospital and unable to look after them. Their father Patrick, who had brought them over, together with Paddy, Anne's brother Sean Smyth (a tractor driver who lived with them) and Giuseppe had gone to the local pub, the Royal Lancer, for a round of drinks. Anne, having tucked up the O'Neill children, was sorting out the day's laundry when she heard the doorbell ring. The caller introduced himself as Detective Chief Inspector Munday and led her into the sitting room where by now there were several other CID men and dogs waiting. Munday asked Anne Maguire if she knew why they were there, and she said she supposed it was to do with the arrest of Gerry Conlon, picked up for the Guildford bombings. Munday, aware of the incriminating references to Anne as a bomb-maker, asked her what she thought about the IRA bombings and she said what she believed – that to kill innocent people was terrible.

Her son Vincent then approached the house, but a policeman told him to move on, to which he replied, 'What do you mean? I live here' and was let in. When he found his mother in the front room crying, he asked her what was happening. 'They think we're making bombs here,' she told him, whereupon Vincent, swearing to his mother for the first time in his life, said, 'You've got to be fucking joking!'

Vincent's brother Patrick arrived next and was also let in. The sight of so many people in the hall at first led him to think there was a party, but when he heard the men asking what he called silly little questions like, 'Where's the bombs? Where d'you hide them?', he and his brother

John 'thought it funny, really funny. I remember John saying, "It's *Candid Camera*", but it wasn't.'

After the police and their dogs had searched unsuccessfully for evidence of any bomb-making equipment, Paddy, Sean Smyth, the newly arrived Giuseppe and Patrick O'Neill, were taken from the pub to Harrow Road police station, while Anne and her three sons left in another police car for Paddington Green station. All eight, now regarded as suspects, underwent lengthy interrogations. When Mr Munday asked Anne if she had ever handled explosives, she replied, 'Oh, Jesus God, sir. I would never touch anything like that. We are not people like that'; and when he asked Paddy what he would say if told that a member of his household was involved in bombings, Paddy replied that his wife was as sick of them as everyone else. The others reacted with similar denials – as well they might, for they were speaking the truth.

Then, to complete this tragi-farce, all eight had their hands swabbed for traces of explosives, just as the hands of the Birmingham Six had been: each hand was wiped with a dry piece of cotton, then again with a swab impregnated with toluene to test for traces beneath the skin; in addition, fingernails were scraped for further traces, and on completion swabs and scrapings were put into plastic bags, labelled and sealed. These were then taken by the police to the government's research laboratory at Woolwich for analysis.

You will hardly credit this but, when the results of the swabs were conveyed to the police, they showed that positive traces of nitroglycerine had been found on the hands or under the fingernails of Paddy, Giuseppe, Sean Smyth, Pat O'Neill and the two Maguire sons Vincent and Patrick. Only the hands of John Maguire and his mother Anne were clear, but later one of the gloves she wore for household cleaning was allegedly found to be contaminated – this despite trained sniffer dogs having searched every room in the house from top to bottom and found nothing. In the light of these publicly convincing but factually absurd findings, a trial was inevitable, and that of the Maguire Seven –

Paddy, Anne, Vincent and Patrick Maguire, Giuseppe Conlon, Sean Smyth and Pat O'Neill – opened at the Old Bailey on 27 January 1976. As with the trial of the Guildford Four, Sir Michael Havers was prosecuting and Mr Justice Donaldson presiding.

There was only one issue at stake: the reliability or otherwise of the TLC (short for Thin Layer Chromatology) tests that had shown traces of nitroglycerine on the defendants' hands. For the prosecution Douglas Higgs told the court, 'I seek to establish that the TLC test is infallible and I believe it to be. We have tested enough by TLC to exclude other substances. In a purely scientific sense the chances of a rogue elephant turning up are one in 10,000. In the real world they are millions to one.' He then produced evidence to show that tests had been conducted on hundreds of people with all sorts of substances and not one had produced the same reaction as nitroglycerine.

Mr Higgs was talking mostly tosh, as his predecessor as chief scientific officer at Woolwich, John Yallop, speaking for the defence, was soon to show. With thirty-four years of experience of explosives behind him, Yallop was the originator of the TLC test. But, he told the court, it had been designed as a means of identifying traces of explosive *where an explosion had actually occurred* and was never intended to be used as the sole test on which to base a particular case. He added that he had tested every household chemical found at the Maguires' house and none based on toluene had yielded spots in a similar position to those yielded by nitroglycerine, but in tests with methanol and alcohol the results were identical to those produced by Players No. 6 and Benson and Hedges cigarettes.[1]

Mr Yallop was to have a second bite at the cherry when, on the day that Donaldson was due to sum up, he remembered a RARDE paper of

---

1   There were rumours at the time that the swabbings had been contaminated with nitroglycerine by the police before forwarding them to RARDE, but unsurprisingly these were never investigated though, knowing what we now know about noble cause corruption, it cannot be discounted as a possibility.

1974 which showed that the TLC *was not* unique for nitroglycerine; another explosive, PETN, produced identical results. This made no impression on Donaldson, who remarked that as no PETN had been found on the defendants' hands, the evidence was irrelevant. When the jury were not there, say McKee and Franey, defence counsel spelled out 'as clearly as etiquette demanded' that Donaldson had entirely missed the point, that the existence of any substance that performed in the same way as nitroglycerine demolished the very uniqueness of TLC on which the prosecution was depending. It was judicial myopia all over again.

When it came to Donaldson's summing-up, the impression left on Robert Kee, Grant McKee, Ros Franey, and indeed myself, was that he showed a preference for the evidence and arguments of the prosecution over those of the defence. One of the most impressive submissions for the defence was that, even if nitroglycerine had been found on their hands, where had it come from? The sniffer dogs had not only searched the Maguires' house from top to bottom but also adjoining premises without finding the source, if there was one, from which the traces on their hands had come. It was not in the house, Donaldson told the jury, so it must have been hidden somewhere else, along with the detonators and timing devices, 'we just don't know where'. This was speculation, all part of a fantasy scenario arising from the positive findings of the swabs.

Then there was the matter of the photograph of Patrick Maguire holding a stick of chalk, which in a pre-trial statement he said had been given to him by his gym master at school. Mr Hayes, another scientific officer called by the prosecution, replied, when it was suggested that it looked like a candle, 'It does not suggest a candle. In my experience there are sticks of gelignite with white wax wrappers eight inches long and one inch in diameter.' Patrick's brother Vincent in the witness box said that he could not remember how he had described it to the police, as they were assaulting him at the time. 'Harvey ran at me with his forearm against my throat up against the wall. He twisted my head. He hit me in the stomach. It hurt and I cried …'

Inevitably this was the moment for Donaldson to embark on the usual judicial mantra familiar to the reader of these pages, the necessity of paying lip service to the snow white characters of the police: 'Do you think,' he asked the jury, 'that he *was* beaten up? You have seen the police officers. It was put to them and they denied using any violence towards Vincent at all.' He went on,

> *You no doubt will consider whether, if he really was beaten up like that, he would not have complained to somebody at the time.* [Just who did Donaldson suppose that a teenage boy was going to complain to? Another policeman who might beat him up again for making the complaint?] *Why is Vincent lying? Is he lying because he regrets now having told the truth about this stick of gelignite?* [Here Donaldson, speculating again, was abusing the language. Vincent was not lying but telling the truth. The only person to say that the object resembled a stick of gelignite was Mr Hayes: Vincent had rightly insisted that it was a piece of chalk.]

Having told the jury that if they had the slightest doubt about the presence of nitroglycerine on the hands of the defendants, they should acquit, he invited them to retire and reach a verdict. They took nearly two days over this, during which a combination of Havers' skills and Donaldson's prejudices dispelled any doubts. All seven totally innocent defendants were found guilty (rightly so, Donaldson told them) and were sentenced as follows: Anne Maguire, cleaning lady and alleged bomb-maker, who had never seen a bomb in her life, to fourteen years' imprisonment, and who, on hearing the sentence, had to be carried screaming from the dock; Giuseppe Conlon, racked by TB, whose only crime was to travel to London to help his son Gerry in his dire predicament; Sean Smyth the lodger and the equally innocent Pat O'Neill, whose one mistake was to drop in on the Maguires to leave his children on the same day as the visit by the Fuzz, twelve years apiece; Vincent Maguire, aged sixteen, five years, and his 13-year-old brother Patrick, four years' youth custody.

The whole trial had been a mockery of justice, but when they applied for leave to appeal, the myopic Lord Justices Roskill and Waller plus Mr Justice Ackner declined to grant it. They had found no irregularities in fact or the law, they said. As they chose to see it, justice had been done and a bunch of IRA desperadoes had been prevented from manufacturing bombs with which to terrify Londoners for a long time to come.

And so the innocent Seven had no option but to settle down and serve their sentences as best they could – during which Guiseppe Conlon died from the TB that was slowly consuming him and Sean Smyth and Pat O'Neill saw the breakdown of their marriages. Vincent and his younger brother Patrick were the first to be released after serving respectively three years in prison and three years' youth custody. To McKee and Franey, Vincent said, 'My mother was nearly blind. She had to wear really strong glasses to see what she was doing. I don't think she could put a screw in a plug, let alone make bombs.' Their release was followed by those of Sean Smyth after seven years, Pat O'Neill after eight and finally Paddy and Annie after nine, who moved back into the same area of north-west London (though not the same house) where they had lived before and where they still live today. But justice continued to be denied them.

The Guildford Four were more fortunate. In the light of the statements and evidence of the Balcombe Street gang, they were granted leave to appeal and awaited the outcome with high hopes.

Their appeal was heard at the Old Bailey (for greater security) on 10 October 1977. After the fiasco of the Maguire appeal, the appellants must have been dismayed to see the ultra conservative Lord Justice Roskill again presiding. Sitting with him was Lord Justice Lawton, who the reader may recall played a useful role in the Iain Hay Gordon case, was later an appeal judge in the Luton Post Office case, and most recently in the first unsuccessful appeal of the Birmingham Six. Once, on a BBC programme called *Out of Court*, Lawton said that he did not think juries got it all that wrong in the sense of convicting the innocent. 'But,' he added, no doubt with a knowing chuckle, 'they frequently get it wrong in acquitting the guilty!' On this occasion he and Roskill were joined by Mr Justice Boreham. Sir Michael Havers again appeared for the Crown.

Of the many errors that Roskill and his colleagues were to make in the handling of the appeal, the first and worst (because almost everything else flowed from it) was their decision that they were going to usurp the function of a jury and themselves become judges of fact – the same complaint raised by Lord Devlin in the Luton case, and also in this one. What lawyers agree Roskill and co. should have done, in the light of the Balcombe Street gang's admissions, was to order a new trial, all the principal participants being still very much alive; then a jury would have had the opportunity to consider *all* the evidence that had led to the convictions of the Guildford Four (no more than their 'confessions') as well as all the evidence arising from the Balcombe Street gang's admissions, and then decide if the verdicts in the original trial of the Guildford Four could be sustained.

Roskill and Lawton (and, for all I know, Boreham) were no fools, so must have considered this for themselves and known that a retrial would almost certainly result in the Guildford Four's acquittals – with them again asserting their innocence and explaining again how their 'confessions' came to be made and the Balcombe Street lot, with a wealth of evidence to prove it, asserting their guilt. But that in its turn would have led to the exposure of the Four having suffered a massive miscarriage of justice, and of the criminal law being brought into disrepute. Anything was better than that. If Roskill, Lawton and Boreham did it their way, assessed the credibility of the new witnesses for themselves, then nothing need be said to disturb the convictions of the Four.

But there was a problem: for not only did the Balcombe Street witnesses deny that they had ever heard of the Guildford Four, but in cross-examination by Havers they showed an intimate knowledge of the bombings at Woolwich and Guildford which the Four in their 'confessions' had never shown. Havers said that Butler's and Duggan's evidence of having taken part in the Woolwich bombing had been convincing and that O'Connell's evidence of having been both at Woolwich and Guildford had the ring of truth, his having shown 'a very close personal knowledge of both bombings'. Roskill was forced to agree. 'We are content to assume that O'Connell's story of his presence [at Guildford] and participation may indeed be true and that Dowd may also have taken part.' The judges were also willing to assume that O'Connell had been present both at Woolwich and Guildford, with Roskill feeling generous enough to say, 'It is difficult to believe that had he not been present on both occasions the knowledge of the detail could have been wholly invented.'

Such generosity on Roskill's part was at first surprising, but became apparent when Sir Michael Havers addressed him. Even if it was agreed that the Balcombe Street men had taken part in the Guildford and Woolwich bombings, he said, *this did not mean that the Guildford Four had not been present too*, and, though the IRA men denied this, they were lying.

The Guildford Four, he said, had been a second eleven,[2] and the new evidence was part of an IRA plot to secure the release of colleagues belonging to the same Active Service Unit.

This was breathtaking in its absurdity, though one can see the reasoning behind it – once again to prevent the possibility of a miscarriage of justice inflicted on the Guildford Four being revealed. It would seem that in putting the idea forward Havers had not bothered to think it through, for if Hill and Armstrong had been at Woolwich but O'Connell, Dowd, Duggan and Butler had been there, too, then no less than six people had been assembled to throw one bomb through a pub window, and if the Guildford Four had also been at Guildford, as Havers now alleged, while Dowd and O'Connell had been accompanied

---

2   The reader will recall that this was the same scenario proposed by Lord Hunter in his findings about Meehan's and Griffiths's roles in the Ayr break-in.

by another man and two women still at large, and two others whom the police say they knew were there but had since gone to Ireland, then that meant it had taken as many as eleven or twelve people to plant a bomb in each of two pubs. It was a Cloud-cuckoo-land scenario which nevertheless Roskill and his colleagues accepted (and may even have been anticipating).

Another absurdity of the second eleven theory was the unlikelihood (the IRA would say, impossibility) of a disciplined group like the London ASU, who never took drugs or drank to excess, associating with layabouts and drifters, two of whom – Armstrong and Richardson – had, after they had allegedly planted the Horse and Groom bomb which had killed five people, gone on a hitch-hiking trip to Folkestone where they had had a spat with a man in a telephone box and had had to summon the police. Indeed, the Balcombe Street gang felt affronted by the very suggestion. But the ludicrousness of this scenario was never aired in court.

Instead, whenever a matter arose which questioned the validity of the joint scenario, Roskill and co. always found reasons to rubbish it. For instance, Havers's theory of a much enlarged team meant that they would have required two cars to take them to Guildford. Dowd's assertion was that he, O'Connell and three accomplices had all fitted into a car he had hired from Swan National in the name of Martin Moffitt. A photostat of the rental agreement survives showing the signature of 'Moffitt' to be in Dowd's hand but – another defect of English law – photostats are not admissible as evidence. However, at about the same time, another car had been hired in the name of a Mr R. C. Moffat whose signature bore no resemblance to Dowd's. Quite unprofessionally, the ingenious Roskill decided that nevertheless this was the second car hired by Dowd to accommodate the enlarged party. In fact, after the hearing Alastair Logan tracked down the real Mr Moffat, who lived in

South Africa and confirmed that it was he who had made his own hirings, thus exposing (but too late for contradiction) Roskill and co.'s incompetence in accepting as proof what was wild speculation.

Again, in the 'confessions' of the Guildford Four, it had been stated that the Horse and Groom bomb had been carried there in a shoe box. This was contrary to Dowd's statement that it had been placed inside what he called 'a brown shoulder-bag of a type popular with students, probably some sort of plastic, imitation leather'. Mr Yallop, Douglas Higgs's predecessor at the government research establishment at Woolwich, was then called and said he had inspected the debris left behind by the Horse and Groom bomb and found among it 'a piece of brown imitation leather which appeared to have originated from the handle of a bag … a bit like the things you get on shoulder straps. In my opinion these pieces … are certainly consistent with it being the bomb container.' This opinion, coming from a distinguished scientist with more than thirty years' experience of explosives, was not supported by Donald Lidstone from the same establishment, but Roskill dismissed both their evidence as 'far too nebulous in character to assist us'. Elsewhere he contemptuously referred to Mr Yallop's testimony as 'certain allegedly scientific evidence of a Mr Yallop'.

As regards Dowd's unique and telling piece of evidence about the two old men and their shopping bags, which had never surfaced at the Guildford Four trial and was known only to the police, Roskill said that 'that knowledge could have been acquired subsequently'. But who from? He did not say, but if the Guildford Four had also been present it could only have been from one of them – which we now know was an impossibility. Roskill was equally dismissive of Dowd's account of another car flashing its lights at Woolwich, confirmed by the police witness, Mr Fairs. And because Dowd had taken part in so many bombing operations that his memory of some events had telescoped into others (Dowd had warned Logan and Still of the likelihood of this), Roskill was able to denigrate him as 'a deplorable witness'. He was supported in this by Michael Havers, who, say McKee and Franey, ' did a supreme job in ensnaring Dowd, exaggerating the inconsistencies until something quite small was made to seem large and significant'.

At some point in the middle of all this Gerry Conlon wrote to his mother:

Well, Mum, I suppose you want to know how the appeal is going. These judges seem to be ultra friendly towards the Crown and very icy towards our counsel. They seem to doubt anything that indicates our innocence but they seem to find no bother with what the Crown says, in fact you can see they are bending over backwards to help them. Mum, on the evidence given by O'Connell, Dowd, Duggan and Butler, we four should be out of prison because there is no doubt whatsoever that these are the people responsible for the Guildford and Woolwich bombings. They say we are connected with them but they can't show or bring any evidence to connect us with them ... They have absolutely nothing to show we even knew they existed, so why are we still in prison? Mum, this is an evil country ...

More determined than ever to sustain the myth of the guilt of the Guildford Four, Roskill voiced the doubts of himself and his two colleagues about Dowd ever having been to Woolwich.

If, as we conclude without hesitation, Dowd was not there, it follows not only that Dowd has lied to the court ... but that O'Connell, Butler and Duggan have also lied in asserting that he was their companion. We have no hesitation in concluding that each of them has lied [and we have reached] the clear conclusion that they were also lying in denying knowledge of Hill and Armstrong with regard to Woolwich.

Indeed, so confident were this injudicious trio of their batty scenario that they could conclude that the claims of Dowd, O'Connell and co. not to know any of the Guildford Four could be 'wholly rejected as unworthy of credence', and therefore the whole case in relation to Guildford based on the new evidence of the IRA collapsed.

Roskill having by now taken wing, there was no stopping him:

The new evidence therefore gives rise to no lurking doubts whatsoever in our minds. We are sure there has been a cunning and skilful attempt to deceive the court by putting forward false evidence.

In the end he concluded,

We are all of the clear opinion that there are no possible grounds for doubting the justice of any of these four convictions or reordering new trials … We therefore propose to dispose of all these applications for leave to appeal by refusing them.

Thus, to preserve the sanctity of the guilt of four innocent people whom they must have known a jury would most probably have freed had they heard the totality of the evidence past and present, Roskill, Lawton and Boreham joined the ranks of Robertson, Hunter, Bridge, Denning and Lane as well as Lord Justices O'Connor and Brown betraying, if not perverting, the course of British justice.

But that was not the end of the affair. A spate of articles and editorials deplored the findings of the court, while Ros Franey and Grant McKee, whose book was still to come, mounted a series of programmes on Yorkshire Television that were equally critical. In addition, a group of some of the most distinguished names in public life came together to urge the Home Secretary to re-open the case: led by Basil Hume, the Roman Catholic Cardinal Archbishop of Westminster (who had long taken a personal interest in the case), they were the two outstanding judges of the late twentieth century, Lords Devlin and Scarman, two former Home Secretaries, Roy Jenkins and Merlyn Rees, and Robert Kee, the author of *Trial And Error*. This 'Deputation', as it came to be called, first had a meeting with the Conservative Home Secretary, Douglas Hurd, in July 1987 at which he rejected their request, but in the light of the new evidence invited the Avon and Somerset police force to make an inquiry into all aspects of the case and the Surrey police force's handling of it.

The Four's solicitors, among them now the indefatigable Gareth Peirce (acting for Conlon) and the long-suffering but financially unrewarded Alastair Logan, also continued their inquiries; and progress was made. The director of the independent Police Foundation, Barry Irving, wrote to the Home Office expressing his concern about the reliability of the Four's 'confessions' and the manner in which they had been obtained – a view which the forensic psychologist Dr Gudjusson, whom Gareth Peirce had brought in, also shared. Carole Richardson's alibi witness, Frank Johnson, initially bullied and then disbelieved by the Surrey police, was reassessed and given credence. And an even greater alibi breakthrough came when Gareth Peirce found among the case papers of the Surrey police the statement made in January 1975 by Charles Burke confirming what Conlon had claimed at his trial, that he had seen Conlon in bed in a London hostel at the time that Conlon in his 'confession' had claimed to be in Guildford. This statement, moreover, had been made long before the Four's trial and was known not only to the Surrey police but also to the Crown Prosecution Service and the Home Office *and had been deliberately withheld from the defence.*

As a result of all this, in 1989 Douglas Hurd backtracked on his earlier decision not to refer the case back to the Court of Appeal. The hearing took place on 19 October 1989 with the Lord Chief Justice, Lord Lane, sitting with Lord Justices Glidewell and Farquharson, and Mr Roy Amlot, QC, appearing for the Crown. In his opening address Mr Amlot dropped what seemed to the general public to be a bombshell but was the inevitable culmination of all that had gone before – the discovery of the corruption of the Surrey police:

It is my onerous duty to have to inform the court that ... evidence of great significance has come to light. That evidence throws such doubt upon the honesty and integrity of a number of Surrey police officers investigating this case in 1974 that the Crown feels unable to say that the conviction of any appellant was safe or satisfactory.

A close examination of the various statements of the many interviews the police had had with the Four had revealed many discrepancies. Notes relating to statements of Armstrong's 'confession', said to be contemporaneous, were not contemporaneous; the typewritten 'confession' on which they relied in court *preceded* the manuscript notes and had also had manuscript improvements inserted into it.

The inescapable conclusion is that no contemporaneous notes were made of each interview, as indeed was suggested by the defence at the trial, and that the officers seriously misled the court.

Similar discrepancies were found in the interview records relating to Paul Hill. At Hill's trial the police had denied that an interview had taken place on a certain day. But the notes concerning that interview had been found, which showed that it had occurred two days after Hill had been charged with murder, yet the notes bore no resemblance to the evidence given by the police as to how Hill came to make a further statement admitting his guilt. In addition, these notes had been withheld from the DPP and prosecuting counsel.

Amlot gave examples of police evidence being concocted and what he called the 'disturbing difference' between the numbers and times of interviews according to the official record and what the officers had said had happened in evidence. He concluded by saying that a full criminal investigation of these misdemeanours had been set in motion by the DPP, but that it would not be right for the Crown to contend that any of the convictions could be sustained.

It must have been painful for Lord Lane, remembering his own misguided dismissal of the 1988 Birmingham Six appeal, to listen to this tale of widespread police corruption which he and his colleagues were always so keen to deny; but on this occasion he was willing to grasp the nettle. Referring to Amlot's 'somewhat anodyne expression that the Surrey police had misled the court', he commented, 'In fact they must have lied.' The appeals would be allowed and the convictions quashed and after nearly sixteen years of wrongful imprisonment. The Guildford Four walked free at last.

A few days later, Carole Richardson was interviewed by the *Daily Mirror* and asked for her comment on a judicial system that had deprived her of half her life. She answered simply yet without rancour, 'For someone to say they're sorry.'[3]

It was what her co-convicted and all those who have ever suffered miscarriages of justice always want and never get (though on one occasion Lord Justice Farquharson was a shining exception). 'Never apologise, never explain for the monumental cock-ups our judicial system has made' should be the judiciary's motto, as they repair to their cosy, privileged Inns of Court world, and, like the ship in Auden's poem,[4] sail calmly on.

The decision to quash the Four's convictions inevitably raised questions about the safety of those of the Maguire Seven, still uncorrected, and it was not until early in 1990, or fourteen years after their wrongful

---

3   In one of his submissions to the Runciman Commission on Criminal
    Procedure, Lord Devlin proposed that in cases where miscarriages of justice
    were acknowledged to have occurred and convictions quashed, an appropriate
    apology should be made by the Lord Chancellor as head of the judiciary. My
    own view is that he is too remote and impersonal a figure, and the proper
    person to apologise should be the presiding Lord Justice of Appeal responsible
    for quashing the conviction. This would have the advantage of immediacy, and
    would benefit from the publicity already generated by the appeal.
4   'Musée des Beaux Arts' (1938).

conviction, that Douglas Hurd, the Home Secretary, appointed a retired High Court judge, Sir John May, to conduct an inquiry into their case. May was so perturbed by what he found that in his report published on 12 July 1990, he recommended that Hurd refer the case back to the Court of Appeal, which Hurd did on the day he received it.

However, it was not until nearly a year later, on 7 May 1991, that they began their month-long deliberations, under the presidency of Lord Justice Stuart-Smith, sitting with Lord Justices Mann and McCowan. In their judgment they cleared the Seven of knowingly handling bulk explosives but added a caveat that some might have innocently acquired nitroglycerine through possible contact with a contaminated towel. The reader should know that this was an apocryphal or imaginary towel, dreamed up by the three judges. It had not been introduced at the Seven's trial, nor had it been located either by the body of police on the premises or by their sniffer dogs which, it will be recalled, had drawn a complete blank throughout the house and its neighbourhood. But positing a towel at all posed the unspoken question as to who had contaminated it and the unspoken answer that it must have been someone in the house – a smear, if you like, in every sense of the word.

The Seven themselves felt shattered, depressed and angry that they had not been given complete and unequivocal clearance, Annie most of all. Robert Kee keeps in close touch with her and tells me that she still has nightmares about the conviction and imprisonment and that, along with Carole Richardson, she feels the only act that could now compensate her for the injustice done would be a full and unqualified apology. But apologies for their errors have never been gifts which members of the British judiciary, long on arrogance but short on humility, have felt incumbent on themselves to bestow.

10

THE CASE OF GEORGE LONG
1978–95

My penultimate case, that of George Long, has an unusual and disturbing twist to it, in that it was his persistent declarations of innocence that, paradoxically, denied him an earlier release. Some time during 1987 George (I use his Christian name, as in the years ahead I got to know him quite well), who had already served nine years of a life sentence for murder, switched on Radio 4 in his cell at Long Lartin prison near Evesham in Worcestershire. George was listening to a current affairs programme in which he happened to hear me saying that the British adversary system of criminal justice is an invitation to corruption by police and judiciary, and that some sort of inquisitorial system, as practised in some European countries, had a better chance of avoiding such pitfalls.

This was music to George's ears, for ever since his arrest and conviction he had denied strenuously to anybody who would listen that he knew anything about the crime of which he had been charged, indeed that he was entirely innocent of it. Nor had he ever forgotten the chilling response to his denial of an assistant governor at Wormwood Scrubs, the prison to which he had been taken after his trial.

'Take that attitude, Long, and you'll never be released.' But he continued to maintain this attitude and, the day after he heard the radio programme, he wrote me a letter stating his innocence. Over the years I have received scores of letters from prisoners or their relatives saying the same thing, but none quite so unassertive as this. He did not ask me to look into his case, or even to show an interest in it. It was almost as if all he wanted was to set the record straight, then I could take it or leave it.

Although I had promised myself for the umpteenth time that I had now retired from the field, there was something about the bare bones of George's letter that convinced me he was telling the truth. So in reply I asked him to tell his solicitors to send me whatever papers they had on the case and then, because Long Lartin was only an hour's drive from my home, made arrangements to visit him. The security arrangements there are tight, and I was again subjected to the routine I remembered from my previous visit when I visited Callaghan and Walker there: of emptying the contents of my pockets into a little tin box, retrievable on exit, of things such as pens, nail file, house and car keys that might encourage George to try to escape.

I was ushered into the canteen and waited. Then George came in, and I bought us cups of coffee. He was of medium height, with a large military-style moustache. In conversation he was as restrained as his letter might have led me to expect; but this in essence was his story.

At the time of his arrest George, then twenty, was living in a flat in Deptford with his epileptic father, his Irish Catholic mother, who had sent him to the local Catholic school and instilled in him her beliefs, and twin sister Margaret and her three children. A year or two earlier he had enlisted in the army but had subsequently been discharged as unsuitable. Since then he had found it difficult to hold down any job, although he was currently employed as a porter at Dulwich hospital. He suffered from acute depression and low self-esteem. He had a problem with drink and drugs and had made one or two unsuccessful attempts at suicide. To compensate for his feelings of inadequacy George often cast himself in a Walter Mitty role, with the qualities of a hero; and it was this, paradoxically, that had led to his undoing.

The murder for which George had been convicted was that of a 14-year-old boy named Garry Wilson, whose body had been found in a back yard off Deptford High Street in November 1978. There were numerous stab wounds on the upper part of his body and lacerations on his legs from shards of glass; he also had a dilated rectum, as though someone had attempted to shove a bottle or other cylindrical object into it, and severe compression of the neck; and he was wearing an Elvis Presley belt.

The crime had outraged and disgusted the local community no less than the IRA pub murders of innocent people in Birmingham and Guildford, and the local police were under pressure to come up with an arrest. Having no clues at all as to whom the murderer might be, they resorted to stopping people in Deptford High Street to see if they had any information. Among those stopped was George's sister Margaret, who related how on the day after the murder, George had shown her and his girlfriend Sonya a knife which he claimed he had seized on the previous night from a man who had tried to murder him. There was not a word of truth in the claim: George had slipped into his Walter Mitty skin to show how courageous he had been to disarm and frustrate a murderous opponent, possibly the man who had killed Garry Wilson.

It was enough, however, for the police to send Detective Inspector Finch to the Longs' flat to interview George, who repeated the story and handed the officer the knife. In the course of the interview Finch asked George whether he liked Elvis Presley and George said he did. This meeting, which took place on 1 December, only ten days after the murder, led nowhere, but nor did any other clues which might have helped the police solve the crime. Christmas came and went, most of January, too, by which time the police were desperate to assuage public anger and charges of ineptitude by producing a suspect. Sifting once again through scores of statements, they came across George's story about being attacked, the fact that Wilson had been wearing an Elvis

Presley belt and that George had said that he liked Elvis Presley. On this flimsy scenario the police left word at Dulwich hospital that they would like to see George after work. He rang back to say he would be at the station at 7 p.m. Thinking the matter of little importance, he had a drink with a friend and did not reach the police station until 8.30 p.m. There he was told (unlawfully) that he would be kept overnight in the cells and interviewed in the morning; nor was he permitted to telephone home to say what had happened to him.

George had never been in trouble before, so this 'softening up' process of being held in custody for no crime that he was aware of, yet of being unable to inform his family who he knew would be worried about him, greatly disturbed him, as indeed it was intended to. He spent a troubled night in the cell with little sleep, and his worries increased when he was left to cool his heels in the early part of the morning. Breakfast was denied him and it was not until 10.30 a.m. that two officers, Detective Sergeant Davanna and Detective Chief Inspector Eager, came to interrogate him. George repeated the story he had first told to Mr Finch about wresting a knife off a stranger who was attacking him, but the time he gave for this did not tally with the time he had given Mr Finch (which, being an invention, he had long forgotten).

In the light of these lies the police were encouraged to believe they were on the right track and for the rest of that day, in a succession of interrogations by two or three officers (mostly Davanna and Eager), who took it in turns to simulate hostility ('You killed that boy, didn't you?') and friendliness ('Just tell us how you did it, George, and we'll see you're all right'). All day they hammered away at him, perfect exemplars of following instructions in the police Manual of Interrogation: 'By one means or another the examiner should impart to the subject the idea that he is certain of his guilt, as any indication of doubt on the examiner's part may defeat his purpose.'

On and on they went, asking the same questions over and over until George became more and more confused, his confusion compounded, as he admitted afterwards, by the fact that he 'did not want to admit to the officers that [he] had lied and bragged about being a brave lad fighting off an attacker'.

By late afternoon he had had enough.

I was left alone in the cell. I was in a state of shock and utterly depressed … I was contemplating what to do when I saw a face looking at me through the cell window. I called out that I wanted to see the CID. I was at that moment prepared to admit to anything that was put to me … to get out of the police interrogation that was continually thrown at me.

And so the officers returned for yet another interview and George 'confessed', as poor hanged Timothy Evans had done, as Iain Hay Gordon and the Birmingham Six and the Guildford Four and scores of other innocents have done, to escape unrelenting police pressure. 'I did it,' he told the officers. 'I killed that boy … I got him by the throat and stabbed him'; and later, 'I kicked him and jumped on him, it was all a blur, my head was humming and I put his belt round his neck and pulled it tight, then I fucked him.'

If, after all they have read in this book so far, there are still readers who think that 'confessions' are only credible if the suspect is truly guilty, they should ponder on the words written by Dr William Sargant in *Battle for the Mind*:

The examiner and the prisoner build up between them complete delusional systems. For the prisoner may be completely innocent but the police examiner is required to continue his examination until he has dragged 'the truth' out of him, which means that he himself must come to believe what has been confessed.

And the prisoner, too, says Sargant, himself comes to believe temporarily in the false confession he has made.

But there is a further litmus test by which, in my experience, the truth or falsity of a confession may be judged. When a guilty man admits to a crime, he generally does so in a straightforward, no frills manner; what he does not do is qualify his admissions with the conditional word 'must'. The 'confessions' of innocents like Margaret Livesey (convicted of murdering her son) and Stephen Miller (convicted in 1990 of the murder of a Cardiff prostitute, though later this conviction was quashed) and George Long are shot through with 'musts', as the Deptford officers found when they came to take a fuller statement from him later.

People say I was seen with him. I must *have been with him.*

I went home and I had blood on me [untrue] so I must *have met the boy and killed him.*

I must *have done it.*

It must *have been me.*

I said I did [put the Elvis Presley belt round his neck] so I must *have.*

After his first 'confession' George was put into a police car and driven round the area of the crime where, the police say, he gave a blow-by-blow account of his actions which he described later as 'absolute rubbish'. Next day George's sister Margaret was allowed to visit him in the presence of a Detective Chief Superintendent Stagg, who urged him to repeat his 'confession'. 'I killed the boy,' he told his sister, who replied, believing him innocent, 'You never. They made you say that. You were with me and Sonya and Danny and Vince that night up the Brown Bear, don't you remember?'

By now confident they had found the right man the police allowed a solicitor, a Mr Haeems, to attend a further interrogation – the sixth that day – in the late afternoon. George elaborated on his guilt, although as he admitted afterwards, 'it was difficult to remember all the lies I had told'. When Mr Haeems asked him how he could be so accurate in his account of the details of the murder, he replied that they had been given to him by the police. Mr Haeems then said that he wished to speak to George alone, and when the officers had left, George told him he was innocent. Mr Haeems called back the Detective Chief Superintendent, to whom George said, 'All that I have told you is lies. I never killed that boy and I wasn't attacked like I said. I made it all up.'

He then made a statement that on the night of the murder he had gone straight home from work and later, because he believed the alibi his sister had given him, spent the rest of the evening in the Brown Bear. It was a disastrous claim, for Margaret had made a genuine mistake about the date, and when Stagg found that it was unsupported, he arrested George for Garry Wilson's murder.

I do not believe that when the Deptford police first summoned George to the station they held any firm beliefs that he was Wilson's murderer. But now, and no doubt to their surprise and gratification, he had fallen into their lap. There were moments in the course of the several interviews they had with him, when they recorded George as crying and shaking and saying he wanted to be put out of the way, that should have given them – and maybe did – pause for thought, especially the following:

> *I am a coward and I want to be just locked up so that the world can't get at me. I never killed the boy. I never met him. I heard he was assaulted. Last night I was frightened. I thought that if I admitted it, you would go easy on me because you were scaring me. I'm frightened of most things and I need people around me. That's all I can say. I have been a liar and a coward all my life. I just want to be locked up. I've prayed for death many times but it never comes.*

Here were clear indications of a severely disturbed personality, and if the Deptford police had been other than what they were, they might have recognised that and acted accordingly. But they were dedicated coppers investigating a particularly squalid murder, and they would have been less than human not to have convinced themselves that they had found the right man. Having previously got nowhere in the case, they could now walk tall in the knowledge that they had put their own and the community's mind at rest.

But for poor, innocent George, the law took its inevitable course: committal, trial, conviction and the usual mandatory sentence of life imprisonment.

You often hear it said of prisons that because of the climate of criminality that permeates most of them, about half of all first offenders soon offend again. But it is also true that in a few cases of long-term offenders, prison matures them – the prime example of this is Caryl Chessman, the 'bird man of Alcatraz' – in a way that might not have happened had they remained outside. This was also true of George, who, deprived of drink and drugs and the utter aimlessness of his previous life, settled down to make the best of his sentence that he could. As a boy he remembered with gratitude the influence of his maternal grandfather, James Collen, who often read to him interesting books and later took him to museums to widen his horizons. On this solid base, George now built. He became a leading light in Long Lartin's amateur theatricals, not only building the sets and props (for he was always good with his hands), but acting in them, taking the lead role in *Les Misèrables* of the prisoner Jean Valjean who spends twenty-five years inside, and that of Chesney Allen in a Flanagan and Allen routine. One of the plays for which he was largely responsible, *Pillar To Post*, was filmed by Melvyn Bragg for the *South Bank Show*. He also spent a lot of time in his cell reading and, because of his evident love and knowledge of books, was at one time made prison librarian, a post he held for seven years. What he steadfastly refused to do was compromise his integrity, so when his sentence came up for review by the parole board each year and he maintained his state of innocence he was repeatedly told that refusal to come to terms with his conviction and sentence would mean that he would be detained indefinitely.

That this was not just an off-the-cuff opinion but Home Office policy was brought home to me forcibly in the early 1990s when I read a letter in *The Times* from the then chairman of the Board of the Association of Prison Visitors, a Mr Julian Ellis. He spoke of a recent occasion when a Home Office official had addressed a gathering of lifers at which she had said that unless a lifer admits guilt, he would not advance through the system. 'Thus', concluded Mr Ellis in his letter, 'a lifer who has not committed a crime is unlikely ever to be released, whereas the guilty who openly admit their crime will progress through the system rapidly.'

I wrote to Julian Ellis, who told me that the Home Office official he had referred to was a Mrs Vicki Harris, and I wrote to her. She replied that consideration of the release of any prisoner was dependent on 'the risk to the public that he or she would commit a further serious offence', but added, 'that particular process must necessarily take as its starting point an assumption that the prisoner was rightly convicted': when I raised the question of possible innocence, she replied that other processes existed to challenge that. Mrs Harris went on to say that there was nothing to prevent a lifer who denied guilt from being released; indeed, some had been, 'when from an assessment of the prisoner's personality and behaviour the ministers find the risk is acceptable'. But where was the risk in granting George parole? He had presented no behavioural problems; he had been a model prisoner.

At the time of this correspondence there was general agreement in Britain that a regrettable proportion of those in prison were innocent of the crimes for which they had been convicted. In their evidence to the Royal Commission on Criminal Justice, then assembled under the chairmanship of Viscount Runciman, the Society of Probation Officers submitted an estimated figure of 700 at any one time; while my friend David Jessel,[1] the creator of many *Rough Justice* programmes for the

---

1   Today one of the Commissioners of the Criminal Cases Review Commission.

BBC and Channel Four, pointed out that if in a prison population of 50,000, 99 per cent were guilty as charged, that left 500 prisoners who should not be there. Whatever figure you take, the extrapolation is troubling.

Recently I published a letter in *The Times* about the Home Office attitude to lifers and sent a copy to Lord Woolf, our present Lord Chief Justice. In reply he said that some of those proclaiming innocence are in fact guilty. Well, in my view not many. For it is well known that once a guilty prisoner settles down to serving his term, he seldom feels the need to assert his innocence. One has to take the claims seriously of lifers like George, who go on denying guilt after ten or twelve years behind bars in preference to expressing remorse for the crime and gaining parole. George has told me that he did consider falsely admitting to the murder of Garry Wilson in order to obtain release, but knew in his heart that he could not go through with it. Yet by 1990, when the average term served by a lifer was around ten years, George had already served twelve.

I published four articles about George's case, two in the *Guardian* and one each in the *Independent* and *The Times*; then others called for his case to be reviewed. London Weekend Television made a programme on it, the investigative journalist Duncan Campbell wrote a piece in the *Guardian* and George's MP, Joan Ruddock, expressed herself forcibly about it to the then Home Secretary, Kenneth Baker – as indeed did I. But for all the effect our joint efforts had to end George's continued incarceration, we might have spared ourselves. It was not until George's future wife arrived on the scene that things really began to move.

Her name was Christine Palmer, an attractive brunette who lived in nearby Evesham with her husband Dave, a sheet metal worker, and their two children, Melanie and Matthew. Chris was then thirty-five and had reached a period of her life when she knew it was time for some self-assessment. Not only was her marriage faltering but she felt the need for personal fulfilment which her previous career as a secretary had failed to give her, though at first she was unsure in what direction. Some sort of social work where she could be of service to others attracted her most, yet she felt put off by the 'do-gooder' aspects of it. In the end she felt most drawn towards the Probation Service, and was taken on as a voluntary associate at Long Lartin.

Chris says that George was the sixth prisoner she had been asked to befriend, but that before she did so, the Chief Probation Officer, Maureen Godfrey, had told her of George's interest in books and plays and said, 'You two ought to get on well together, and I'm sure you'll be able to take his mind off his case', adding, 'They all say they're innocent, you have to take what they say with a pinch of salt – but there's something about George …' But Chris found, as I had, that talking about his case was the last thing George had on his mind, although he said he would be happy to do so if she wanted. Instead he told her about his grandfather James Collen, and how he had taken George under his wing, which had led on to the plays that George had become involved in and the books that both were reading. The time passed in a flash. But for Chris that first visit had meant something more. 'When I left,' she told me, 'I knew I was in trouble. I couldn't get George out of my mind.'

On subsequent visits George did tell her about his case, just as he had done to me, coolly and unassertively, yet so convincingly that she had not the glimmer of a doubt that he was speaking the truth. Their relationship grew ever closer in the weeks and months ahead, and finally in the autumn Chris realised that the only way she could help George to reclaim his liberty was to resign from the Probation Service and devote all her energies to campaigning on his behalf.

Quite ignorant of miscarriages of justice and the means of correcting them, Chris began by browsing in bookshops in search of titles and authors of books on the subject. Initially this led her to the names of two well-known campaigners, Robert Kee and his book on the Maguires and Guildford Four, and to Bob Woffinden, who was then completing his book on Hanratty. She wrote to both and both replied. Robert, she said, was unfailingly helpful and encouraging, while Bob Woffinden put her on to the London solicitor Geoffrey Bindman, who instructed Dr MacKeith of the Bethlem hospital, one of the new and growing band of forensic psychologists, to look into George's case and report on it. Before the report was completed, however, George and Chris felt that because of other commitments Bindman did not seem able to devote as much time to George's case as they felt it deserved, so, with an introduction from Robert Kee, they asked Gareth Peirce of Birnbergs if she would be prepared to take the case on. They could not have made a better choice, for once Gareth has committed herself to a case, she believes in keeping it moving.

As a result of MacKeith's very thorough report, which was now available, Gareth lost no time in preparing a submission to the Home Secretary asking him to consider a referral to the Court of Appeal. It was a formidable document, pointing out the numerous factors that cast doubts on the credibility of the so-called 'confession'. First, there had been no corroboration of guilt from any other source (which in Scotland would have made the confession inadmissible as evidence); secondly, the names of three witnesses who had seen Garry Wilson at the relevant time but without George had not been disclosed to the defence; thirdly, the police had made no contemporaneous notes of the various statements attributed to George but relied on their memories to write them up afterwards; fourthly, there was no record of George being offered breaks for refreshments or toilet facilities, not even in the early statements, or of the presence of a solicitor; and lastly, a Deptford police officer who had viewed an LWT television programme on the case had come forward to state what had not been revealed before, that the interviewing officers were concerned enough about George's mental state to put him on suicide watch.

Then came this:

Dr MacKeith found that at the relevant time Mr Long was suffering from a depressive neurosis that amounted to a degree of depression out of the ordinary, arising in part out of Mr Long's personality and part out of personal factors arising in his life at that time which included dismissal from the army the previous year, rejection by a girlfriend the previous week and a dependency upon alcohol.

Mr Long did inflict upon himself and his life a number of self-destructive acts. His interviews in the police station are riddled with deeply depressive talk, even at the time he retracts his admissions ... his terminology exhibits hopelessness about himself and his own condition ... A person who is so depressed might fail to defend himself when accused and might even welcome the spurious remedy of being locked away.

In conclusion,

Dr MacKeith has been able to piece together his diagnosis from the records of interviews when ... Mr Long was discharged from the Army, and from prison induction reports at Wormwood Scrubs. These demonstrate over the course of a year a constant theme, namely that his mental state and psychological functioning were seriously impaired at the time.

Two other forensic psychologists wrote concurring reports, all of them more than enough for the Court of Appeal to order a hearing. This took place before Lord Taylor, the Lord Chief Justice, over a period of three days in July 1995. Chris came up from Evesham on the train each day and George looked so dapper in a grey suit that another appellant mistook him for a solicitor. Robert Kee and I were there on the last day to hear the judgment, about which Chris and George were very apprehensive. They need have had no qualms. Sixteen years after sentence George's conviction was quashed and Gareth Peirce took us all back to her house for celebratory champagne and strawberries and cream. Before leaving for the station, George managed to transfer some clothes he had brought up in a bag marked 'HM Prison' into a plain black bag leant to him by Gareth. At Evesham they picked up Chris's car and drove to her house. That night they hardly went to bed at all, munching bread and cheese, answering numerous telephone calls of congratulation from friends and well-wishers. The sense of euphoria lasted until dawn when they finally sought sleep. George's reaction the next day to what had happened was the same as Carole Richardson's: 'Couldn't someone have apologised?'

There's a postscript to this story. After Chris had obtained her divorce from Dave, she and George were married in Evesham Register Office. Robert Kee, my wife Moira and I were among the many guests. At the reception I asked George if they had invited any of Long Lartin's prison officers as guests, and he said yes, they had asked two whom he liked, but they had felt obliged to decline. However, he added, every now and then he ran into some of the Long Lartin staff shopping in Evesham and was amused by their discomfiture at coming face to face with him, uncertain as to how to react. For quite a time after his release, says George, he did not dare cross the road without Chris, having lost all sense of time and distance.

George now lives a happy and fulfilled life with Chris in Evesham, sustained by his Catholic faith. There was a moment early in his imprisonment, however, when he came close to losing it. This was when the Catholic chaplain at Wormwood Scrubs, after hearing his first confession, reminded him he had omitted any contrition for murder. 'My explanation,' George told me 'didn't seem to satisfy him – which showed me he had become part of the Establishment.'

George has regular work as a welder and Chris as P.A. in a firm of Accountants. They take summer holidays in distant places, often the

Mediterranean, last year the Hebrides. George can never qualify for a state pension because of his time inside, but the bulk of the compensation he was awarded is still intact and invested in bonds as security for the future.

11

THE TWO SCOTS GUARDSMEN
1992–

The last – the very last and one of the very worst – cases I looked into had its origins in a letter I received in January 1998 from an old friend then living in Edinburgh, retired General Sir Michael Gow of the Scots Guards. Mike and I had had some dealings a few years previously when he was commander-in-chief of the British Army of the Rhine and had written to tell me of having recently met Hitler's principal wartime aide-de-camp, an army officer called Schulze-Cossens whom Mike thought might make a good subject for a television interview. I was sufficiently fired by the suggestion to make contact with Schulze-Cossens and then fly out to Dusseldorf where he lived to see what he might have to say. Sadly, I had to abort the project, for apart from taking me on a rather spooky visit to an upstairs room full of Hitler memorabilia – a gold watch inscribed with the Führer's signature and a pair of gold cufflinks he had also given him, many autographed photographs of them and others together – Schulze-Cossens seemed reluctant to talk about his former employer – although whether this was because he was unobservant by nature or, more probably, as a good ADC he felt it would be disloyal to reveal to a stranger (and former enemy) his master's characteristics and foibles, it would be hard to say. At least I was spared confirmation of the disclosure made to me by both Field Marshal von Manstein and *his* ADC, that the worst thing about Hitler socially was his halitosis.

This time Mike Gow was hoping to interest me in a quite different matter. 'I wonder if you are aware,' his letter began, 'of two young Scots Guardsmen who were involved in an incident in Northern Ireland as a result of which they were charged and found guilty of murder.' He went on to say that an information pack had been prepared by a Scots Guards committee in London, and he had asked them to send me a copy. 'Why I am bothering you is because I think that here is a case near to your heart.' Would I let him know if I could do anything to help?

Having always felt a little regretful at having let Mike down on the matter of Schulze-Cossens, and having some family connections with the Scots Guards, I felt that the least I could do was acquaint myself with the bare bones of the case – although as there had been no accusations of miscarriages of justice, I doubted if I could take things any further. My view was strengthened by a statement in the information pack that the committee was not challenging the conduct of the trial or verdict, simply stating that as the two Guardsmen, James Fisher and Mark Wright, had now been in prison for more than five years (longer than any other soldiers in Northern Ireland convicted of a similar offence), it was time they were released. The stumbling block, it transpired, was the then Secretary of State for Northern Ireland, Mo Mowlam, who had made it known that she did not think they had served enough time for such a heinous offence for their case to be reviewed.

Just what was the situation in which they found themselves and how heinous was the offence? I realised that I was being sucked further into the case than I had ever intended but if I was to be of any support to Mike Gow and the Scots Guards committee, that was inevitable. So I asked the committee if I could be sent a copy of the transcript of the summing-up of the trial judge, Lord Justice Kelly, sitting without a jury (because of the impossibility of finding twelve local citizens whose views were not prejudiced for or against one section of the community or other) in what became known as a Diplock Court. And when I had read it, I found to my surprise, and against the opinion of the committee, that what seemed to have been a very grave miscarriage of justice had taken place.

On 4 September 1992, when Fisher was twenty-three and Wright eighteen, they were part of a four-man army foot patrol operating in the predominantly Republican New Lodge area of Belfast. The third member of the patrol was Guardsman Darren Williams and its leader was Lance Sergeant Mark Swift of the Irish Guards. Civil unrest in Northern Ireland was at its height, and during the five months that the Scots Guards First Battalion had been stationed at the Girdwood Park barracks, they had come under sustained IRA attacks: there had been eighteen incidents of shooting, in one of which a Guardsman named Shackleton had been killed.

More than twenty of the IRA attacks had come from what became known as coffee-jar bombs, made from ordinary glass coffee jars filled with shrapnel, Semtex and a detonator and thrown at the patrols from behind a wall or a parked car; often the bombs were placed in plastic shopping bags with handles which acted as slings for gaining height and distance. These attacks, about which the patrols had been warned repeatedly, had been particularly prevalent in the area of Belfast in which they were operating.

One of the first tasks of the patrol that morning was to give cover to a police search of Flat 5B in a block known as Templar House, where an 18-year-old youth, Peter McBride, already an unmarried father of two, lived with his mother. At about 10 a.m., on their way back to the Gird-wood Park barracks, the men entered Trainfield Street, where they saw a young man approaching them rapidly from the other direction. This, though they did not know it, was Peter McBride. Questioned by RUC officers later that night, Swift described him as scruffy-looking and blond-haired. 'He was startled to see me. He had what seemed to me a suspicious object under his jacket supported by his right arm. He seemed very nervous.'

Swift's reaction should have been to search McBride (and when I came to interview him myself, he told me he would regret not having done so until his dying day). Instead, in accordance with routine instructions, he asked McBride for his name and address. When he gave them to him, Swift naturally wondered if there was any connection with his presence now and the search of his flat a couple of hours earlier. Was McBride concealing some object, a weapon perhaps, that he had been able to retrieve from the flat before or after the search? Swift attempted to call base on his radio link, but because of the volume of traffic on the line, was unable to get through. So he turned to McBride and said, 'I'm now going to search you. Empty your pockets on the wall.'

McBride's reaction was to make a lunge at Swift, tearing the soldier's radio mike out of his ear, and vault over a garden wall. Swift attempted to rugby-tackle him but lost his balance and shouted to the patrol, 'Grab him!'

As McBride vaulted the wall, said Swift in his statement to the RUC that night, 'a bag came from under his jacket with what appeared to be a coffee jar'. Asked what made him think it was a coffee jar he replied, 'Because the shape of it through the thin, plastic bag looked to me to be a coffee jar.' Was the bag transparent? he was asked, to which he replied, 'Opaque white, opaque.'

Seconds later, Fisher and Wright saw what Swift had seen: McBride carrying a white plastic bag containing a cylinder which seemed to them too to have the contours of a coffee jar. Having chased him for two or three streets Fisher and Wright found that, because of the weight of their body armour, McBride was gaining on them. Convinced that he was carrying a coffee-jar bomb with which, sooner or later, he might attack them or others, they decided to act spontaneously in accordance with their yellow card army instructions. These allow a soldier to open fire 'if a person is about to commit an act likely to endanger life and there is no way to avert the danger'. At any moment, for all they knew, McBride might dive behind a parked car and throw the bomb at them.

They shouted out several times, as they were obliged to, 'Army! Halt or I'll fire.' McBride could not have thought they were bluffing, yet, with his life now in imminent danger, he ran on. The two soldiers opened fire. Hit by two bullets but still carrying the plastic bag, McBride was observed by Fisher and Wright disappearing into a house in Upper Meadow Street, whose door was left ajar, enabling him to take refuge. He went through the house, dripping blood with every step, and dropped the plastic bag and its contents either deliberately or accidentally on the way. Then he came out of the back door into an alleyway where he collapsed and died soon afterwards.

In his interrogation by the RUC, Swift was asked if he had questioned Fisher and Wright as to why they had opened fire. 'No,' he replied, 'they told me the fellow had a coffee jar in the bag. This also corresponded with what I thought myself.' Asked if he knew where the bag had got to, Swift said it must be in the house. He himself had tried to enter the house but had been driven away by several screaming, abusive women. 'I said to the police, search the house', but this was not done until more than an hour later, which would have given ample time to spirit away the plastic bag and the coffee-jar bomb which three of the four-man patrol, rightly or wrongly, believed was in it. The fourth member of the patrol, Guardsman Williams, said that when McBride ran away he did not come into his line of sight.

Such was the story of the Scots Guards patrol, told and confirmed by the men who had taken part in the incident – soldiers without a blemish on their records and for whose characters and integrity their commanding officer, Colonel Spicer, had the highest regard. Swift (today still in the army and recently promoted to Colour Sergeant) was then on his fourth tour of duty in Northern Ireland, regarded by his peers as one of the outstanding non-commissioned officers there. Mike Gow told me that in his view the patrol had followed the army's yellow card instructions to the letter, and, had he been in their place, he would have acted exactly as they did.

Republican opinion in Belfast, however, was another matter. In their eyes an innocent, unarmed local boy who had no proven connection with terrorist activities had been hunted like an animal through the streets of where he lived and then brutally shot in the back by the soldiers of the occupying power: throughout his community there was a sense of outrage and anger, tempered with widespread sympathy for his mother, who had lost an only son. Charges must be brought against Fisher and Wright, but charges of what? Manslaughter might have been acceptable to both sides, but in Northern Ireland at that time manslaughter was not an option: it had to be murder or nothing, and as nothing was politically not an option either, murder it had to be.

The Northern Ireland Crown Prosecution Service now set about preparing its case against Fisher and Wright and interviewed one or two witnesses prepared to give evidence which contradicted Lance Sergeant Swift's version of events. So Swift, who by then was serving at Pirbright, was ordered to report to the adjutant of the Scots Guards battalion at Windsor to hear what this amounted to. In the adjutant's office he found himself confronted by two plain clothes CID officers from the RUC whose attitude he described as ill-mannered and hostile. Only one of them did the talking, he said. This man referred to the statement Swift had made to the RUC on the night of the shooting in which he had said that McBride had torn his ear piece out of his ear as he was about to search him, and ran away. This (according to Swift) the RUC man said was a lie. Some witnesses had said that they had seen Swift search McBride, so would Swift now make a further statement to conform with that? Swift's reaction (he told me) was anger and disbelief, disbelief that people could have doubted the truth of what he had said, disbelief that the RUC could have believed them. For a time, Swift said, his questioner continued to press him in the way police interrogators do, stressing that Swift was telling lies, with Swift, aware of being in the presence of a senior officer, the adjutant, endeavouring to keep his anger under control. Finally he told his questioner with some heat that nothing would induce him to alter his original statement or make a second one, and he returned to Pirbright.

When the trial of Fisher and Wright opened in the High Court on 10 February 1995, Swift, who looked like the key to the whole case, was not called as a witness. For obvious reasons the prosecution had no reason to call him, but why didn't the defence call him? It seemed such a crucial omission that I raised the question with Mr Telford of the Belfast solicitors for the defence, McCartan, Turkington and Breen. He gave me several reasons why not, which I said at the time had to be respected. But I have come increasingly to believe (and in this I have since gained the support of two former Chiefs of the General Staff, Field-Marshalls Lord Bramall and Inge) that if Fisher and Wright were to have had a fair trial, then the presence of Swift in the witness box over-rode all of these. Had the court accepted Swift's evidence about not searching McBride, I think it would have been impossible for Lord Justice Kelly to bring in his guilty verdict – a jury almost certainly would not have done so. And Guardsman Williams, who could have confirmed that McBride was not searched, was not called as a witness either.

With no Lance Sergeant Swift or Guardsman Williams (whose joint evidence Lord Justice Kelly said he much regretted had not been called) to muddy the waters and honest enough to admit that the occupants of the streets where the incident took place might be hostile to the British army and capable of making it worse for the accused, Kelly nevertheless preferred the evidence of the three witnesses to that of Fisher and Wright.

All three said in court that they had seen McBride being searched. George Yendell said he was outside his house at 85 Spamount Road (which adjoins Trainfield Street) repairing a taxi when he saw 'a fella standing with his hands out and one soldier searching him'. He also said that when McBride ran past him, he had something in his right hand which was waving about but could have had something solid in it, 'either a white bag or a cloth'. *Yet he had made two previous statements to the police, one on the day of the shooting and another six months later, in neither of which had he made any mention of seeing McBride searched.* Why the need for a third statement?

Yendell's brother-in-law John McMullan was the next witness to be called. He claimed to have been standing on the pavement quite close to Yendell and seen McBride being searched by one of three soldiers. He claimed that the soldier who was doing the searching 'went right up his arm, right along his other arm, right down his back and down his legs' and illustrated this with his own body in the witness box. He also said that during the chase he had heard one of the soldiers shout, 'Shoot the bastard' (highly unlikely given the strictness of patrol discipline), something he had also failed to mention in either of his earlier statements. In the second of these, made, like Yendell's, six months after the shooting, he had said that McBride was holding a white paper bag in his hand. 'It looked like one you could get a bun in.'

The third civilian witness of the alleged search was an 18-year-old girl, Arlene McKee, a friend of McBride – a fact which might have made her evidence suspect in the eyes of a jury, though seemingly not in those of Lord Justice Kelly. There were several things questionable about her evidence. She said she was standing outside her father's house at 104 Spamount Street (though she lived elsewhere) having a smoke when Peter passed her coming along Spamount Street (in the opposite direction from which the patrol said he was coming). Next she said that *from where she was standing only five feet away from the patrol* she saw *two soldiers* search McBride. This was simply not credible (as Swift, had he been called, would have confirmed), as army instructions for a search insist that only *one man*, preferably the leader, did the search, while the others faced outward with rifles at the ready, to give him cover. Swift and Williams had also claimed in statements that the streets that morning were deserted, which to them meant no bystanders at all; and so, in retrospect, there are reasons to suppose that Yendell, McMullen and McKee were not where they claimed to be.

After admitting that McBride was carrying a white plastic bag which could have contained something else as well as the packet of crisps she said she did see, McKee was obliged to admit under cross-examination to a number of criminal convictions: thirteen for shoplifting, two for receiving, one for handling stolen goods, one for disorderly behaviour and one for failing to surrender to bail. These admissions alone might well have led a jury to doubt her evidence, though not seemingly Lord Justice Kelly. And when he came to outline the Crown case, with which he agreed, he said that the Crown held that McBride was carrying neither a coffee-jar bomb nor a bag. On the claim about the coffee-jar bomb, it surprises me that I, an amateur, have to remind both the Crown and Kelly that in law, as in life, it is not possible to prove a negative. Fisher and Wright certainly thought he was, for reasons which should not have been so cavalierly discounted; while the Crown's denial that McBride was carrying a bag is inexplicable, it having been admitted by all three witnesses the Crown had put forward.

Leaving aside Kelly's preference for the combined evidence of Yendell, McMullan and McKee, which on any reading was flimsy compared to that of Fisher and Wright, he clearly had not thought through the consequences of his belief that McBride had been thoroughly searched. *For if he had been thoroughly searched and no coffee-jar bomb or other weapon had been found on him, the patrol would have had no further reason, cause or duty to detain him, and would have been bound (and perhaps thankful) to have let him go on his way.* For if that had been the situation, no radio mike would have been pulled out of Swift's ear, no chase would have taken place, no warnings to stop would have been given, no shots would have been fired and Peter McBride would be alive today. The logic is unassailable; yet Kelly, stumbling unthinkingly on a *non sequitur*, was too blind to see it. And the absence of that scenario was proof positive that no search had taken place, and also confirmed the strength of Fisher's and Wright's beliefs, right or wrong, that McBride was carrying a coffee-jar bomb.

Having spent the bulk of his summing up quoting judgments of similar cases which he claimed enabled him to form the view he did, Kelly wove a scenario of his own:

> *The whole image of the case most strongly depicted nothing more than that of a cheeky young man after an impudent and improper confrontation with Sergeant Swift running away as hard as he possibly could to escape being caught by the pursuing soldiers, because of this impropriety and nothing more.*

Nothing more? Nothing to hide? Then why did he sever Swift's radio link with his base? Why did he run away, and go on running when he must have known for certain that his life was at risk? *Nothing more?*

At the end, then, with all obstacles to believing the soldiers' evidence out of the way, Kelly felt free to blacken their good names. He was quite satisfied, he said, that Fisher and Wright realised what adverse inference could be brought against them if they admitted to having seen McBride searched in Trainfield Street, and so they had lied about it: they had also lied when they said they first saw the bag being carried by McBride when he began to run away from them. 'There was no reasonable possibility that Fisher could have held an honest belief that McBride was carrying a coffee-jar bomb ...' Why, then, did Kelly think the soldiers opened fire? For the sheer fun of it? He lacked the *nous* to tell us.

Yet he did say one good thing. Before passing sentence of life imprisonment he did query, as many other judges have done, whether such an unrealistic and inapposite sentence should be maintained. Had not the time come for Parliament to consider the substitution of the single crime of culpable homicide for the present categories of murder and manslaughter, together with the abolition of the mandatory life sentence for murder, with all its artificiality? 'Indeed, trial judges might be given the flexibility to impose more condign punishment on those who commit culpable homicide, ranging from non-custodial sentences to imprisonment unlimited in terms of years.'

But that was for the future. The mandatory life sentence was passed and Fisher and Wright were shamefully carted off to spend long years in Maghaberry prison and everyone could sleep easy in their beds that night, knowing now that the city would be free of Republican lootings and burnings and murders for at least one night and maybe others.

As inevitable as the life sentence was Fisher's and Wright's appeal, which was heard before Sir Brian Hutton, the local Lord Chief Justice, on 21 December 1995. I did not have to read far into Hutton's summing-up, for on page 2 he categorically repeats Kelly's assertion that McBride was not carrying a coffee-jar bomb. And if he noticed Kelly's *non sequitur*, he must have chosen to disregard it. The rest was a rubber-stamping of the evidence and findings of the trial.

For the next five years Fisher and Wright served their life sentences in Maghaberry jail, where they were regarded as model prisoners, uncomplaining of the injustice that had been inflicted upon them, but conforming with prison discipline and the prison regime. It was only after they had entered their sixth year of incarceration that first army and then public interest was aroused. Martin Bell, the former war correspondent and then independent MP for Tatton accepted an invitation from the Scots Guards committee to become its patron, Tam Dalyell, the veteran Scottish MP gave his support, and Mike Gow wrote his letter to me.

On 7 March 1998 I wrote the first of several articles in the *Daily Mail* outlining the case, in which I said I thought that if Swift had been called as a witness the verdict might have been very different, but also, on legal advice, adding that there could be no criticism of the defence lawyers for not calling him. Then, on 23 May, I published a piece in the *Spectator* magazine floating the idea that Kelly's perverse judgment could have been unconsciously motivated by fear of IRA mayhem. I expected some reaction to this from the Northern Ireland judiciary, such as a charge of contempt of court, but there was none. However, on this occasion, because the article was sent in a last-minute rush, I did not include a paragraph absolving the defence team of any criticism. As a result, McCartan, Turkington and Breen threatened a libel suit against me and the *Spectator*, in which all but one of the defence advocates joined, with the result that the *Spectator's* insurers agreed to settle for £40,000 damages. The exception was the senior counsel for Fisher, Peter Smith, QC, who, I suspected, regarded what I had said, or omitted to say, as fair comment on a matter of public interest. Yet when I telephoned him recently to ask whether he thought the two Guardsmen had had a fair trial, he said to my surprise, 'Now you've put me on the spot', and when I pressed him, said, to my further surprise, that professional etiquette forbade him to comment. At least, he could not bring himself to say he thought they *had* had a fair trial.

By now the great and the good had been alerted to what had been happening, and on 23 June and again on 21 July Lord Campbell of Alloway, QC, introduced a debate on the matter in the House of Lords. In the June debate Field Marshal Lord Inge, immune from any comebacks from McCartan, Turkington and Breen, said he thought that a very grave injustice had been done and that the decision not to call Swift was incredible.

Lord Napier and Ettrick spoke in the same vein, while Lord Westbury called the Guardsmen's proven culpability fatally flawed.[1] In the July debate Field Marshal Bramall said the two Guardsmen could have made a split-second error of judgement and should now be released.

---

1   Ex-Guardsman Darren Williams submitted an affidavit just before the debate saying that as McBride ran away, he observed a white plastic bag in his hand tightly rolled round a cylindrical object. This was what Fisher and Wright claimed to have seen as well, but in his statement to the RUC on the night of the shooting Williams had said that McBride was not in his line of sight. He remained insistent, however, both on the day of the shooting and in his affidavit that McBride had not been searched.

Lord Chalfont, chairman of the All Party Defence Group, called the verdict 'unwise, unsafe, unsound', while Lord Vivian, who had served in Northern Ireland, described it as a gross miscarriage of justice; and without taking a vote, the 150 peers present agreed to recommend to the Queen that she exercise the Royal Prerogative of Mercy.

On 2 September 1988 the two Guardsmen were at last given their freedom. The next day I wrote in the *Daily Mail* that the choice now was whether to grant them a retrial, with Swift made a compellable witness, or to refer the case to the Criminal Cases Review Commission.

In November the Army Board announced that in its view the killing of McBride had been an error of judgement and it recommended the Guardsmen's reinstatement. McBride's mother sought a judicial review, in which Mr Justice Kerr in Belfast claimed that the Board's decision 'wholly contradicted the findings of Lord Justice Kelly who had ruled that McBride had been unlawfully killed', and he ordered a differently constituted Army Board to reconsider the decision. It duly did so, but came up with the same decision, which I supported. This led a *Guardian* journalist, Roy Greenslade who, in repeating the claim that McBride had been searched, called the decision 'scandalous' and said that I had besmirched my 'otherwise honourable record' in supporting it. For him, and for many left-wingers, justice would appear to be divisible: OK for illiterates with low IQs like Timothy Evans, but not for wronged Scots Guardsmen.

The situation at present (February 2002) is that the Guardsmen's solicitors have forwarded a preliminary submission on the case to the Criminal Cases Review Commission, who have requested all relevant documents and are now waiting to appoint a case worker; they will then consider whether to submit a detailed dossier asking for the Northern Ireland Court of Appeal to quash the verdict. Justice demands that they do so without delay, but whether they can find the courage to admit that Fisher and Wright were wrongfully convicted, and are therefore entitled to compensation for nearly six years of wrongful imprisonment, remains to be seen.

12

CONCLUSIONS

So what are the lessons to be drawn from the cases I have looked into in this book? Firstly, to be grateful for the procedural improvements that have come about since the introduction of the Police and Criminal Evidence Act (PACE) in 1984, as a result of which there is now a statutory obligation for interrogations of suspects in police stations to be tape-recorded and/or for a duty solicitor to be present to represent the interests of the suspect. One consequence, thankfully, has been that 'confession' evidence has all but disappeared, although there is still nothing to prevent police officers alleging real or imaginary confessions in the backs of police cars or at the point of arrest, as was at one time tried on unsuccessfully by certain officers in the West Midlands force.

The adversary system, however, to which we are wedded, is another matter. As part of my research for this last chapter, I wrote to the ministries of justice and/or leading newspapers in the countries of western Europe (Spain, Portugal, France, Germany, Austria, Italy, Belgium, the Netherlands, Denmark, Sweden, Norway) which operate different systems to ascertain whether they are plagued, as we are, by reports of alleged miscarriages of justice running from year to year, decade to decade. None had, and some seemed faintly surprised at my raising so novel a question. A free press exists in all these countries, so had campaigners felt that miscarriages had occurred on any scale, they would have had the means and the channels to draw attention to them.

Yet in Britain during my lifetime the papers have never seemed to have been free of campaigns to review the cases of allegedly innocent prisoners and even as I write in February 2002, there are several queuing in the pipeline: Alami and Botweh, convicted of bombing the Israeli Embassy in July 1994, yet in whose innocence Gareth Peirce firmly believes; Sion Jenkins, convicted of the murder of his step-daughter in July 1998, whose case, having failed at appeal, is now being considered by the CCRC; Susan May, found guilty of having murdered her aunt in March 1993; Sally Clarke, who was found guilty in November 1999 of killing her two babies on separate occasions and whose case is also now with the CCRC; and Michael Stone, whose case I discussed in the prologue.

The adversary system is a comparatively late development in English law, so let me take a brief look at its origins. Until well into the eighteenth century criminal cases were heard without benefit of counsel, so that the trial judge was both examiner and cross-examiner, as he still is in France today. This, explained William Hawkins in his *Pleas of the Crown* in 1721, was just as it should be. 'The very speech, gesture and countenance of those who are guilty, when they speak for themselves', he wrote, 'may often help to disclose the truth which would probably not be so well discovered from the artificial defence of those speaking for them.' This, where the accused is a compellable witness, is in essence the inquisitorial system as practised on the Continent today.

In France in the eighteenth century they had already established the system of the examining magistrate, or *juge d'instruction*, sifting out prosecution witnesses. In England, where there was no such sifting process, all sorts of vagabonds – reward seekers, those with a score to settle, accomplices turning King's evidence – would appear for the Crown; and it was to protect the accused against the likes of these, at a time when you could be hanged for petty theft, that defence counsel began to emerge. Often, having demolished the Crown witnesses, they found there was no case to answer and therefore no cause for their clients to speak; and from there it was a succession of steps first to the accused being granted permission not to speak (the right to silence), then to his being forbidden to speak and finally, under the Criminal Evidence Act at the end of the nineteenth century, to his being permitted to speak if he wanted to. Next it was decided that the accused could not be convicted on the word of an accomplice alone, and that was the start of the Rules of Evidence with which we are saddled today, and which to many seem even more complex than the rules of cricket or golf. And gradually over the years counsel became what they are today, the dominant figures in court.

And so, in the words of Charles Langbein, Professor of Law at Chicago University, the adversary system came about, 'slowly, incrementally, without plan or theory', until it became the top-heavy, artificial and essentially childish creature it is today. It is a system in which the accused, in one way the most important person in court, in that he/she has more to gain or lose than anyone else, is somehow seen to be the least important (the more so when not called to testify), an object rather than a subject; in which the prosecution often fail to supply to the defence, as they are obliged to, evidence that might be helpful to them; in which a spurious sense of drama is created which encourages counsel to strike postures and attitudes and even indulge in sarcasm; in which counsel see it as one of their tasks to destroy the credibility of the other side's witnesses, whether on an issue germane to the verdict or not; in which some questions which could provide a shortcut to the truth are not allowed to be asked and others which are asked are not allowed to be answered; in which the evidence of witnesses is shaped by what the prosecution and defence want them to say, or what they think prosecution and defence want them to say; in which other witnesses whose evidence might help to shape the jury's verdict are not called for fear they will say the wrong thing; in which police evidence given or suppressed can and (as I have shown) does lead to the conviction of the innocent; and in which the skills of counsel can and in many cases have

(Norman Birkett in the Brighton Trunk murder case, Nicky Fairbairn, QC, in Scotland) set free the guilty. Is this really the best we can do? If we were devising a new system of justice today from scratch, would it ever occur to us to dream up something either so complicated or so inefficient?

Nor is the problem one confined just to this country. Other major countries which also practise the adversary system – the United States, Canada and Australia – suffer from it, too. As I have already discussed in my chapter on the Lindbergh–Hauptmann case, Professors Bedau and Radelet have shown the spread of miscarriages and wrongful executions in the US; while in neighbouring Canada, following a particularly dubious conviction, an organisation calling itself the Association in Aid of the Wrongly Convicted (AIDWYC) was formed in 1993 to 'reduce the likelihood of future miscarriages of justice and secondly to review and overturn wrongful convictions'. AIDWYC has since put forward proposals for reforms of criminal law procedure to prevent similar miscarriages which the Federal Minister of Justice has accepted. At the time of writing (February 2002) AIDWYC is investigating thirty-five dubious cases. The idea of such an organisation being set up in any country of western Europe is laughable.

In Australia one of the most vociferous opponents of the adversary system is lawyer Evan Whitton, and in the *Australian* of 2 March 2000 he listed the names of judges and others in a variety of judicatures who think as he (and I) do:

Justice Geoffrey Davies, Queensland Court of Appeal: 'The adversary system operates unfairly in that both in specific cases and by its general operation it causes injustice to those who are affected by it.'
Nicholas Cowdrey, QC, New South Wales Director of Public Prosecutions: 'The adversary system is not directed to the ascertainment of truth, despite our pretences to the contrary ... In our system a lawyer with a client works hard to avoid justice being done or, even worse, the truth being discovered.'

Judge Harold Rothwax, New York: 'Our system is a maze of elaborate and impenetrable barriers to truth … suppressing evidence is suppressing truth … Without truth there can be no justice.'

Sir Laurence Street, a former New South Wales Chief Justice: 'Truth and justice require a moderation of the extreme adversary system and the abolition of rules for concealing evidence.'

John Dobies, a distinguished Sydney lawyer: 'Once we are in court we play this game called Courtroom. The idea is to win this game.'

Geoffrey Robertson, Australian-born British QC and author of The Justice Game: 'Is it a game? Yes. Should it be? No.'[1]

Stuart Littlemore, QC: 'You feel you've really done something when you get the guilty off.'

Professor William Pizzi, former US prosecutor: 'Even those who work the system don't respect it.'

And *Denis Burke, Chief Minister and Attorney-General of Australia's Northern Territory:* 'Our justice system *per se* is totally, totally corrupt.'

Is the corruption Burke has in mind, one wonders, that which runs like a thread through the pages of this book, of the police fabricating evidence to make a conviction stick, of judges believing police evidence and emphasising that belief to juries, and of juries, who mostly regard the police as society's guardians, accepting their word in preference to that of defendants?

If so, here lies the opportunity for the first and most important reform: in all the most serious criminal cases – rape, murder, etc. – a neutral legal figure should be appointed, preferably a senior QC analogous to the *juge d'instruction* in France, to oversee and supervise all early police inquiries – for it is mostly there, as I have shown (see Evans, Gordon, the Birmingham Six, Guildford Four, etc.) that 'noble cause corruption'

---

1   In *The Justice Game* Robertson expresses contempt for the adversary system, yet surprisingly proposes no alternative.

takes place. This suggestion follows a recommendation submitted to the Runciman Commission by those two wise men Lords Devlin and Scarman, and also has the support of one of this country's most eminent defence lawyers, Michael Mansfield, QC. Michael tells me that this is already beginning to come about with the Northern Ireland Ombudsman investigating the Omagh bombing, digging out documents and logs which had hitherto been concealed. He also feels, as I do, that the antique practice of the administration of justice being partly the responsibility of the Home Office and partly that of the Lord Chancellor is now outdated as well as inefficient. The time has come to join most other countries in the establishment of a Ministry of Justice, with the current minister appointing the QC to supervise police investigations.

And after that, what? As an exemplar of rigorous and successful cross-examination Michael Mansfield believes in maintaining the adversary system in court because he thinks that is the only way that justice can be achieved. So, on balance, does Gareth Peirce. So, too, does Lord Justice Auld, who says in his recent report on criminal procedure that he found no support for an alternative system (and was thereby saved the bother of studying its merits). The one thing of which I am certain – but which in an adversary system is inevitable – is the foolishness of a defendant's right to silence. If there is sufficient evidence to justify taking an accused to trial, it must surely follow that he should be obliged to give an account of himself, as he is in inquisitorial systems, and if he refuses, the court will be entitled to draw its own conclusions. The American rule against self-incrimination has always seemed to me ridiculous. The more the guilty are encouraged to admit their guilt, the swifter can justice be delivered.

And then there is the question of the importance of the lay element in trials, juries or otherwise. In Germany and other countries, the lay element is supplied in criminal courts by the presiding judge, a trained professional, sitting with two lay judges and, in the most serious criminal cases, juries. In France, the *juge d'instruction* does all the spade work on a case, then forwards his dossier to either the *Tribunal Correctional*, where three judges sit without jury or to the highest court of all, the *Cour d'Assises*, where nine jurors sit alongside five judges who must agree by a majority vote on both verdict and sentence. These French courts have a conviction rate of 90–95 per cent, as compared to Crown Court trials in England and Wales, which currently have no more than a 56 per cent conviction rate of contested pleas.

On these facts alone, I would urge those like Lord Lamont and other lawyers who continually denigrate the French system, and those like Sir John Stevens, the current Commissioner of the Metropolitan Police, who want to see more of the guilty convicted, to ask themselves whether the adoption of an inquisitorial system here is not just desirable but a matter of urgency. And while it is true that the French Ministry of Justice has admitted to occasional miscarriages of justice (four in the last twelve years) they are on nothing like the scale that has occurred here.

In my view the successful French conviction rate comes about because the inquisitorial approach, which began with the investigations of the *juge*, is continued in the court of trial, which means that the questioning of witnesses is not done by partisan counsel whose roles are confined to opening and closing speeches but by the presiding judge – although at any time counsel may ask the judge to put questions they think he has omitted to ask. This has several advantages. Firstly, it avoids the pseudo-dramatic atmosphere of the adversary trial. One reason you see no courtroom dramas emanating from countries with the inquisitorial system is that the system, being low-key, does not lend itself to that. Secondly, the questioning of witnesses in a quiet, firm but non-partisan way often produces a more fruitful response than by a more hostile approach. Thirdly, the system saves time, for it obviates the need for prosecution and defence to cover, often at tedious length, the same ground and thus potentially muddle the jury. And lastly, the trial itself does not come grinding to a halt, as often happens here, when the jury are shuffled out of court so that the judge can decide what is or is not admissible evidence. In a system whose object is to find the truth, there is very little evidence – so long as it is deemed relevant – that is not admissible.

Another attractive feature of the inquisitorial system is the way in which expert witnesses are treated. Under the adversary system prosecution and defence each produce their own tame psychiatrist, pathologist, engineer or whatever, and by skilful questioning along narrow lines, invariably make them seem to contradict one another (as they did in the Yorkshire Ripper case, in which the Crown experts claimed that Peter Sutcliffe was sane while the defence experts said that he was not). In the inquisitorial system it is the custom of the court to call as many expert witnesses as the court or counsel request and through the painstaking eliciting of information try to reach a consensus. This is surely a more effective method of arriving at the truth then the adversary approach, which can be both humiliating for the expert witness and confusing for the jury.

Of all the judicatures in the countries of western Europe which practise the inquisitorial system no two are exactly the same. It would take another book to say which or which combinations would suit us best.[2] But after what I have written about the frailties of the adversary system, as practised by four of the most advanced countries in the world, I would hope that our law makers and practitioners will at long last consider seriously the benefits of change. My final word is that justice can be better dispensed by means of trial by discovery rather than through trial by conflict.

The reader will have noticed that in these pages I have been pretty rough on some of our judges, especially the prosecution-minded, and I think deservedly, although there are many I like and admire. Yet apart from strictures on individuals, I know many lawyers and others who feel

2   And let those who are so critical of the inquisitorial system ask themselves whether, if there is a fault, it could be less that of the system than of its practitioners, and whether, if it were adopted here, we would not operate it more efficiently.

that they are drawn from too narrow a section of society – public school and Oxbridge men, with all the social attitudes that these engender.

Let me recall two passages in this book. The first is the comment of Bryan Magee, former MP, on attending the appeal of Cooper and McMahon before Lord Justices Roskill and Lawton and Mr Justice Wien (see page 166):

> *Their general demeanor was like that of elderly club men determined that it should be clearly understood that they were men of the world, fully alive to all the tricks of your Tom, Dick and Harry; yet their actual questions and comments revealed that they had not the remotest notion what sort of a world it was that these East End people they were listening to actually lived in, or how to evaluate their characters and the plausibility of what they said.*

The second quote comes from Mr Justice (now Lord) Donaldson in his summing-up before sentencing the Guildford Four to life imprisonment when he said, 'I would not have made a confession but maybe Armstrong is different to me' – typical of the condescending attitude with which judges have traditionally viewed the judged.

I agree with those lawyers, Michael Mansfield among them, who believe that judges in future should be chosen from a wider cross-section of society. Also that they should not be recruited exclusively from the ranks of QCs and others who simply apply, but, as in some European countries, enjoy a separate career structure, including a long period of learning and training. First they should take office as recorders at around the age of thirty, then become fully-fledged judges until retirement at sixty or sixty-five, perhaps moving to the Appeal Court later in their careers. One judge in recent times of common sense northern stock was James Pickles, and, while thought to be a little eccentric on some issues, his presence and remarks on the Bench made a refreshing change to the attitudes of such as Lane, Roskill, Lawton, Bridge and

Donaldson. We could do with more of his ilk and a corresponding diminution of the other.

There are other reforms I would like to see, some of which I put forward at the first ever Bar conference in London in 1986, and again at the international Bar conference in New Zealand that followed it. Like Michael Mansfield, I favour the establishment of a Ministry of Justice (we must be almost the only advanced country in the world not to have one); also the modernisation of courtroom dress and language, which tends to give the Bench an inflated importance which is bad for it, bad for us and bad for justice. Maybe there was a time when it was necessary for judges to dress up in outlandish gear both to emphasise their authority and as a cloak for their anonymity. But not, surely, any more? Gentlemen gave up wigs in the eighteenth century, bishops in the nineteenth and it was a nineteenth-century Lord Chief Justice, Lord Denman, who called them the silliest things in England. The debate continues to this day, yet still our judges continue to parade before us as so many Mrs Tiggywinkles. If the Bench can abandon wigs to talk to children in child abuse cases, lest the sight of them give the children the heebie-jeebies, then they can also dispose of them when talking to adults. For Bar and Bench alike, surely no more is required than a gown (coloured for the Bench, black for the Bar) and white bands.

A further reform might be the modernisation of court language. Why *albeit* instead of *although*, why *avocation* instead of *job*, what need is there for *resiling* and *ex parte* and *res ipsa loquitur*? Why do Bar and Bench refer to judges as 'learned' other than to inflate their status? And why address them as 'my lord' and 'your lordship' when they are mostly no more than knights. What is wrong with 'your honour', dignified and unpretentious?

I am also in favour of the televising of certain trials so that justice may be seen to be done by more than the handful that are permitted to watch and listen from the public gallery. A few years ago, a three-man Bar Council committee under the chairmanship of Jonathan Caplan, QC, visited several countries where the televising of some trials was permitted. In all of them, against their expectations, they found that the practice had in no way adversely affected the administration of justice – in just the same way as the fears of those like Mrs Thatcher who for so long opposed the televising of Parliament on the grounds that it would change for the worse the atmosphere of the House by encouraging Members to play to the gallery, were seen to be unfounded. What proved true for Parliament would also be true for the courts, where the only role television can play is one of eavesdropper. The argument that witnesses who were nervous of giving evidence would be made even more so if they knew they were being televised, the committee found to be without foundation: cameras and lights are so unobtrusive these days that few people would even be aware of when they were operating.

But the committee did recommend certain procedures. The trials covered should be of general public interest and, because of the many *longueurs* in the average trial, only edited versions of the day's proceedings, similar to *Today in Parliament*, should be shown each night, orchestrated by whatever broadcasting authority had been licensed to cover it. To prevent nobbling, shots of the jury would not be allowed, nor shots of the judge reacting to the evidence. A narrator would link the various extracts together. Trials that might have been covered in the past are those of Stephen Ward and Jeremy Thorpe, the Birmingham Six and the Guinness defendants, and the libel actions of Jeffrey Archer against the *Star* and of Lord Aldington against Count Nikolai Tolstoy: a window on these would have enabled thousands, if not millions, to see for the first time how the law in action works and at the same time fulfill the BBC's charter to educate, inform and entertain. Regrettably, the Caplan Committee's recommendations were not taken up at the time (although the Scottish Bench permitted one short and not very satisfactory series), but I am hopeful that demand for it will come again.

Let me end by repeating what I wrote in 1965 at the end of my book on the trial of Stephen Ward and still believe to be true:

It is time not only for the rules of the game to be revised but also, if people like Stephen Ward[3] are to have a just trial in future, to ask ourselves whether the game we have chosen is the one we wish to go on playing.

---

3   And, I might add, Timothy Evans, Derek Bentley, Patrick Meehan, Cooper and McMahon, Iain Gordon, the Birmingham Six, the Guildford Four, George Long, the two Scots Guardsmen, and many others known, as was said of the unidentified dead in the First World War, only to God.

APPENDIX

The abuse of Hugh Callaghan, one of the Birmingham Six, whose allega-
tions against the police, alongside those of the others Mr Justice Bridge dis-
missed as bizarre and grotesque; but to me, and I trust the reader, bear all
the hallmarks of truth.

As soon as we arrived at the station one of the policemen picked up a
phone from the reception desk. He was so excited he was panting.
'We've got him! We've got Callaghan!' He gave the thumbs-up sign to
policemen who passed him; I heard him mention something about 'the
sixth one'. I said to myself, Christ, they can't be serious! Me! I couldn't
believe it.

I was brought into a small, brightly lit interviewing room with just a
table and some chairs. It smelt of smoke and bad air, and it was freezing
cold. I was given a cup of foul-smelling coffee, which I couldn't drink.
It was supposed to sober me up; but the shock I got when they carted
me off was enough.

The two officers identified themselves – both of them were detectives, one a sergeant, the second a constable. 'We want to talk to you.'
There were few formalities. I replied to questions about my identity,
where I lived, my age, and my place of work. Beyond this I was told little
of what I was to expect. I was full of apprehension. What on earth was

going to happen to me? I didn't even know if I was formally arrested. The word 'arrested' wasn't used; I don't remember being cautioned either. One of them took control and asked all the questions. He fired them at me rapidly and threateningly; he shouted and verbally abused me and my family, making the customary derogatory remarks about Irish people. He started to shout at me about people being blown up with bombs. I said I had nothing to do with bombs. I wouldn't recognise an explosive device if I was shown one.

I was totally confused and frightened. I was still dumbfounded at the very idea of being taken in for questioning about any crime, never mind such a dreadful one as this. My denials were strenuous, but I could hear my voice faltering. Why would I want to blow up Birmingham people? I was a family man living and settled in Birmingham since 1947. I had a 16-year-old daughter, a Birmingham girl like any other. The very thought of planting a bomb in a pub that could take the life of a young person just like her, or of any person, revolted me. I told them over and over again where I was, and who I was with, but they refused to believe me. I was slapped across the face. 'Don't give us that shit, Callaghan. You were there and you're going to tell all about it.'

I was asked about my movements on the evening of the twenty-first. I told them I went to New Street station to see off five people from home who were going to Belfast; that I went for a drink in a nearby pub, Yates's Wine Lodge, and met a friend I hadn't seen for a long time, John Fannon; and that the police came in to tell us there had been explosions in nearby pubs. That, I said, was all I knew about the bombs. I was able to give plenty of details, with witnesses who could verify my movements during the day and in the evening.

They had the names of the five men I left at the station. I was asked for details about them. At that stage I didn't know for certain that they had been arrested, though I guessed by now that they probably were. None of them were people I regularly met, I explained. I couldn't give them one complete address: I knew the street or the district but not the number of their houses. I was older by ten years or more than Billy

Power, Gerry Hunter and Paddy Hill. But my lack of information only added to their suspicions …

More questions followed. A lot of accusations were thrown at me about myself and the other five being in the IRA. They suggested I knew a lot more than I was prepared to admit. They were 'going to get the truth' from me, however long it took. I wanted to scream. I felt helpless. We were not in the IRA; I knew nothing about the bombs. I heard myself repeating the same words over and over again.

Throughout the whole process neither of them appeared to be taking notes. I wouldn't have minded, since I had nothing to hide. They never really seemed to be listening to my answers. My shocked reactions to much of what they were suggesting, and my emphatic denials, didn't impress them one bit. It appeared to me that their minds were already made up. They kept interrupting me; one question rolled into another, giving me no time to reply. I sensed they were trying to confuse me, to make me contradict myself. Everything I said was twisted around, and they kept calling me a liar, at one point suggesting that I could have killed my own daughter. I couldn't believe what I was hearing.

The officer who led the interview raised his voice louder and louder, banging his fist on the table. I think he got a kick out of seeing me terrified out of my wits by him and his aggression. He sneered at me and seemed to detest my fear. I hated violent behaviour. Even in these circumstances I found it difficult to shout back. It wasn't in me.

There was never a moment to think or compose myself. I felt it was all part of their plan to psychologically undermine my certainty about my own innocence. The same accusations were repeated over and over. My head was thumping and my whole body was sweating; I was trembling all over, and I just wanted to escape. I needed sleep. It was all becoming a bad dream.

At some point a sheet of paper was flung down in front of me. 'You're involved in all this. It says so here in Billy Power's statement. Read it.' I wasn't up to reading anything. The piece of paper could have been blank. 'I don't care what that says. It's not true. None of us had anything to do with those bombings.' As they had already obtained one confession, implicating me up to the hilt, they told me, it was all straightforward: I should now make a statement, sign a confession. 'I'm not signing anything. I had nothing to do with bombs,' I shouted. I was becoming hysterical. Both looked very angry and frustrated. They appeared for a while to be getting nowhere.

After a few hours of sheer terror, they eventually informed me that I was being moved to another station. I was hoping they would allow me some sleep first, but I was out of luck. In the small hours of Saturday morning I was taken to Sutton Coldfield, and I was placed in a cell underneath the station. 'A fucking pigsty is too good for you,' a policeman shouted in from the desk outside my cell.

The cell door was left open. The only furniture was a bed, which I was not allowed to lie on. I was instructed to stand upright. If they saw me close my eyes they would shout in at me, 'No sleeping!' I tried a few times to sit on the bed; each time I did someone would yell, 'What are you doing? Get up!' The last time I had slept was Thursday night, and this was now early Saturday morning. Outside the cell were two armed policemen. One of them kept clicking his gun and pretending to aim it in my direction. The second one was a dog handler. The Alsatian wandered in and out of the cell, and he encouraged it to come close to me, sniffing and growling. I was afraid to move. They warned me that if I moved or closed my eyes the dog would attack. Throughout my life I was always very frightened of Alsatian dogs. I knew I was being psychologically and physically terrorised. My heart was pounding with fear.

Standing there in the cell, the time seemed interminable. Every once in a while a policeman would look in and shout out some more abuse at me.

Around eleven o'clock on Saturday morning I was called back briefly by the same officers who interrogated me the night before. I felt like a compliant zombie, subdued, frightened, confused and by now very very tired. I kept wishing for sleep and a nice cold drink. I was taken to be swabbed by a forensic scientist whose name, I later found out, was

Lloyd. My hands were shaking; they felt sweaty and were unwashed. He never looked at me during the whole process and did not speak to me or anyone else. He conducted the business efficiently, from what I was able to observe. I hoped he was an honest man.

I was then returned to the interviewing room to be confronted by my interrogators again. I told them I had a duodenal ulcer, which I half hoped would make them go a bit easy on me. I sat opposite one of the officers at a table answering routine questions about my age and address that I had already answered several hours before. He kept kicking me hard on the shins. The pain was excruciating. Every time I flinched he kicked me again. I couldn't say any more. If I spoke I would be kicked, and if I remained silent I would be kicked. One thing I knew and that was that I wouldn't dare to complain. It was a terrifying half an hour before they left me and I was returned to my cell.

Back again to the interviewing room, this time with a fresh team of detectives. There were three or four men there. I quickly gathered by their attitude and the expression on their faces that this was the 'heavy mob', sent in to finish the job. This was no simple case of rough treatment and then being let go: these people were trying to pin something very serious on me and the other five men. I knew too that I would not be able to take much from them. Their very presence terrified me. But Christ, I was innocent, and I would keep saying it!

By now I desperately needed time to myself. I was losing control; I was losing my resolve not to admit anything. A few more hours with these men and I felt I would give up. I asked for something to eat; they said the canteen was closed. I was sick and weak from lack of sleep, food and drink. I was told to strip, and I was left naked for several minutes; then I was told to dress again, and strip again. The humiliation was unbearable; I have always been a private person. My embarrassment amused all of them, who stood looking and laughing contemptuously.

Three or four men circled me while I remained sitting on a chair. Sometimes they didn't speak, just circled round my back, coming up close to me, breathing on my face and hissing and whispering vile threats and abuse into my ears. Then they would suddenly shout and make me jump. My stomach was churning, and I was crying. When I was at my weakest they whipped the chair from under me.

When I had still just a blanket around me and was feeling very vulnerable and exposed, one of them raised his fist to me. 'You will make a fucking statement or we will bash you around this cell.' I begged him not to hit me. I pleaded with him to believe my story, which I kept saying I could prove. He wasn't interested; the only thing that was going to satisfy him was a confession. I asked for a drink – I couldn't eat now. My mouth was parched. I could hardly speak above a whisper. Eventually they let me go to the toilet, and I scooped up water in my hands from the sink.

At some point an exasperated officer grabbed me bodily and pinned me against the wall. Strange, animal-like noises emanated from him; his eyes were wild, like a man about to kill. My head hit the wall and bounced back. I was dizzy; I thought I was going to get sick. I really believed he was going to kill me – at least it would have been an escape from this terror.

Another policeman realised that his colleague was going too far. He pulled him from me, rescuing me like an impartial referee. He put his hand on my shoulder and spoke very quietly. 'I'm not like him.' He walked me back to the table; I was like a lamb. 'Come on, mate, you'll do it for me.' I had never experienced such terror or pressure in my life before. I knew before God that neither I nor any of the others had any part in planting bombs. I just couldn't take any more. I begged them once more to believe me, but I just wanted it over with and to be left alone. At my lowest ebb, they seized their opportunity, and I conceded. I agreed to sign a confession.

I was led through the 'confession'. I hardly spoke or made any contribution to it. I nodded my agreement occasionally about places I was really in and the people I had spoken to; as far as I was aware the rest was a complete fabrication. They suggested names of people who were my accomplices in this evil crime. I offered no details about the explosions –

because I couldn't. It was of no consequence to them. My only part in this cruel farce was to put my name to it. I did – knowing it all to be a lie. I was getting them off my back, if only for a while. I convinced myself that as soon as I got to see a solicitor I could deny all this. I would explain the circumstances; I even contemplated complaining about the treatment I received. I now know that this was a very naïve belief indeed.

They read the statement back to me. I wasn't even listening. It was like a bad dream that I would eventually awake from. The statement was placed in front of me. I didn't read it, and in a million years couldn't have read it. At that moment I would have signed anything. With a policeman's hand over mine, 'to steady my hand', he said, I signed it in two places. The second section was read back to me, but I wasn't taking it in. It stated, as I learnt later to my cost, that 'I have read the above statement and have been told that I can correct, alter or add anything I wish. This statement is true. I have made it of my own free will.'

By the time this business was concluded I was totally exhausted and defeated. They all had a smug look of satisfaction on their faces. I wept with despair as the significance of what I had done began to overwhelm me.

The very minute I signed they grabbed the statement and left. I was at last left alone. I had no desire to think or contemplate anything now. I wept continuously …

That evening and night I alternated between anger and despair. Why were we picked out? Was it simply because we were Irish? I went through elaborate justifications for signing. Who could stand up to that terror? I decided that a good solicitor was my only hope. I resolved that I would ask for a solicitor in the morning. I would tell the solicitor that the statement was a pack of lies, that I was forced to sign it, that everything in it was made up. It all seemed logical and simple. Yet it failed to console me …

By the small hours of the morning I became more alert, and I was obsessed with one thing. I must be allowed to retract that statement. If it wasn't retracted we could all end up in great trouble. I knew Billy had signed something, and I guessed he did so under the same pressure as I had experienced. I had no idea whether any of the others had signed. I couldn't wait for them to open my cell door. I was bursting to tell them my decision. I actually felt mentally stronger and more determined about my intentions. I had two objectives: to see a solicitor and retract that statement.

I shut my eyes and remained sitting upright on the foot of the bed. When daylight came I was, I thought, ready for them. But it didn't work out as I had planned. I had yet to receive anything to drink. I was dying for a decent cup of tea. I was whisked off in an unmarked car, pushed in the back between two plain-clothes men with two others in front. I recognised one of the officers as the one who had led the interview. I had, of course, no idea where I was going. Sitting in the back between the two policemen I immediately said, 'You can't use that statement. It's false. I was forced to sign it, and none of it is true. I was forced to involve Gerry Hunter in something he didn't do.' My heart was beating as I spoke. I was petrified, but I hoped I sounded convincing enough.

My remarks drew an instant reaction. The brakes were slammed on, and the policeman sitting in the front passenger seat produced a gun from under his coat. He leaned right over the seat and pointed the gun to my stomach. 'You stick to that statement,' he said. I didn't stir. I knew he meant business. I was trapped in this car and trapped again by that statement.

The drive to the Queen's Road station seemed interminable. Yet it was only a short distance. I knew the area well and it was obvious to me they were taking a long route. They stopped by the lake in Selford Park en route, and one said to the other, 'Let's throw the bastard in the lake.' I was terrified and didn't move or look in any direction. I knew these men were by now capable of anything. I believed the slightest agitation from me would have made them carry out their threat. Later they drove on to Queen's Road police station. By the time I reached there I didn't know what other evil they might have in store for me. The psychological torture seemed unending and getting worse.

Handcuffed to a radiator back in Queen's Road station, I was questioned again by two very unattractive, sneering detectives, whose comments during the interview showed me how crude and ignorant they were. I again said I didn't want the statement I signed used; I asked for it to be retracted. They just ignored me. 'Right then, Callaghan. Who is the head man in your cell? Who is the captain, the brigadier? What about you? Are you a captain?' It was laughable ...

I remained handcuffed throughout this interview, though I cannot think what danger I could possibly have been. My mouth was dry, my stomach was empty, and I needed a shower. My body and hair were sweaty. I felt foul. I asked for a drink and a biscuit, but, as ever, my request fell on deaf ears.

When the detectives left I still hadn't succeeded in retracting my statement, and now I was told I was going to be charged. The charge was murder.

SOURCES

Callaghan, Hugh, *Cruel Fate: One Man's Triumph over Injustice* (Dublin: Poolbeg Press, 1993) The Birmingham Six

Devlin, Patrick, *The Criminal Prosecution in England* (London: Oxford University Press, 1960)

Hunter, John, *Report by the Hon. Lord Hunter into the Whole Circumstances of the Murder of Mrs Rachel Ross at Ayr in July 1969* (Edinburgh: HMSO, 1982)

Hyde, H. Montgomery (ed.), *Trial of Christopher Craig and Derek William Bentley* (Notable British Trials series, London: William Hodge, 1954)

Jesse, F. Tennyson (ed.), *The Trials of Evans and Christie* (Notable British Trials series, London: William Hodge, 1957)

Kee, Robert, *Trial and Error: The Maguires, the Guildford Pub Bombings and British Justice* (London: Hamish Hamilton, 1986)

Kennedy, Ludovic, *Ten Rillington Place* (London: Victor Gollancz, 1961) The Evans–Christie case
— *The Trial of Stephen Ward* (London: Victor Gollancz, 1964)
— *A Presumption of Innocence: The Amazing Case of Patrick Meehan* (London: Victor Gollancz, 1976)
— (ed.), *Wicked Beyond Belief: The Luton Murder Case* (London:

Granada, 1980) The Luton Post Office Murder Case

— *The Airman and the Carpenter: The Lindbergh Baby Kidnapping and Murder Case and the Framing of Richard Hauptmann* (London: Collins, 1985)

— article in the *Sunday Times* (25 February 1990) on the Birmingham Six case

McKee, Grant, and Franey, Ros, *Time Bomb* (London: Bloomsbury, 1988) The Guildford Four and Maguire Seven cases

Mullin, Chris, *Error of Judgement: The Birmingham Bombings* (London: Chatto & Windus,1986)

Parris, John, *Scapegoat: The Inside Story of the Trial of Derek Bentley* (London: Duckworth, 1991)

Pickles, James, *Straight from the Bench* (London: Phoenix House, 1987)

Radelet, Michael L. and Bedau, Hugo Adam, and Putnam, Constance E., *In Spite of Innocence: Erroneous Convictions in Capital Cases* (Boston: Northeastern University Press, 1992)

Rose, David, *In the Name of the Law: The Collapse of Criminal Justice* (London: Jonathan Cape, 1996)

Sargant, William, *Battle for the Mind: A Physiology of Conversion and Brain-washing* (New York: Doubleday, 1957)

Trow, M. J., *Let Him Have It, Chris: The Murder of Derek Bentley* (London: Constable, 1990)

Police and Criminal Evidence Act (PACE) (London: HMSO, 1984)

Report: Presented to Parliament by Command of Her Majesty, July 1993/Royal Commission on Criminal Justice Runciman Commission Report

The Australian (2 March 2000)

Daily Mail (7 March and 3 September 1988)

Spectator (23 May 1988)

Toronto Globe and Mail (16 February 2002)

INDEX

Rice-Davies, Mandy 45, 46, 47, 48,
  51–7, 65
Richardson, Carole 247, 248, 257,
  268, 274
  alibi 251, 272
  false confession 249–50
Rifkind, Malcolm 145
right to silence 306, 309
Rillington Place murder 21–40
Robertson, Geoffrey 308
Robertson, Lord *Ill* 4, 147–9, 151,
  152–3, 154, 242
Rogers, Ginger 205
Rolph, C. H. 144
Roosevelt, Eleanor 220
Rose-Smith, Brian 251
Roskill, Lord Justice *Ill* 6
  Guildford Four 248, 265, 266, 267,
    268, 269, 270, 271
  Luton Post Office murder 164,
    166, 170, 242, 312
  Maguire Seven 265
Ross, Abraham 108–12, 113–14, 136,
  141, 142, 143
  identification parade 117–18, 138,
    152
  at trial 128–30, 133
  voice identification 135, 137, 153
Ross, Rachel 108–12, 113–14, 150
Ross, William 138, 141, 142, 145, 146
Rossellini, Isabella 225
Rothwax, Judge Harold 308
Roughea, William 4
Rowe, Asst Chief Constable *Ill* 21,
  250
Royal Commission on Criminal
  Justice 6, 19, 246, 284–5, 309

Ruddock, Joan 285
Runciman, Viscount 6, 19, 246,
  284–5, 309
Runyon, Damon 205
Russell, Head Constable 78, 89–90
Russell, Josie, Lin and Megan 6–9
Ruxton, Dr Buck 3

S

Sacco, Nicola 175
Samuelson, Anthony 15–16
Sargant, Tom 160, 166
Sargant, Dr William 37, 69, 127,
  280
Savundra, Dr Emil 50, 53, 54–5, 56
Scaduto, Anthony 197, 221, 223
Scapegoat (Scaduto) 197, 221
Scarman, Lord 228, 271, 309
Schoeffler, Anna *see* Hauptmann,
  Anna
Schwarzkopf, Colonel Norman
  Ill 25, 183, 204, 207, 213
Scots Guardsmen 291–303, 315
Scotsman 101, 140, 141
Scott, David 140, 153
Scott, George 21
Scott, John 150
Scott Henderson, John 35–6, 37, 39,
  242
Scottish Daily News 143
Scottish Daily Record 141
Sharp, Brian 236
Shawcross, Lord 85
Silverman, Sidney 36
Silvers, Robert 223
Simmons, Detective Chief
  Superintendent *Ill* 22, 249, 250